PRAISE FOR *THINK LIKE A PROGRAMMER*

"The author is obviously very knowledgeable and experienced with teaching hard concepts to new learners, and this shows in his no-nonsense, down-to-earth but enjoyable writing style."
—ADRIAN WOODHEAD, SLASHDOT

"Spraul has taught intro computer science classes for over fifteen years and it shows. He does a great job showing the theory using concrete examples, and rightfully puts a great deal of emphasis on programming exercises to strengthen the concepts."
—ARIANE COFFIN, WIRED.COM'S GEEKMOM

"This is one of the most helpful books I've read, due to the fact that it guides you towards designing a system for yourself, as opposed to encouraging a mindset where there can be only one correct method."
—LUCAS WESTERMANN, FULL CIRCLE MAGAZINE

"The book is well written, with tons of excellent advice and solid, well-thought-out examples. If you're willing to devote some time to studying the material, you'll soon find yourself equipped with an impressive array of problem-solving strategies and, maybe, a new outlook on programming."
—PHIL BULL, AUTHOR OF THE OFFICIAL UBUNTU DOCUMENTATION

"I guarantee if you work through the entire book, you will stretch your brain."
—DAVID BOLTON, ABOUT.COM C/C++/C#

"The advice is simple, straightforward, and practical. It's an easy—and valuable—read."
—JAMES E. POWELL, ENTERPRISE SYSTEMS

THINK LIKE A PROGRAMMER

An Introduction to Creative Problem Solving

by V. Anton Spraul

no starch press

San Francisco

Fourth printing

19 18 17 16 15   4 5 6 7 8 9

ISBN-10: 1-59327-424-6
ISBN-13: 978-1-59327-424-5

Publisher: William Pollock
Production Editor: Alison Law
Cover Design: Charlie Wylie
Interior Design: Octopod Studios
Developmental Editor: Keith Fancher
Technical Reviewer: Dan Randall
Copyeditor: Julianne Jigour
Compositor: Susan Glinert Stevens
Proofreader: Ward Webber

For information on distribution, translations, or bulk sales, please contact No Starch Press, Inc. directly:

No Starch Press, Inc.
245 8th Street, San Francisco, CA 94103
phone: 415.863.9900; info@nostarch.com
www.nostarch.com

Library of Congress Cataloging-in-Publication Data

Spraul, V. Anton.
  Think like a programmer : an introduction to creative problem solving / V. Anton Spraul.
      pages cm
  ISBN 978-1-59327-424-5 (pbk.) -- ISBN 1-59327-424-6 (pbk.)
1. Computer programming. 2. Creative thinking. 3. Problem solving. I. Title.
  QA76.6.S685 2012
  005.1--dc23
                                2012020396

BRIEF CONTENTS

CONTENTS IN DETAIL

3
SOLVING PROBLEMS WITH ARRAYS 55

4
SOLVING PROBLEMS WITH POINTERS AND
DYNAMIC MEMORY 81

ACKNOWLEDGMENTS

No book is truly the work of one author, and I've received lots of help on *Think Like a Programmer*.

I'm grateful to everyone at No Starch Press, especially Keith Fancher and Alison Law, who edited, shaped, and shepherded the book throughout its production. I must also thank Bill Pollock for his decision to sign me up in the first place—I hope he is as pleased with the result as I am. The folks at No Starch have been unfailingly kind and helpful in their correspondence with me. I hope one day to meet them in person and see to what degree they resemble their cartoon avatars on the company website.

Dan Randall did a wonderful job as technical editor. His numerous suggestions beyond the technical review helped me strengthen the manuscript in many areas.

On the home front, the most important people in my life, Mary Beth and Madeline, provided love, support, and enthusiasm—and, crucially, time to write.

Finally, to all the students of programming I've had over the years: Thank you for letting me be your teacher. The techniques and strategies described in this book were developed through our joint efforts. I hope we've made the journey easier for the next generation of programmers.

INTRODUCTION

Do you struggle to write programs, even though you think you understand programming languages? Are you able to read through a chapter in a programming book, nodding your head the whole way, but unable to apply what you've read to your own programs? Are you able to comprehend a program example you've read online, even to the point where you could explain to someone else what each line of the code is doing, yet you feel your brain seize up when faced with a programming task and a blank screen in your text editor?

You're not alone. I have taught programming for over 15 years, and most of my students would have fit this description at some point in their instruction. We will call the missing skill *problem solving*, the ability to take a given problem description and write an original program to solve it. Not all programming requires extensive problem solving. If you're just making minor modifications to an existing program, debugging, or adding testing code, the programming may be so mechanical in nature that your creativity is never tested. But all programs require problem solving at some point, and all good programmers can solve problems.

Problem solving is hard. It's true that a few people make it look easy—the "naturals," the programming world's equivalent of a gifted athlete, like Michael Jordan. For these select few, high-level ideas are effortlessly translated into source code. To make a Java metaphor, it's as if their brains execute Java natively, while the rest of us have to run a virtual machine, interpreting as we go.

Not being a natural isn't fatal to becoming a programmer—if it were, the world would have few programmers. Yet I've seen too many worthy learners struggle too long in frustration. In the worst cases, they give up programming entirely, convinced that they can never be programmers, that the only good programmers are those born with an innate gift.

Why is learning to solve programming problems so hard?

In part, it's because problem solving is a different activity from learning programming syntax and therefore uses a different set of mental "muscles." Learning programming syntax, reading programs, memorizing elements of an application programming interface—these are mostly analytical "left brain" activities. Writing an original program using previously learned tools and skills is a creative "right brain" activity.

Suppose you need to remove a branch that has fallen into one of the rain gutters on your house, but your ladder isn't quite long enough for you to reach the branch. You head into your garage and look for something, or a combination of things, that will enable you to remove the branch from the gutter. Is there some way to extend the ladder? Is there something you can hold at the top of the ladder to grab or dislodge the branch? Maybe you could just get on the roof from another place and get the branch from above. That's problem solving, and it's a creative activity. Believe it or not, when you design an original program, your mental process is quite similar to that of the person figuring out how to remove the branch from the gutter and quite different from that of a person debugging an existing for loop.

Most programming books, though, focus their attention on syntax and semantics. Learning the syntax and semantics of a programming language is essential, but it's only the first step in learning how to program in that language. In essence, most programming books for beginners teach how to read a program, not how to write one. Books that do focus on writing are often effectively "cookbooks" in that they teach specific "recipes" for use in particular situations. Such books can be quite valuable as time savers, but not as a path toward learning to write original code. Think about cookbooks in the original sense. Although great cooks own cookbooks, no one who relies upon cookbooks can be a great cook. A great cook understands ingredients, preparation methods, and cooking methods and knows how they can be combined to make great meals. All a great cook needs to produce a tasty meal is a fully stocked kitchen. In the same way, a great programmer understands language syntax, application frameworks, algorithms, and software engineering principles and knows how they can be combined to make great programs. Give a great programmer a list of specifications, turn him loose with a fully stocked programming environment, and great things will happen.

In general, current programming education doesn't offer much guidance in the area of problem solving. Instead, it's assumed that if programmers are given access to all of the tools of programming and requested to write enough programs, eventually they will learn to write such programs and write them well. There is truth in this, but "eventually" can be a long time. The journey from initiation to enlightenment can be filled with frustration, and too many who start the journey never reach the destination.

Instead of learning by trial and error, you can learn problem solving in a systematic way. That's what this book is all about. You can learn techniques to organize your thoughts, procedures to discover solutions, and strategies to apply to certain classes of problems. By studying these approaches, you can unlock your creativity. Make no mistake: Programming, and especially problem solving, is a creative activity. Creativity is mysterious, and no one can say exactly how the creative mind functions. Yet, if we can learn music composition, take advice on creative writing, or be shown how to paint, then we can learn to creatively solve programming problems, too. This book isn't going to tell you precisely what to do; it's going to help you develop your latent problem-solving abilities so that you will know what you should do. This book is about helping you become the programmer you are meant to be.

My goal is for you and every other reader of this book to learn to systematically approach every programming task and to have the confidence that you will ultimately solve a given problem. When you complete this book, I want you to *think like a programmer* and to *believe that you are a programmer.*

About This Book

Having explained the necessity of this book, I need to make a few comments about what this book is and what it is not.

Prerequisites

This book assumes you are already familiar with the basic syntax and semantics of the C++ language and that you have begun writing programs. Most of the chapters will expect you to know specific C++ fundamentals; these chapters will begin with a review of those fundamentals. If you are still absorbing language basics, don't worry. There are plenty of great books on C++ syntax, and you can learn problem solving in parallel to learning syntax. Just make sure you have studied the relevant syntax before attempting to tackle a chapter's problems.

Chosen Topics

The topics covered in this book represent areas in which I have most often seen new programmers struggle. They also present a broad cross-section of different areas in early and intermediate programming.

I should emphasize, however, that this is not a "cookbook" of algorithms or patterns for solving specific problems. Although later chapters discuss how to employ well-known algorithms or patterns, you should not use this book as a "crib sheet" to get you past particular problems or focus on just the chapters that directly relate to your current struggles. Instead, I would work through the entire book, skipping material only if you lack the prerequisites needed to follow the discussion.

Programming Style

A quick note here about the programming style employed in this book: This book is not about high-performance programming or running the most compact, efficient code. The style I have chosen for the source code examples is intended to be readable above all other considerations. In some cases, I take multiple steps to accomplish something that could be done in one step, just so the principle I'm trying to demonstrate is made clear.

Some aspects of programming style will be covered in this book—but larger issues, like what should or should not be included in a class, not small issues, like how code should be indented. As a developing programmer, you will of course want to employ a consistent, readable style in all of the work you do.

Exercises

The book includes a number of programming exercises. This is not a textbook, and you won't find answers to any of the exercises in the back. The exercises provide opportunities for you to apply the concepts described in the chapters. Whether you choose to try any of the exercises is, of course, up to you, but it is essential that you put these concepts into practice. Simply reading through the book will accomplish nothing. Remember that this book is not going to tell you exactly what to do in each situation. In applying the techniques shown in this book, you will develop your own ability to discover what to do. Furthermore, growing your confidence, another primary goal of this book, requires success. In fact, that's a good way to know when you have worked through enough exercises in a given problem area: when you are confident that you can tackle other problems in the area. Lastly, programming exercises should be *fun*. While there may be moments where you'd rather be doing something else, working out a programming problem should be a rewarding challenge.

You should think of this book as an obstacle course for your brain. Obstacle courses build strength, stamina, and agility and give the trainer confidence. By reading through the chapters and applying the concepts to as many exercises as you can, you're going to build confidence and develop problem-solving skills that can be used in any programming situation. In the future, when you are faced with a difficult problem, you'll know whether you should try going over, under, or through it.

Why C++?

The programming examples in this text are coded using C++. Having said that, this book is about solving problems with programs, not specifically about C++. You won't find many tips and tricks specific to C++ here, and the general concepts taught throughout this book can be employed in any programming language. Nevertheless, you can't discuss programming without discussing programs, and a specific language had to be chosen.

C++ was selected for a number of reasons. First, it's popular in a variety of problem areas. Second, because of its origins in the strictly procedural C language, C++ code can be written using both the procedural and object-oriented paradigms. Object-oriented programming is so common now that it could not be omitted from a discussion on problem solving, but many fundamental problem-solving concepts can be discussed in strictly procedural programming terms, and doing so simplifies both the code and the discussion. Third, as a low-level language with high-level libraries, C++ allows us to discuss both levels of programming. The best programmers can "hand-wire" solutions when required and make use of high-level libraries and application programming interfaces to reduce development time. Lastly, and partly as a function of the other reasons listed, C++ is a great choice because once you have learned to solve problems in C++, you have learned to solve problems in any programming language. Many programmers have discovered how the skills learned in one language easily apply to other languages, but this is especially true for C++ because of its cross-paradigm approach and, frankly, because of its difficulty. C++ is the real deal—it's programming without training wheels. This is daunting at first, but once you start succeeding in C++, you'll know that you're not going to be someone who can do a little coding—you're going to be a programmer.

1

STRATEGIES FOR PROBLEM SOLVING

This book is about problem solving, but what is problem solving, exactly? When people use the term in ordinary conversation, they often mean something very different from what we mean here. If your 1997 Honda Civic has blue smoke coming from the tailpipe, is idling roughly, and has lost fuel efficiency, this is a problem that can be solved with automotive knowledge, diagnosis, replacement equipment, and common shop tools. If you tell your friends about your problem, though, one of them might say, "Hey, you should trade that old Honda in for something new. Problem solved." But your friend's suggestion wouldn't really be a *solution* to the problem—it would be a way to *avoid* the problem.

Problems include constraints, unbreakable rules about the problem or the way in which the problem must be solved. With the broken-down Civic, one of the constraints is that you want to fix the current car, not purchase a new car. The constraints might also include the overall cost of the repairs, how long the repair will take, or a requirement that no new tools can be purchased just for this repair.

When solving a problem with a program, you also have constraints. Common constraints include the programming language, platform (does it run on a PC, or an iPhone, or what?), performance (a game program may require graphics to be updated at least 30 times a second, a business application might have a maximum time response to user input), or memory footprint. Sometimes the constraint involves what other code you can reference: Maybe the program can't include certain open-source code, or maybe the opposite—maybe it can use only open source.

For programmers, then, we can define *problem solving* as writing an original program that performs a particular set of tasks and meets all stated constraints.

Beginning programmers are often so eager to accomplish the first part of that definition—writing a program to perform a certain task—that they fail on the second part of the definition, meeting the stated constraints. I call a program like that, one that appears to produce correct results but breaks one or more of the stated rules, a *Kobayashi Maru*. If that name is unfamiliar to you, it means you are insufficiently familiar with one of the touchstones of geek culture, the film *Star Trek II: The Wrath of Khan*. The film contains a subplot about an exercise for aspiring officers at Starfleet Academy. The cadets are put aboard a simulated starship bridge and made to act as captain on a mission that involves an impossible choice. Innocent people will die on a wounded ship, the *Kobayashi Maru*, but to reach them requires starting a battle with the Klingons, a battle that can only end in the destruction of the captain's ship. The exercise is intended to test a cadet's courage under fire. There's no way to win, and all choices lead to bad outcomes. Toward the end of the film, we discover that Captain Kirk modified the simulation to make it actually winnable. Kirk was clever, but he did not solve the dilemma of the *Kobayashi Maru*; he avoided it.

Fortunately, the problems you will face as a programmer are solvable, but many programmers still resort to Kirk's approach. In some cases, they do so accidentally. ("Oh, shoot! My solution only works if there are a hundred data items or fewer. It's supposed to work for an unlimited data set. I'll have to rethink this.") In other cases, the removal of constraints is deliberate, a ploy to meet a deadline imposed by a boss or an instructor. In still other cases, the programmer just doesn't know how to meet all of the constraints. In the worst cases I have seen, the programming student has paid someone else to write the program. Regardless of the motivations, we must always be diligent to avoid the Kobayashi Maru.

Classic Puzzles

As you progress through this book, you will notice that although the particulars of the source code change from one problem area to the next, certain patterns will emerge in the approaches we take. This is great news because this is what eventually allows us to confidently approach any problem, whether we have extensive experience in that problem area or not. Expert problem solvers are quick to recognize an *analogy*, an exploitable similarity between a solved problem and an unsolved problem. If we recognize that a feature of problem A is analogous to a feature of problem B and we have already solved problem B, we have a valuable insight into solving problem A.

In this section, we'll discuss classic problems from outside the world of programming that have lessons we can apply to programming problems.

The Fox, the Goose, and the Corn

The first classic problem we will discuss is a riddle about a farmer who needs to cross a river. You have probably encountered it previously in one form or another.

PROBLEM: HOW TO CROSS THE RIVER?

A farmer with a fox, a goose, and a sack of corn needs to cross a river. The farmer has a rowboat, but there is room for only the farmer and one of his three items. Unfortunately, both the fox and the goose are hungry. The fox cannot be left alone with the goose, or the fox will eat the goose. Likewise, the goose cannot be left alone with the sack of corn, or the goose will eat the corn. How does the farmer get everything across the river?

The setup for this problem is shown in Figure 1-1. If you have never encountered this problem before, stop here and spend a few minutes trying to solve it. If you *have* heard this riddle before, try to remember the solution and whether you were able to solve the riddle on your own.

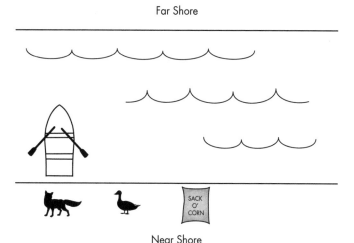

Figure 1-1: The fox, the goose, and the sack of corn. The boat can carry one item at a time. The fox cannot be left on the same shore as the goose, and the goose cannot be left on the same shore as the sack of corn.

Few people are able to solve this riddle, at least without a hint. I know I wasn't. Here's how the reasoning usually goes. Since the farmer can take only one thing at a time, he'll need multiple trips to take everything to the far shore. On the first trip, if the farmer takes the fox, the goose would be left with the sack of corn, and the goose would eat the corn. Likewise, if the farmer took the sack of corn on the first trip, the fox would be left with the goose, and the fox would eat the goose. Therefore, the farmer must take the goose on the first trip, resulting in the configuration shown in Figure 1-2.

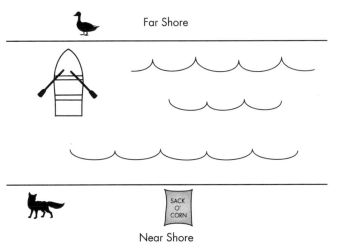

Figure 1-2: The required first step for solving the problem of the fox, the goose, and the sack of corn. From this step, however, all further steps appear to end in failure.

So far, so good. But on the second trip, the farmer must take the fox or the corn. Whatever the farmer takes, however, must be left on the far shore with the goose while the farmer returns to the near shore for the remaining item. This means that either the fox and goose will be left together or the goose and corn will be left together. Because neither of these situations is acceptable, the problem appears unsolvable.

Again, if you have seen this problem before, you probably remember the key element of the solution. The farmer has to take the goose on the first trip, as explained before. On the second trip, let's suppose the farmer takes the fox. Instead of leaving the fox with the goose, though, the farmer *takes the goose back* to the near shore. Then the farmer takes the sack of corn across, leaving the fox and the corn on the far shore, while returning for a fourth trip with the goose. The complete solution is shown in Figure 1-3.

This puzzle is difficult because most people never consider taking one of the items back from the far shore to the near shore. Some people will even suggest that the problem is unfair, saying something like, "You didn't say I could take something back!" This is true, but it's also true that nothing in the problem description suggests that taking something back is prohibited.

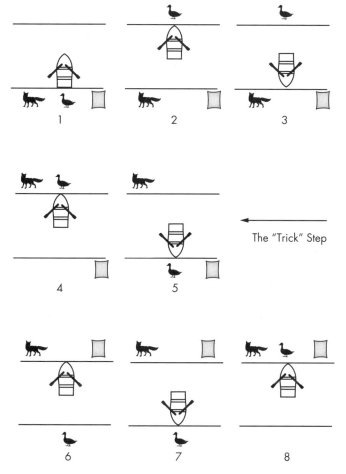

The "Trick" Step

Figure 1-3: Step-by-step solution to the fox, goose, and corn puzzle

Think about how much easier the puzzle would be to solve if the possibility of taking one of the items back to the near shore was made explicit: *The farmer has a rowboat **that can be used to transfer items in either direction**, but there is room only for the farmer and one of his three items.* With that suggestion in plain sight, more people would figure out the problem. This illustrates an important principle of problem solving: If you are unaware of all possible actions you could take, you may be unable to solve the problem. We can refer to these actions as operations. By enumerating all the possible operations, we can solve many problems by testing every combination of operations until we find one that works. More generally, by restating a problem in more formal terms, we can often uncover solutions that would have otherwise eluded us.

Let's forget that we already know the solution and try stating this particular puzzle more formally. First, we'll list our constraints. The key constraints here are:

1. The farmer can take only one item at a time in the boat.
2. The fox and goose cannot be left alone on the same shore.
3. The goose and corn cannot be left alone on the same shore.

This problem is a good example of the importance of constraints. If we remove any of these constraints, the puzzle is easy. If we remove the first constraint, we can simply take all three items across in one trip. Even if we can take only two items in the boat, we can take the fox and corn across and then go back for the goose. If we remove the second constraint (but leave the other constraints in place), we just have to be careful, taking the goose across first, then the fox, and finally the corn. Therefore, if we forget or ignore any of the constraints, we will end up with a Kobayashi Maru.

Next, let's list the operations. There are various ways of stating the operations for this puzzle. We could make a specific list of the actions we think we can take:

1. Operation: Carry the fox to the far side of the river.
2. Operation: Carry the goose to the far side of the river.
3. Operation: Carry the corn to the far side of the river.

Remember, though, that the goal of formally restating the problem is to gain insight for a solution. Unless we have already solved the problem and discovered the "hidden" possible operation, taking the goose back to the near side of the river, we're not going to discover it in making our list of actions. Instead, we should try to make operations generic, or parameterized.

1. Operation: Row the boat from one shore to the other.
2. Operation: If the boat is empty, load an item from the shore.
3. Operation: If the boat is not empty, unload the item to the shore.

By thinking about the problem in the most general terms, this second list of operations will allow us to solve the problem without the need for an "ah-hah!" moment regarding the trip back to the near shore with the goose. If we generate all possible sequences of moves, ending each sequence once it violates one of our constraints or reaches a configuration we've seen before, we will eventually hit upon the sequence of Figure 1-3 and solve the puzzle. The inherent difficulty of the puzzle will have been sidestepped through the formal restatement of constraints and operations.

Lessons Learned

What can we learn from the fox, the goose, and the corn?

Restating the problem in a more formal manner is a great technique for gaining insight into a problem. Many programmers seek out other programmers to discuss a problem, not just because other programmers may have the answer but also because articulating the problem out loud often triggers new and useful thoughts. Restating a problem is like having that discussion with another programmer, except that you are playing both parts.

The broader lesson is that thinking about the problem may be as productive, or in some cases more productive, than thinking about the solution. In many cases, the correct approach to the solution *is* the solution.

Sliding Tile Puzzles

The sliding tile puzzle comes in different sizes, which, as we'll see later, offers a particular solving mechanism. The following description is for a 3×3 version of the puzzle.

PROBLEM: THE SLIDING EIGHT

A 3×3 grid is filled with eight tiles, numbered 1 through 8, and one empty space. Initially, the grid is in a jumbled configuration. A tile can be slid into an adjacent empty space, leaving the tile's previous location empty. The goal is to slide the tiles to place the grid in an ordered configuration, from tile 1 in the upper left.

The goal of this problem is shown in Figure 1-4. If you've never tried a puzzle like this before, take the time to do so now. Plenty of sliding puzzle simulators can be found on the Web, but for our purposes it's better if you use playing cards or index cards to make your own game on a tabletop. A suggested starting configuration is shown in Figure 1-5.

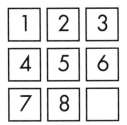

Figure 1-4: The goal configuration in the eight-tile version of the sliding tile puzzle. The empty square represents the empty space into which an adjacent tile may slide.

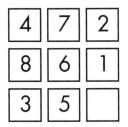

Figure 1-5: A particular starting configuration for the sliding tile puzzle

This puzzle is quite different from the farmer with his fox, goose, and corn. The difficulty in that problem came from overlooking one of the possible operations. In this problem, that doesn't happen. From any given configuration, up to four tiles may be adjacent to the empty space, and any of those tiles can be slid into the empty space. That fully enumerates all possible operations.

The difficulty in this problem arises instead from the long chain of operations required by the solution. A series of sliding operations may move some tiles to their correct final positions while moving other tiles out of position, or it may move some tiles closer to their correct positions while moving others farther away. Because of this, it's difficult to tell whether any particular operation would make progress toward the ultimate goal. Without being able to measure progress, it's difficult to formulate a strategy. Many people who attempt a sliding tile puzzle simply move the tiles around randomly, hoping to hit upon a configuration from which a path to the goal configuration can be seen.

Nevertheless, there are strategies for sliding tile puzzles. To illustrate one approach, let's consider the puzzle for a smaller grid that is rectangular but not square.

PROBLEM: THE SLIDING FIVE

A 2×3 grid is filled with five tiles, numbered 4 through 8, and one empty space. Initially, the grid is in a jumbled configuration. A tile can be slid into an adjacent empty space, leaving the tile's previous location empty. The goal is to slide the tiles to place the grid in an ordered configuration, from tile 4 in the upper left.

You may have noticed that our five tiles are numbered 4 through 8 instead of 1 through 5. The reason for this will become clear shortly.

Although this is the same basic problem as the sliding eight, it is much easier with only five tiles. Try the configuration shown in Figure 1-6.

If you play around with these tiles for just a few minutes, you will probably hit upon a solution. From playing around with small-count tile puzzles, I have developed a particular skill. It is this one skill, coupled with an observation we will discuss shortly, that I use to solve all sliding tile puzzles.

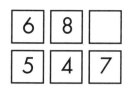

Figure 1-6: A particular starting configuration for a reduced, 2×3 sliding tile puzzle

I call my technique *the train*. It's based on the observation that a circuit of tile positions that includes the empty space forms a train of tiles that can be rotated anywhere along the circuit while preserving the relative ordering of the tiles. Figure 1-7 illustrates the smallest possible train of four positions. From the first configuration, the 1 can slide into the empty square, the 2 can slide into the space vacated by the 1, and finally the 3 can slide into the space vacated by the 2. This leaves the empty space adjacent to the 1, which allows the train to continue and, thus, the tiles to be effectively rotated anywhere along the train path.

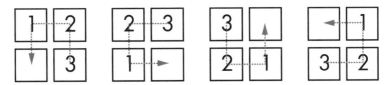

Figure 1-7: A "train," a path of tiles that begins adjacent to the empty square and can slide like a train of cars through the puzzle

Using a train, we can move a series of tiles while maintaining their relative relationship. Now let's return to the previous 2×3 grid configuration. Although none of the tiles in this grid is in its correct final position, some tiles are adjacent to the tiles they need to border in the final configuration. For example, in the final configuration, the 4 will be above the 7, and currently those tiles are adjacent. As shown in Figure 1-8, we can use a six-position train to bring the 4 and 7 to their correct final positions. When we do that, the remaining tiles are nearly correct; we just need to slide the 8 over.

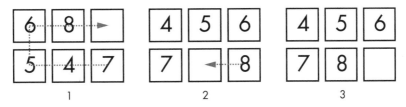

Figure 1-8: From configuration 1, two rotations along the outlined "train" bring us to configuration 2. From there, a single tile slide results in the goal, configuration 3.

So how does this one technique allow us to solve any sliding tile puzzle? Consider our original 3×3 configuration. We can use a six-position train to move the adjacent 1 and 2 tiles so that the 2 and 3 are adjacent, as shown in Figure 1-9.

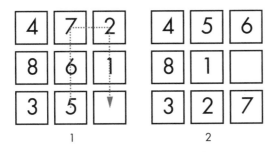

Figure 1-9: From configuration 1, tiles are rotated along the outlined "train" to reach configuration 2.

This puts 1, 2, and 3 in adjacent squares. With an eight-position train, we can shift the 1, 2, and 3 tiles to their correct final positions, as shown in Figure 1-10.

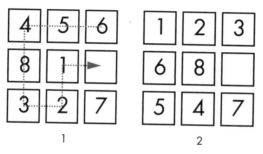

Figure 1-10: From configuration 1, tiles are rotated to reach configuration 2, in which tiles 1, 2, and 3 are in their correct final positions.

Notice the positions of tiles 4–8. The tiles are in the configuration I gave for the 2×3 grid. This is the key observation. Having placed tiles 1–3 in their correct positions, we can solve the rest of the grid as a separate, smaller, and easier puzzle. Note that we have to solve an entire row or column for this method to work; if we put tiles 1 and 2 in the correct positions but tile 3 is still out of place, there is no way to move something into the upper-right corner without moving one or both of the other upper-row tiles out of place.

This same technique can be used to solve even larger sliding tile puzzles. The largest common size is a 15-tile puzzle, a 4×4 grid. This can be solved piecemeal by first moving tiles 1–4 to their correct position, leaving a 3×4 grid, and then moving the tiles of the leftmost column, leaving a 3×3 grid. At that point, the problem has been reduced to an 8-tile puzzle.

Lessons Learned

What lessons can we learn from the sliding tile puzzles?

The number of tile movements is large enough that it is difficult or impossible to plan out a complete solution for a sliding tile puzzle from the initial configuration. However, our inability to plan a complete solution does not prevent us from making strategies or employing techniques to systematically solve the puzzle. In solving programming problems, we are sometimes faced with situations where we can't see a clear path to code the solution, but we must never allow this to be an excuse to forgo planning and systematic approaches. It's better to develop a strategy than to attack the problem through trial and error.

I developed my "train" technique from fiddling around with a small puzzle. Often, I use a similar technique in programming. When faced with an onerous problem, I experiment with a reduced version of the problem. These experiments frequently produce valuable insights.

The other lesson is that sometimes problems are divisible in ways that are not immediately obvious. Because moving a tile affects not only that tile but also the possible moves that can be made next, one might think that a sliding tile puzzle must be solved all in one step, not in stages. Looking for a way to divide a problem is usually time well spent. Even if you are unable to find a clean division, you may learn something about the problem that helps you to solve it. When solving problems, working with a specific goal in mind is always better than random effort, whether you achieve that specific goal or not.

Sudoku

The sudoku game has become enormously popular through appearances in newspapers and magazines and also as a web-based and phone-based game. Variations exist, but we will briefly discuss the traditional version.

PROBLEM: COMPLETING A SUDOKU SQUARE

A 9×9 grid is partially filled with single digits (from 1–9), and the player must fill in the empty squares while meeting certain constraints: In each row and column, each digit must appear exactly once, and further, in each marked 3×3 area, each digit must appear exactly once.

If you have played this game before, you probably already have a set of strategies for completing a square in the minimum time. Let's focus on the key starting strategy by looking at the sample square shown in Figure 1-11.

	9	1		6		7		
				8	2		3	9
5		3				2		
			9	1	3		6	2
		2	4		6	8		
1	4		8	2	5			
		9				5		7
6	7		1	5				
		5		4		6	9	

Figure 1-11: An easy sudoku square puzzle

Sudoku puzzles vary in difficulty, their difficulty determined by the number of squares left to be filled. By this measure, this is a very easy puzzle. As 36 squares are already numbered, there are just 45 that must be filled to complete the puzzle. The question is, which squares should we attempt to fill in first?

Remember the puzzle constraints. Each of the nine digits must appear once in every row, in every column, and in every 3×3 area marked by the heavy borders. These rules dictate where we should begin our efforts. The 3×3 area in the middle of the puzzle already has numbers in eight of its nine squares. Therefore, the square in the very center can have only one possible value, the one value not already represented in another square in that 3×3 area. That's where we should start solving this puzzle. The missing number in that area is 7, so we would place that in the middle square.

With that value in place, note that the centermost column now has values in seven of its nine squares, which leaves only two squares remaining, each of which has to have a value not already in the column: The two missing numbers are 3 and 9. The constraint on this column would allow us to put either number in either place, but notice that 3 is already present in the third row and 9 is already present in the seventh row. Therefore, the row constraints dictate that 9 go in the third row of the middle column and 3 go in the seventh row of the middle column. These steps are summarized in Figure 1-12.

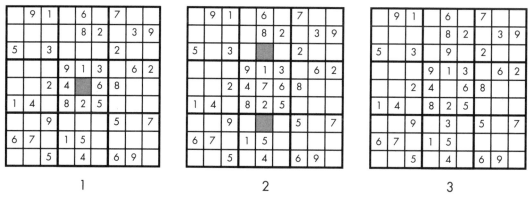

Figure 1-12: The first steps in solving the sample sudoku puzzle

We won't solve the entire puzzle here, but these first steps make the important point that we search for squares that have the lowest number of possible values—ideally, just one.

Lessons Learned

The main lesson from sudoku is that we should look for the most constrained part of the problem. While constraints are often what make a problem difficult to begin with (remember the fox, the goose, and the corn), they may also simplify our thinking about the solution because they eliminate choices.

Although we will not discuss artificial intelligence specifically in this book, there is a rule for solving certain types of problems in artificial intelligence called the "most constrained variable." It means that in a problem where you are trying to assign different values to different variables to meet constraints, you should start with the variable that has the most constraints, or put another way, the variable that has the lowest number of possible values.

Here's an example of this sort of thinking. Suppose a group of coworkers wants to go to lunch together, and they've asked you to find a restaurant that everyone will like. The problem is, each of the coworkers imposes some kind of constraint on the group decision: Pam is a vegetarian, Todd doesn't like Chinese food, and so on. If your goal is to minimize the amount of time it takes to find a restaurant, you should start by talking to the coworker with the most onerous restrictions. If Bob has a number of broad food allergies, for example, it would make sense to start by finding a list of restaurants where he knows he can eat, rather than starting with Todd, whose dislike of Chinese food can be easily mitigated.

The same technique can often be applied to programming problems. If one part of the problem is heavily constrained, that's a great place to start because you can make progress without worrying that you are spending time on work that will later be undone. A related corollary is that you should start with the part that's obvious. If you can solve part of the problem, go ahead and do what you can. You may learn something from seeing your own code that will stimulate your imagination to solve the rest.

The Quarrasi Lock

You may have seen each of the previous puzzles before, but you should not have seen the last one in this chapter unless you have read this book previously, because I've made this one up myself. Read carefully because the wording of this problem is a little complicated.

PROBLEM: OPENING THE ALIEN LOCK

A hostile alien race, the Quarrasi, has landed on Earth, and you've been captured. You've managed to overpower your guards, even though they are enormous and tentacled, but to escape the (still grounded) spaceship, you have to open the massive door. The instructions for opening the door are, oddly enough, printed in English, but it's still no piece of cake. To open the door, you have to slide the three bar-shaped Kratzz along tracks that lead from the right receptor to the left receptor, which lies at the end of the door, 10 feet away.

That's easy enough, but you have to avoid setting off the alarms, which work as follows. On each Kratzz are one or more star-shaped crystal power gems known as Quinicrys. Each receptor has four sensors that light up if the number of Quinicrys in the column above is even. An alarm goes off if the number of lit sensors is ever exactly one. Note that each receptor's alarm is separate: You can't ever have exactly one sensor lit for the left receptor or for the right receptor. The good news is that each alarm is equipped with a suppressor, which keeps the alarm from sounding as long as the button is pressed. If you could press both suppressors at once, the problem would be easy, but you can't since you have short human arms rather than long Quarassi tentacles.

Given all of this, how do you slide the Kratzz to open the door without activating either alarm?

The starting configuration is shown in Figure 1-13, with all three Kratzz in the right receptor. For clarity, Figure 1-14 shows a bad idea: Sliding the uppermost Kratzz to the left receptor causes an alarm state in the right receptor. You might think that we could avoid the alarm with the suppressor, but remember that we just moved the upper Kratzz to the left receptor, so we're 10 feet away from the right receptor's suppressor.

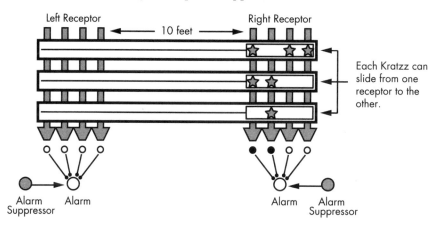

Figure 1-13: Starting configuration for the Quarrasi lock problem. You must slide the three Kratzz bars, currently in the right receptor, to the left receptor without setting off either alarm. A sensor is lit when an even number of star-shaped Quinicrys appear in the column above, and an alarm sounds if exactly one connected sensor lights up. Suppressors can keep an alarm from sounding, but only for the receptor where you are standing.

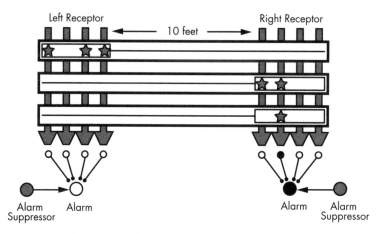

Figure 1-14: The Quarrasi lock in an alarm state. You just slid the upper Kratzz to the left receptor, so the right receptor is out of reach. The second sensor for the right alarm is lit because an even number of Quinicrys appears in the column above, and an alarm sounds when exactly one of its sensors is lit.

Before moving on, take some time to study this problem, and try to develop a solution. Depending on your point of view, this problem is not as hard as it looks. Seriously, think about it before moving on!

Have you thought about it? Were you able to come up with a solution? There are two possible paths to an answer here. The first path is trial and error: attempting various Kratzz moves in a methodical way and backing up to previous steps when you reach an alarm state until you find a series of moves that succeeds.

The second path is realizing that the puzzle is a trick. If you haven't seen the trick yet, here it is: This is just the fox, goose, and corn problem in an elaborate disguise. Although the rules for the alarm are written generally, there are only so many combinations for this specific lock. With only three Kratzz, we just have to know which combinations of Kratzz in a receptor are acceptable. If we label the three Kratzz *top*, *middle*, and *bottom*, then the combinations that create alarms are "top and middle" and "middle and bottom." If we rename *top* as *fox*, *middle* as *goose*, and *bottom* as *corn*, then the troublesome combinations are the same as in the other problem, "fox and goose" and "goose and corn."

This problem is therefore solved in the same way as the fox, goose, and corn problem. We slide the middle Kratzz (goose) over to the left receptacle. Then, we slide the top (fox) to the left, holding the left alarm's suppressor as we put the top (fox) into place. Next, we start sliding the middle (goose) back to the right receptacle. Then, we slide the bottom (corn) to the left, and finally, we slide the middle (goose) to the left once again, opening the lock.

Lessons Learned

The chief lesson here is the importance of recognizing analogies. Here, we can see that the Quarrasi lock problem is analogous to the fox, goose, and corn problem. If we discover that analogy early enough, we can avoid most of the work of the problem by translating our solution from the first problem rather than creating a new solution. Most analogies in problem solving won't be so direct, but they will happen with increasing frequency.

If you had trouble seeing the connection between this problem and the fox, goose, and corn problem, that's because I deliberately included as much extraneous detail as possible. The story that sets up the Quarrasi problem is irrelevant, as are the names for all of the alien technology, which serve to heighten the sense of unfamiliarity. Furthermore, the odd/even mechanism of the alarm makes the problem seem more complicated than it is. If you look at the actual positioning of the Quinicrys, you can see that the top Kratzz and the bottom Kratzz are opposites, so they don't interact in the alarm system. The middle Kratzz, however, interacts with the other two.

Again, if you didn't see the analogy, don't worry. You'll start to recognize them more after you put yourself on alert for them.

General Problem-Solving Techniques

The examples we have discussed demonstrate many of the key techniques that are employed in problem solving. In the rest of this book, we'll look at specific programming problems and figure out ways to solve them, but first we need a general set of techniques and principles. Some problem areas have specific techniques, as we'll see, but the rules below apply to almost any situation. If you make these a regular part of your problem-solving approach, you'll always have a method to attack a problem.

Always Have a Plan

This is perhaps the most important rule. You must always have a plan, rather than engaging in directionless activity.

By this point, you should understand that having a plan is always possible. It's true that if you haven't already solved the problem in your head, then you can't have a plan for implementing a solution in code. That will come later. Even at the beginning, though, you should have a plan for how you are going to find the solution.

To be fair, the plan may require alteration somewhere along the journey, or you may have to abandon your original plan and concoct another. Why, then, is this rule so important? General Dwight D. Eisenhower was famous for saying, "I have always found that plans are useless, but planning is indispensable." He meant that battles are so chaotic that it is impossible to predict everything that could happen and have a predetermined response for every outcome. In that sense, then, plans are useless on the battlefield (another military leader, the Prussian Helmuth von Moltke, famously said that "no plan survives first contact with the enemy"). But no army can succeed without planning and organization. Through planning, a general learns what his army's capabilities are, how the different parts of the army work together, and so on.

In the same way, you must always have a plan for solving a problem. It may not survive first contact with the enemy—it may be discarded as soon as you start to type code into your source editor—but you must have a plan.

Without a plan, you are simply hoping for a lucky break, the equivalent of the randomly typing monkey producing one of the plays of Shakespeare. Lucky breaks are uncommon, and those that occur may still require a plan. Many people have heard the story of the discovery of penicillin: A researcher named Alexander Fleming forgot to close a petri dish one night and in the morning found that mold had inhibited the growth of the bacteria in the dish. But Fleming was not sitting around waiting for a lucky break; he had been experimenting in a thorough and controlled way and thus recognized the importance of what he saw in the petri dish. (If I found mold growing on something I left out the night before, this would not result in an important contribution to science.)

Planning also allows you to set intermediate goals and achieve them. Without a plan, you have only one goal: solve the whole problem. Until you have solved the problem, you won't feel you have accomplished anything. As you have probably experienced, many programs don't do anything useful until they are close to completion. Therefore, working only toward the primary goal inevitably leads to frustration, as there is no positive reinforcement from your efforts until the end. If instead, you create a plan with a series of minor goals, even if some seem tangential to the main problem, you will make measurable progress toward a solution and feel that your time has been spent usefully. At the end of each work session, you'll be able to check off items from your plan, gaining confidence that you will find a solution instead of growing increasingly frustrated.

Restate the Problem

As demonstrated especially by the fox, goose, and corn problem, restating a problem can produce valuable results. In some cases, a problem that looks very difficult may seem easy when stated in a different way or using different terms. Restating a problem is like circling the base of a hill that you must climb; before starting your climb, why not check out the hill from every angle to see whether there's an easier way up?

Restatement sometimes shows us the goal was not what we thought it was. I once read about a grandmother who was watching over her baby granddaughter while knitting. In order to get her knitting done, the grandmother put the baby next to her in a portable play pen, but the baby didn't like being in the pen and kept crying. The grandmother tried all sorts of toys to make the pen more fun for the baby, until she realized that keeping the baby in the pen was just a means to an end. The goal was for the grandmother to be able to knit in peace. The solution: Let the baby play happily on the carpet, while the grandmother knits inside the pen. Restatement can be a powerful technique, but many programmers will skip it because it doesn't directly involve writing code or even designing a solution. This is another reason why having a plan is essential. Without a plan, your only goal is to have working code, and restatement is taking time away from writing code. With a plan, you can put "formally restate the problem" as your first step; therefore, completing the restatement officially counts as progress.

Even if a restatement doesn't lead to any immediate insight, it can help in other ways. For example, if a problem has been assigned to you (by a supervisor or an instructor), you can take your restatement to the person who assigned the problem and confirm your understanding. Also, restating the problem may be a necessary prerequisite step to using other common techniques, like reducing or dividing the problem.

More broadly, restatement can transform whole problem areas. The technique I employ for recursive solutions, which I share in a later chapter, is a method to restate recursive problems so that I can treat them the same as iterative problems.

Divide the Problem

Finding a way to divide a problem into steps or phases can make the problem much easier. If you can divide a problem into two pieces, you might think that each piece would be half as difficult to solve as the original whole, but usually, it's even easier than that.

Here's an analogy that will be familiar if you have already seen common sorting algorithms. Suppose you have 100 files you need to place in a box in alphabetical order, and your basic alphabetizing method is effectively what we call an insertion sort: You take one of the files at random, put it in the box, then put the next file in the box in the correct relationship to the first file, and then continue, always putting the new file in its correct position relative to the other files, so that at any given time, the files in the box are alphabetized. Suppose someone initially separates the files into 4 groups of roughly equal size, A–F, G–M, N–S, and T–Z, and tells you to alphabetize the 4 groups individually and then drop them one after the other into the box.

If each of the groups contained about 25 files, then one might think that alphabetizing 4 groups of 25 is about the same amount of work as alphabetizing a single group of 100. But it's actually far *less* work because the work involved in inserting a single file grows as the number of files already filed grows—you have to look at each file in the box to know where the new file should be placed. (If you doubt this, think of a more extreme version—compare the thought of ordering 50 groups of 2 files, which you could probably do in under a minute, with ordering a single group of 100 files.)

In the same way, dividing a problem can often lower the difficulty by an order of magnitude. Combining programming techniques is much trickier than using techniques alone. For example, a section of code that employs a series of if statements inside a while loop that is itself inside a for loop will be more difficult to write—and to read—than a section of code that employs all those same control statements sequentially.

We'll discuss specific ways to divide problems in the chapters that follow, but you should always be alert to the possibility. Remember that some problems, like our sliding tile puzzle, often hide their potential subdivision. Sometimes the way to find a problem's divisions is to reduce the problem, as we'll discuss shortly.

Start with What You Know

First-time novelists are often given the advice "write what you know." This doesn't mean that novelists should try only to craft works around incidents and people they have directly observed in their own lives; if this were the case, we could never have fantasy novels, historical fiction, or many other popular genres. But it means that the further away a writer gets from his or her own experience, the more difficult writing may be.

In the same way, when programming, you should try to start with what you already know how to do and work outward from there. Once you have divided the problem up into pieces, for example, go ahead and complete any pieces you already know how to code. Having a working partial solution may spark ideas about the rest of the problem. Also, as you may have noticed, a common theme in problem solving is making useful progress to build confidence that you will ultimately complete the task. By starting with what you know, you build confidence and momentum toward the goal.

The "start with what you know" maxim also applies in cases where you haven't divided the problem. Imagine someone made a complete list of every skill in programming: writing a C++ class, sorting a list of numbers, finding the largest value in a linked list, and so on. At every point in your development as a programmer, there will be many skills on this list that you can do well, other skills you can use with effort, and then the other skills that you don't yet know. A particular problem may be entirely solvable with the skills you already have or it may not, but you should fully investigate the problem using the skills already in your head before looking elsewhere. If we think of programming skills as tools and a programming problem as a home repair project, you should try to make the repair using the tools already in your garage before heading to the hardware store.

This technique follows the principles we have already discussed. It follows a plan and gives order to our efforts. When we begin our investigation of a problem by applying the skills we already have, we may learn more about the problem and its ultimate solution.

Reduce the Problem

With this technique, when faced with a problem you are unable to solve, you reduce the scope of the problem, by either adding or removing constraints, to produce a problem that you do know how to solve. We'll see this technique in action in later chapters, but here's a basic example. Suppose you are given a series of coordinates in three-dimensional space, and you must find the coordinates that are closest to each other. If you don't immediately know how to solve this, there are different ways you could reduce the problem to seek a solution. For example, what if the coordinates are in two-dimensional space, instead of three-dimensional space? If that doesn't help, what if the points lie along a single line so that the coordinates are just individual numbers (C++ doubles, let's say)? Now the question essentially becomes, in a list of numbers, find the two numbers with the minimum absolute difference.

Or you could reduce the problem by keeping the coordinates in three-dimensional space but have only three values, instead of an arbitrary-sized series. So instead of an algorithm to find the smallest distance between any two coordinates, it's just a question of comparing coordinate A to coordinate B, then B to C, and then A to C.

These reductions simplify the problem in different ways. The first reduction eliminates the need to compute the distance between three-dimensional points. Maybe we don't know how to do that yet, but until we figure that out, we can still make progress toward a solution. The second reduction, by contrast, focuses almost entirely on computing the distance between three-dimensional points but eliminates the problem of finding a minimal value in an arbitrary-sized series of values.

Of course, to solve the original problem, we will eventually need the skills involved in both reductions. Even so, reduction allows us to work on a simpler problem even when we can't find a way to divide the problem into steps. In effect, it's like a deliberate, but temporary, Kobayashi Maru. We know we're not working on the full problem, but the reduced problem has enough in common with the full problem that we will make progress toward the ultimate solution. Many times, programmers discover they have all the individual skills necessary to solve the problem, and by writing code to solve each individual aspect of the problem, they see how to combine the various pieces of code into a unified whole.

Reducing the problem also allows us to pinpoint exactly where the remaining difficulty lies. Beginning programmers often need to seek out experienced programmers for assistance, but this can be a frustrating experience for everyone involved if the struggling programmer is unable to accurately describe the help that is needed. One never wants to be reduced to saying, "Here's my program, and it doesn't work. Why not?" Using the problem-reduction technique, one can pinpoint the help needed, saying something like, "Here's some code I wrote. As you can see, I know how to find the distance between two three-dimensional coordinates, and I know how to check whether one distance is less than another. But I can't seem to find a general solution for finding the pair of coordinates with the minimum distance."

Look for Analogies

An *analogy*, for our purposes, is a similarity between a current problem and a problem already solved that can be exploited to help solve the current problem. The similarity may take many forms. Sometimes it means the two problems are really the same problem. This is the situation we had with the fox, goose, and corn problem and the Quarrasi lock problem.

Most analogies are not that direct. Sometimes the similarity concerns only part of the problems. For example, two number-processing problems might be different in all aspects except that both of them work with numbers requiring more precision than that given by built-in floating point data types; you won't be able to use this analogy to solve the whole problem, but if you've already figured out a way to handle the extra precision issue, you can handle that same issue the same way again.

Although recognizing analogies is the most important way you will improve your speed and skill at problem solving, it is also the most difficult skill to develop. The reason it is so difficult at first is that you can't look for analogies until you have a storehouse of previous solutions to reference.

This is where developing programmers often try to take a shortcut, finding code that is similar to the needed code and modifying from there. For several reasons, though, this is a mistake. First, if you don't complete a solution yourself, you won't have fully understood and internalized it. Put simply, it's very difficult to correctly modify a program that you don't fully understand. You don't need to have written code to fully understand, but if you could not have written the code, your understanding will be necessarily limited. Second, every successful program you write is more than a solution to a current problem; it's a potential source of analogies to solve future problems. The more you rely on other programmers' code now, the more you will have to rely on it in the future. We'll talk in depth about "good reuse" and "bad reuse" in Chapter 7.

Experiment

Sometimes the best way to make progress is to try things and observe the results. Note that experimentation is not the same as guessing. When you guess, you type some code and hope that it works, having no strong belief that it will. An experiment is a controlled process. You hypothesize what will happen when certain code is executed, try it out, and see whether your hypothesis is correct. From these observations, you gain information that will help you solve the original problem.

Experimentation may be especially helpful when dealing with application programming interfaces or class libraries. Suppose you are writing a program that uses a library class representing a vector (in this context, a one-dimensional array that automatically grows as more items are added), but you've never used this vector class before, and you're not sure what happens when an item is deleted from the vector. Instead of forging ahead with solving the original problem while uncertainties swirl inside your head, you could create a short, separate program just to play around with the vector class and to specifically try out the situations that concern you. If you spend a little time on the "vector demonstrator" program, it might become a reference for future work with the class.

Other forms of experimentation are similar to debugging. Suppose a certain program is producing output that is backward from expectations—for example, if the output is numerical, the numbers are as expected, but in the reverse order. If you don't see why this is occurring after reviewing your code, as an experiment, you might try modifying the code to deliberately make the output backward (run a loop in the reverse direction, perhaps). The resulting change, or lack of change, in the output may reveal the problem in your original source code or may reveal a gap in your understanding. Either way, you're closer to a solution.

Don't Get Frustrated

The final technique isn't so much a technique, but a maxim: Don't get frustrated. When you are frustrated, you won't think as clearly, you won't work as efficiently, and everything will take longer and seem harder. Even worse, frustration tends to feed on itself, so that what begins as mild irritation ends as outright anger.

When I give this advice to new programmers, they often retort that while they agree with my point in principle, they have no control over their frustrations. Isn't asking a programmer not to get frustrated at lack of success like asking a little boy not to yell out if he steps on a tack? The answer is no. When someone steps on a tack, a strong signal is immediately sent through the central nervous system, where the lower depths of the brain respond. Unless you know you're about to step on the tack, it's impossible to react in time to countermand the automatic response from the brain. So we'll let the little boy off the hook for yelling out.

The programmer is not in the same boat. At the risk of sounding like a self-help guru, a frustrated programmer isn't responding to an external stimulus. The frustrated programmer isn't angry with the source code on the monitor, although the programmer may express the frustration in those terms. Instead, the frustrated programmer is angry at himself or herself. The source of the frustration is also the destination, the programmer's mind.

When you allow yourself to get frustrated—and I use the word "allow" deliberately—you are, in effect, giving yourself an excuse to continue to fail. Suppose you're working on a difficult problem and you feel your frustration rise. Hours later, you look back at an afternoon of gritted teeth and pencils snapped in anger and tell yourself that you would have made real progress if you had been able to calm down. In truth, you may have decided that giving in to your anger was easier than facing the difficult problem.

Ultimately, then, avoiding frustration is a decision you must make. However, there are some thoughts you can employ that will help. First of all, never forget the first rule, that you should always have a plan, and that while writing code that solves the original problem is the goal of that plan, it is not the only step of that plan. Thus, if you have a plan and you're following it, then you are making progress and you must believe this. If you've run through all the steps on your original plan and you're still not ready to start coding, then it's time to make another plan.

Also, when it comes down to getting frustrated or taking a break, you should take a break. One trick is to have more than one problem to work on so that if this one problem has you stymied, you can turn your efforts elsewhere. Note that if you successfully divide the problem, you can use this technique on a single problem; just block out the part of the problem that has you stuck, and work on something else. If you don't have another problem you can tackle, get out of your chair and do something else, something that keeps your blood flowing but doesn't make your brain hurt: Take a walk, do the laundry, go through your stretching routine (if you're signing up to be a programmer, sitting at a computer all day, I highly recommend developing a stretching routine!). Don't think about the problem until your break is over.

Exercises

Remember, to truly learn something you have to put it into practice, so work as many exercises as you can. In this first chapter, of course, we're not yet discussing programming, but even so, I encourage you to try some exercises out. Think of these questions as warm-ups for your fingers before we start playing the real music.

1-1.   Try a medium-difficulty sudoku puzzle (you can find these all over the Web and probably in your local newspaper), experimenting with different strategies and taking note of the results. Can you write a general plan for solving a sudoku?

1-2.   Consider a sliding tile puzzle variant where the tiles are covered with a picture instead of numbers. How much does this increase the difficulty, and why?

1-3.   Find a strategy for sliding tile puzzles different from mine.

1-4. Search for old-fashioned puzzles of the fox, goose, and corn variety and try to solve them. Many of the great puzzles were originated or popularized by Sam Loyd, so you might search for his name. Furthermore, once you uncover (or give up and read) the solution, think of how you could make an easier version of the puzzle. What would you have to change? The constraints or just the wording?

1-5. Try to write some explicit strategies for other traditional pencil-and-paper games, like crosswords. Where should you start? What should you do when you're stuck? Even simple newspaper games, like "Jumble," are useful for contemplating strategy.

2

PURE PUZZLES

In this chapter, we'll start dealing with actual code. While intermediate programming knowledge will be needed for later chapters, the programming skills required in this chapter are as simple as can be. That doesn't mean that all of these puzzles will be easy, only that you should be able to focus on the problem solving and not the programming syntax. This is problem solving at its purest. Once you figure out what you want to do, translating your thoughts into C++ code will be straightforward. Remember that reading this book, in itself, provides limited benefit. You should work through any problem that appears nontrivial to you as we discuss it, trying to solve it yourself before reading about my approach. At the end of the chapter, try some of the exercises, many of which will be extensions of the problems we discuss.

Review of C++ Used in This Chapter

This chapter uses the basic C++ with which you should already be familiar, including the control statements if, for, while and do-while, and switch. You may not yet be comfortable writing code to solve original problems with these statements—that's what this book is about, after all. You should, however, understand the syntax of how these statements are written or have a good C++ reference handy.

You should also know how to write and call functions. To keep things simple, we'll use the standard streams cin and cout for input and output. To use these streams, include the necessary header file, iostream, in your code, and add using statements for the two standard stream objects:

```
#include <iostream>
using std::cin;
using std::cout;
```

For brevity, these statements won't be shown in the code listings. Their inclusion is assumed in any program that uses them.

Output Patterns

In this chapter, we will work through three main problems. Because we'll be making extensive use of the problem division and reduction techniques, each of these main problems will spawn several subproblems. In this first section, let's try a series of programs that produce patterned output in a regular shape. Programs like these develop loop-writing skills.

PROBLEM: HALF OF A SQUARE

Write a program that uses only two output statements, cout << "#" and cout << "\n", to produce a pattern of hash symbols shaped like half of a perfect 5 x 5 square (or a right triangle):

```
#####
####
###
##
#
```

Here's another great example of the importance of constraints. If we ignore the requirement that we can use only two output statements, one that produces a single hash symbol and one that produces an end-of-line, we can write a Kobayashi Maru and solve this problem trivially. With that constraint in place, however, we'll have to use loops to solve this problem.

You may already see the solution in your head, but let's assume that you don't. A good first weapon is reduction. How can we reduce this problem to a point where it's easy to solve? What if the pattern was a whole square instead of half of a square?

PROBLEM: A SQUARE
(HALF OF A SQUARE REDUCTION)

Write a program that uses only two output statements, cout << "#" and cout << "\n", to produce a pattern of hash symbols shaped like a perfect 5x5 square:

```
#####
#####
#####
#####
#####
```

This may be enough to get us going, but suppose we didn't know how to tackle this either. We could reduce the problem further, making a single line of hash symbols instead of the square.

PROBLEM: A LINE
(HALF OF A SQUARE FURTHER REDUCTION)

Write a program that uses only two output statements, cout << "#" and cout << "\n", to produce a line of five hash symbols:

```
#####
```

Now we have a trivial problem that can be solved with a for loop:

```
for (int hashNum = 1; hashNum <= 5; hashNum++) {
    cout << "#";
}
cout << "\n";
```

From here, return to the previous reduction, the full square shape. The full square is simply five repetitions of the line of five hash symbols. We know how to make repeating code; we just write a loop. So we can turn our single loop into a double loop:

```
for (int row = 1; row <= 5; row++) {
    for (int hashNum = 1; hashNum <= 5; hashNum++) {
        cout << "#";
    }
    cout << "\n";
}
```

We've placed all of the code from the previous listing in a new loop so that it repeats five times, producing five rows, each row a line of five hash symbols. We're getting closer to the ultimate solution. How do we modify the code so that it produces the half-square pattern? If we look at the last listing and compare it to our desired half-square output, we can see that the problem is in the conditional expression hashNum <= 5. This conditional produces the same line of five hash symbols on each row. What we require is a mechanism to adjust the number of symbols produced on each row so that the first row gets five symbols, the second row gets four, and so on.

To see how to do this, let's make another reduced program experiment. Again, it's always easiest to work on the troublesome part of a problem in isolation. For a moment, let's forget about hash symbols and just talk about numbers.

PROBLEM: COUNT DOWN BY COUNTING UP

Write a line of code that goes in the designated position in the loop in the listing below. The program displays the numbers 5 through 1, in that order, with each number on a separate line.

```
for (int row = 1; row <= 5; row++) {
    cout << ❶ expression << "\n";
}
```

We must find an *expression* ❶ that is 5 when row is 1, 4 when row is 2, and so on. If we want an expression that decreases as row increases, our first thought might be to stick a minus sign in front of the values of row by multiplying row by –1. This produces numbers that go down, but not the desired numbers. We may be closer than we think, though. What's the difference between the desired value and the value given by multiplying row by –1? Table 2-1 summarizes this analysis.

Table 2-1: Computation of Desired Value from Row Variable

Row	Desired Value	Row * –1	Difference from Desired Value
1	5	–1	6
2	4	–2	6
3	3	–3	6
4	2	–4	6
5	1	–5	6

The difference is a fixed value, 6. This means the expression we need is row * -1 + 6. Using a little algebra, we can simplify this to 6 - row. Let's try it out:

```
for (int row = 1; row <= 5; row++) {
    cout << 6 - row << "\n";
}
```

Great—it works! If this hadn't worked, our mistake probably would have been minor, because of the careful steps we have taken. Again, it's very easy to experiment with a block of code that is this small and simple. Now let's take this expression, and use it to limit the inner loop:

```
for (int row = 1; row <= 5; row++) {
    for (int hashNum = 1; hashNum <= 6 - row; hashNum++) {
        cout << "#";
    }
    cout << "\n";
}
```

Using the reduction technique requires more steps to get from the description to the completed program, but each step is easier. Think of using a series of pulleys to lift a heavy object: You have to pull the rope farther to get the same amount of lift, but each pull is much easier on your muscles.

Let's tackle another shape problem before moving on.

PROBLEM: A SIDEWAYS TRIANGLE

Write a program that uses only two output statements, cout << "#" and cout << "\n", to produce a pattern of hash symbols shaped like a sideways triangle:

```
#
##
###
####
###
##
#
```

We're not going to go through all the steps we used on the previous problem, because we don't need to. This "Sideways Triangle" problem is analogous to the "Half of a Square" problem, so we can use what we have learned from the latter in the former. Remember the "start with what you know" maxim? Let's start by listing skills and techniques from the "Half of a Square" problem that can be applied to this problem. We know how to:

- Display a row of symbols of a particular length using a loop

- Display a series of rows using nested loops

- Create a varying number of symbols in each row using an algebraic expression instead of a fixed value

- Discover the correct algebraic expression through experimentation and analysis

Figure 2-1 summarizes our current position. The first row shows the previous "Half of a Square" problem. We see the desired pattern of hash symbols (a), the line pattern (b), the square pattern (c), and the number sequence (d) that will transform the square pattern to the half-a-square pattern. The second row shows the current "Sideways Triangle" problem. We again see the desired pattern (e), the line (f), a rectangle pattern (g), and a number sequence (h).

At this point, we will have no problem producing (f) because it is almost the same as (b). And we should be able to produce (g) because it is just (c) with more rows and one fewer symbol per row. Finally, if someone were to give us the algebraic expression that would produce the number sequence (h), we would have no difficulty creating the desired pattern (e).

Thus, most of the mental work required to create a solution for the "Sideways Triangle" problem has already been done. Furthermore, we know exactly what mental work remains: figuring out an expression to produce the number sequence (h). So that's where we should direct our attention. We could either take the finished code for the "Half of a Square"

```
#####              #####   5
####               #####   4
###        #####   #####   3
##                 #####   2
#                  #####   1

(a)        (b)     (c)     (d)

#                  ####    1
##                 ####    2
###                ####    3
####       ####    ####    4
###                ####    3
##                 ####    2
#                  ####    1

(e)        (f)     (g)     (h)
```

Figure 2-1: Various components needed to solve the shape problems

problem and experiment until we can produce the desired numbered sequence or take a guess and make a table like Table 2-1 to see whether that jogs our creativity.

Let's try experimenting this time. In the "Half of a Square" problem, subtracting the row from a larger number worked well, so let's see what numbers we get by running row in a loop from 1 to 7 and subtracting row from 8. The result is shown in Figure 2-2 (b). That's not what we want. Where do we go from here? In the previous problem, we needed a number that went down instead of up, so we subtracted our loop variable from a greater number. In this problem, we need to go up first and then down. Would it make sense to subtract from a number in the middle? If we replace the 8 - row in the previous code with 4 - row, we get the result in Figure 2-2 (c). That's not right either, but it looks like it could be a useful pattern if we don't look at the minus signs on the last three numbers. What if we used the absolute value function to remove those minus signs? The expression abs(4 - row) produces the results in Figure 2-2 (d). We're so close now—I can almost taste it! It's just that we are going down first and then up when we need to go up first and then down. But how do we get from the number sequence we have to the number sequence we need?

Let's try looking at the numbers in Figure 2-2 (d) in a different way. What if we count the empty spaces instead of the hash marks, as shown in Figure 2-2 (e)? Column (d) *is* the right pattern of values if we count the empty spaces. To get the right number of hash marks, think of each row as having four boxes, and then subtract the number of empty spaces. If each row has four boxes of which abs(4 - row) are empty spaces, then the number of boxes with hash marks will be given by 4 - abs(4 - row). That works. Plug it in, and try it out.

(a)	(b)	(c)	(d)	(e)
1	7	3	3	#
2	6	2	2	##
3	5	1	1	###
4	4	0	0	####
3	3	-1	1	###
2	2	-2	2	##
1	1	-3	3	#

Figure 2-2: Various components needed to solve the "Sideways Triangle" problem

We have avoided most of the work for this problem through analogy and have solved the rest through experimentation. This one-two punch is a great approach when a new problem is very similar to another you can already solve.

Input Processing

The previous programs only produced output. Let's change things up and try programs that are all about processing the input. Each of these programs shares one constraint: The input will be read character by character, and the program must process each character before reading the next one. In other words, the programs will not store the characters in a data structure for later processing but process as they go.

In this first problem, we'll perform identification number validation. In the modern world, almost everything has an identification number, such as an ISBN or a customer number. Sometimes these numbers have to be entered by hand, which introduces the potential for error. If a mistakenly entered number doesn't match any valid identification number, the system can easily reject it. But what if the number is wrong, yet valid? For example, what if a cashier, attempting to credit your account for a product return, enters another customer's account number? The other customer would receive your credit. To avoid this situation, systems have been developed to detect mistakes in identification numbers. They work by running the identification number through a formula that generates one or more extra digits, which become part of an extended identification number. If any of the digits are changed, the original part of the number and the extra digits will no longer match, and the number can be rejected.

PROBLEM: LUHN CHECKSUM VALIDATION

The Luhn formula is a widely used system for validating identification numbers. Using the original number, double the value of every other digit. Then add the values of the individual digits together (if a doubled value now has two digits, add the digits individually). The identification number is valid if the sum is divisible by 10.

Write a program that takes an identification number of arbitrary length and determines whether the number is valid under the Luhn formula. The program must process each character before reading the next one.

The process sounds a little complicated, but an example will make everything clearer. Our program will only validate an identification number, not create the check digit. Let's walk through both ends of the process: computing a check digit and validating the result. This process is demonstrated in Figure 2-3. In part (a), we compute the check digit. The original identification number, 176248, is shown in the dashed-line box. Every other digit, starting from the rightmost digit of the original number (which, after the addition of the check digit, will be the second rightmost), is doubled. Then each digit is added together. Note that when doubling a digit results in a two-digit number, each of those digits is considered separately. For example, when 7 is doubled to produce 14, it's not *14* that is added to the checksum, but *1* and *4* individually. In this case, the checksum is 27, so the check digit is 3 because that's the digit value that would make the overall sum 30. Remember, the checksum of the final number should be divisible by 10; in other words, it should end in 0.

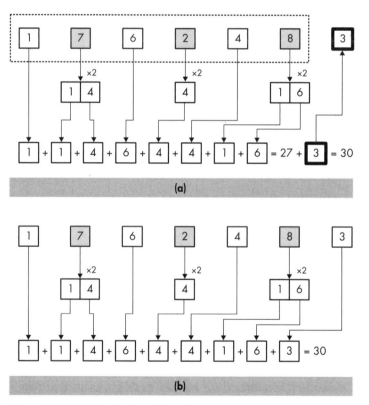

Figure 2-3: The Luhn checksum formula

In part (b), we validate the number 1762483, which now includes the check digit. This is the process we will be using for this problem. As before, we double every second digit, starting with the digit to the left of the check digit, and add the values of all digits, including the check digit, to determine the checksum. Because the checksum is divisible by 10, this number validates.

Breaking Down the Problem

The program that will solve this problem has several separate issues we will have to handle. One issue is the doubling of digits, which is tricky because doubled digits are determined from the right end of the identification number. Remember, we're not going to read and store all of the digits and *then* process. We're going to process as we go. The problem is that we'll be getting the digits left to right, but we really need them right to left in order to know which digits to double. We would know which digits to double if we knew how many digits were in the identification number, but we don't because the problem states that the identification number is of arbitrary length. Another issue is that doubled numbers 10 and greater must be treated according to their individual digits. Also, we have to determine when we've read the whole identification number. Finally, we have to figure out how to read the number digit by digit. In other words, the user is going to enter one long number, but we want to read it as though the digits were entered as separate numbers.

Because we always want to have a plan, we should make a list of these issues and tackle them one by one:

- Knowing which digits to double
- Treating doubled numbers 10 and greater according to their individual digits
- Knowing we've reached the end of the number
- Reading each digit separately

To solve problems, we'll be working on individual pieces before writing a final solution. Thus, there is no need to work on these issues in any particular order. Start with the issue that looks the easiest or, if you want a challenge, the one that looks the most difficult. Or just start with the one that's the most interesting.

Let's begin by tackling the doubled digits that are 10 and greater. This is a situation where problem constraints make things easier rather than more difficult. Computing the sum of the digits of an arbitrary integer could be a good amount of work by itself. But what is the range of possible values here? If we start with individual digits 0–9 and double them, the maximum value is 18. Therefore, there are only two possibilities. If the doubled value is a single digit, then there's nothing more to do. If the doubled value is 10 or greater, then it must be in the range 10–18, and therefore the first digit is always 1. Let's do a quick code experiment to confirm this approach:

```cpp
   int digit;
   cout << "Enter a single digit number, 0-9: ";
   cin >> digit;
❶  int doubledDigit = digit * 2;
   int sum;
❷  if (doubledDigit >= 10) sum = ❸1 + doubledDigit % 10;
   else sum = doubledDigit;
❹  cout << "Sum of digits in doubled number: " << sum << "\n";
```

The % operator is called the modulo operator. *For positive integers, it returns the remainder of integer division. For example, 12 % 10 would be 2 because after dividing 10 into 12, the 2 is left over.*

This is straightforward code: the program reads the digit, doubles it ❶, sums the digits of the doubled number ❷, and outputs the sum ❹. The heart of the experiment is the calculation of the sum for a doubled number that is greater than 10 ❸. As with the calculation of the number of hash marks needed for a particular row in our shapes problems, isolating this calculation to a short program of its own makes experimentation easy. Even if we don't get the correct formula at first, we're sure to find it quickly.

Before we scratch this issue off our list, let's turn this code into a short function we can use to simplify future code listings:

```
int doubleDigitValue(int digit) {
    int doubledDigit = digit * 2;
    int sum;
    if (doubledDigit >= 10) sum = 1 + doubledDigit % 10;
    else sum = doubledDigit;
    return sum;
}
```

Now let's work on reading the individual digits of the identification number. Again, we could tackle a different issue next if we wanted, but I think this issue is a good choice because it will allow us to type the identification number naturally when testing the other parts of the problem.

If we read the identification number as a numeric type (int, for example), we'd just get one long number and have a lot of work ahead of us. Plus, there's a limit to how big an integer we can read, and the question says the identification number is of arbitrary length. Therefore, we'll have to read character by character. This means that we need to make sure we know how to read a character representing a digit and turn it into an integer type we can work with mathematically. To see what would happen if we took the character value and used it in an integer expression directly, take a look at the following listing, which includes sample output.

```
  char digit;
  cout << "Enter a one-digit number: ";
❶ digit = cin.get();
  int sum = digit;
  cout << "Is the sum of digits " << sum << "? \n";

❷ Enter a one-digit number: 7
  Is the sum of digits 55?
```

Note that we use the get method ❶ because the basic extraction operator (as in cin >> digit) skips whitespace. That's not a problem here, but as you'll see, it would cause trouble later. In the sample input and output ❷, you see the problem. All computer data is essentially numeric, so individual characters are represented by integer character codes. Different operating systems may use different character code systems, but in this text we'll focus on the common ASCII system. In this system, the character 7 is stored as the character code value 55, so when we treat the value as an integer, 55 is what we get. We need a mechanism to turn the *character* 7 into the *integer* 7.

PROBLEM: CONVERT CHARACTER DIGIT TO INTEGER

Write a program that reads a character from the user representing a digit, 0 through 9. Convert the character to the equivalent integer in the range 0–9, and then output the integer to demonstrate the result.

In the shape problems of the previous section, we had a variable with one range of values that we wanted to convert to another range of values. We made a table with columns for the original values and desired values and then checked the difference between the two. This is an analogous problem, and we can use the table idea again, as in Table 2-2.

Table 2-2: Character Codes and Desired Integer Values

Character	Character Code	Desired Integer	Difference
0	48	0	48
1	49	1	48
2	50	2	48
3	51	3	48
4	52	4	48
5	53	5	48
6	54	6	48
7	55	7	48
8	56	8	48
9	57	9	48

The difference between the character code and the desired integer is always 48, so all we have to do is subtract that value. You might have noticed that this is the character code value for the zero character, 0. This will always be true because character code systems always store the digit characters in order, starting from 0. We can therefore make a more general, and more readable, solution by subtracting the character 0 rather than using a predetermined value, like 48:

```
char digit;
cout << "Enter a one-digit number: ";
cin >> digit;
int sum = digit - '0';
cout << "Is the sum of digits " << sum << "? \n";
```

Now we can move on to figuring out which digits to double. This part of the problem may take several steps to figure out, so let's try a problem reduction. What if we initially limited ourselves to a fixed-length number? That would confirm our understanding of the general formula while making progress toward the ultimate goal. Let's try limiting the length to six; this is long enough to be a good representation of the overall challenge.

PROBLEM: LUHN CHECKSUM VALIDATION, FIXED LENGTH

Write a program that takes an identification number (including its check digit) of length six and determines whether the number is valid under the Luhn formula. The program must process each character before reading the next one.

As before, we can reduce even further to make getting started as easy as possible. What if we changed the formula so that none of the digits is doubled? Then the program only has to read the digits and sum them.

PROBLEM: SIMPLE CHECKSUM VALIDATION, FIXED LENGTH

Write a program that takes an identification number (including its check digit) of length six and determines whether the number is valid under a simple formula where the values of each digit are summed and the result checked to see whether it is divisible by 10. The program must process each character before reading the next one.

Because we know how to read an individual digit as a character, we can solve this fixed-length, simple checksum problem pretty easily. We just need to read six digits, sum them, and determine whether the sum is divisible by 10.

```
char digit;
int checksum = 0;
cout << "Enter a six-digit number: ";
for (int position = 1; position <= 6; position ++) {
   cin >> digit;
   checksum += digit - '0';
}
cout << "Checksum is " << checksum << ". \n";
if (checksum % 10 == 0) {
   cout << "Checksum is divisible by 10. Valid. \n";
} else {
   cout << "Checksum is not divisible by 10. Invalid. \n";
}
```

From here, we need to add the logic for the actual Luhn validation formula, which means doubling every other digit starting from the second digit from the right. Since we are currently limiting ourselves to six-digit numbers, we need to double the digits in positions one, three, and five, counting from the left. In other words, we double the digit if the position is odd. We can identify odd and even positions using the modulo (%) operator because the definition of an even number is that it is evenly divisible by two. So if the result of the expression position % 2 is 1, position is odd and we should double. It's important to remember that *doubling* here means both doubling the individual digit and also summing the digits of the doubled number if the doubling results in a number 10 or greater. This is where our previous function really helps. When we need to double a digit according to the Luhn formula, we just send it to our function and use the result. Putting this together, just change the code inside the for loop from the previous listing:

```
for (int position  = 1; position  <= 6; position++) {
   cin >> digit;
   if (position % 2 == 0) checksum += digit - '0';
      else checksum += doubleDigitValue(digit - '0');
}
```

We've accomplished a lot on this problem so far, but there are still a couple of steps to go before we can write the code for arbitrary-length identification numbers. To ultimately solve this problem, we need to divide and conquer. Suppose I asked you to modify the previous code for numbers with 10 or 16 digits. That would be trivial—you'd only have to change the 6 used as the upper bound of the loop to another value. But suppose I asked you to validate seven-digit numbers. That would require a small additional modification because if the number of digits is odd and we are doubling every digit starting from the second on the right, the first digit *on the left* is no longer doubled. In this case, you need to double the even positions: 2, 4, 6, and so on. Putting aside that issue for the moment, let's figure out how to handle any even-length number.

The first issue we face is determining when we have reached the end of the number. If the user enters a multidigit number and presses ENTER and we're reading the input character by character, what character is read after the last digit? This actually varies based on the operating system, but we'll just write an experiment:

```
cout << "Enter a number: ";
char digit;
while (true) {
   digit = cin.get();
   cout << int(digit) << " ";
}
```

This loop runs forever, but it does the job. I typed in the number 1234 and pressed ENTER. The result was 49 50 51 52 10 (based on ASCII; this will vary based on the operating system). Thus, 10 is what I'm looking for. With that information in hand, we can replace the for loop in our previous code with a while loop:

```
   char digit;
   int checksum = 0;
❶ int position = 1;
   cout << "Enter a number with an even number of digits: ";
❷ digit = cin.get();
   while ❸(digit != 10) {
    ❹if (position % 2 == 0) checksum += digit - '0';
      else checksum += doubledDigitValue(digit - '0');
    ❺digit = cin.get();
    ❻position++;
   }
   cout << "Checksum is " << checksum << ". \n";
   if (checksum % 10 == 0) {
      cout << "Checksum is divisible by 10. Valid. \n";
   } else {
      cout << "Checksum is not divisible by 10. Invalid. \n";
   }
```

In this code, position is no longer the control variable in a for loop, so we must initialize ❶ and increment it separately ❻. The loop is now controlled by the conditional expression ❸, which checks for the character code value that signals the end-of-line. Because we need a value to check the first time we go through the loop, we read the first value before the loop begins ❷ and then read each subsequent value inside the loop ❺, after the processing code.

Again, this code will handle a number of any even length. To handle a number of any odd length, we'd need only to modify the processing code, reversing the logic of the if statement condition ❹ in order to double the numbers at the even positions, rather than the odd positions.

That, at least, exhausts every possibility. The length of the identification number must be odd or even. If we knew the length ahead of time, we would know whether to double the odd positions or the even positions in the number. We don't have that information, however, until we have reached the end of the number. Is a solution impossible given these constraints? If we know how to solve the problem for an odd number of digits and for an even number of digits but don't know how many digits are in the number until we've read it completely, how can we solve this problem?

You may already see the answer to this problem. If you don't, it's not because the answer is difficult but because it is hidden in the details. What we could use here is an analogy, but we haven't seen an analogous situation so far. Instead, we'll make our own analogy. Let's make a problem that is explicitly about this very situation and see whether staring the problem in the face helps us find a solution. Clear your mind of preconceptions based on the work so far, and read the following problem.

PROBLEM: POSITIVE OR NEGATIVE

Write a program that reads 10 integers from the user. After all the numbers have been entered, the user may ask to display the count of positive numbers or the count of negative numbers.

This is a simple problem, one that doesn't seem to have any complications at all. We just need one variable that counts the positive numbers and another variable that counts the negative numbers. When the user specifies the request at the end of the program, we just need to consult the proper variable for the response:

```
int number;
int positiveCount = 0;
int negativeCount = 0;
for (int i = 1; i <= 10; i++) {
   cin >> number;
   if (number > 0) positiveCount++;
   if (number < 0) negativeCount++;
}
char response;
cout << "Do you want the (p)ositive or (n)egative count? ";
cin >> response;
if (response == 'p')
   cout << "Positive count is " << positiveCount << "\n";
if (response == 'n')
    out << "Negative count is " << negativeCount << "\n";
```

This shows the method we need to use for the Luhn checksum problem: Keep track of the running checksum both ways, as if the identification number is an odd length and again as if it is an even length. When we get to the end of the number and discover the true length, we'll have the correct checksum in one variable or the other.

Putting the Pieces Together

We've now checked off everything on our original "to-do" list. It's time to put everything together and solve this problem. Because we've solved all of the subproblems separately, we know exactly what we need to do and can use our previous programs as reference to produce the final result quickly:

```
char digit;
int oddLengthChecksum = 0;
int evenLengthChecksum = 0;
int position = 1;
cout << "Enter a number: ";
digit = cin.get();
while (digit != 10) {
```

```
        if (position % 2 == 0) {
            oddLengthChecksum += doubleDigitValue(digit - '0');
            evenLengthChecksum += digit - '0';
        } else {
            oddLengthChecksum += digit - '0';
            evenLengthChecksum += doubleDigitValue(digit - '0');
        }
        digit = cin.get();
        position++;
    }
    int checksum;
❶  if ((position - 1) % 2 == 0) checksum = evenLengthChecksum;
    else checksum = oddLengthChecksum;
    cout << "Checksum is " << checksum << ". \n";
    if (checksum % 10 == 0) {
        cout << "Checksum is divisible by 10. Valid. \n";
    } else {
        cout << "Checksum is not divisible by 10. Invalid. \n";
    }
```

Note that when we check to see whether the length of the input number is odd or even ❶, we subtract 1 from position. We do this because the last character we read in the loop will be the terminating end-of-line, not the last digit of the number. We could also have written the test expression as (position % 2 == 1), but that's more confusing to read. In other words, it's better to say "if position - 1 is even, use the even checksum" than "if position is odd, use the even checksum" and have to remember why that makes sense.

This is the longest code listing we've looked at so far, but I don't need to annotate everything in the code and describe how each part works because you've already seen each part in isolation. This is the power of having a plan. It's important to note, though, that *my* plan is not necessarily *your* plan. The issues I saw in the original description of the problem and the steps I took to work through those issues are likely to differ from what you would've seen and done. Your background as a programmer and the problems you have successfully completed determine which parts of the problem are trivial or difficult and thus what steps you need to take to solve the problem. There may have been a point in the previous section where I took what looked like a needless detour to figure out something that was already obvious to you. Conversely, there may have been a point where I nimbly skipped over something that was tricky for you. Also, if you'd worked through this yourself, you might have come up with an equally successful program that looked quite different from mine. There is no one "right" solution for a problem, as any program that meets all constraints counts as a solution, and for any solution, there is no one "right" way of reaching it.

Seeing all the steps that we took to reach the solution, along with the relative brevity of the final code, you might be tempted to try to trim steps in your own problem-solving process. I would caution against this impulse. It's always better to take more steps than to try to do too much at once, even if some steps seem trivial. Remember what the goals are in problem solving. The primary goal is, of course, to find a program that solves the stated problem and meets all constraints. The secondary goal is to find that program in the minimal amount of time. Minimizing the number of steps isn't a goal, and no one has to know how many steps you took. Consider trying to reach the summit of a steep hill that has a shallow but long and winding path. Ignoring the path and climbing the hill directly from the base to the peak will certainly require fewer steps than following the path—but is it faster? The most likely outcome of a direct climb is that you give up and collapse.

Also remember the last of my general rules for problem solving: *Avoid frustration.* The more work you try to do in each step, the more you invite potential frustration. Even if you back off a difficult step and break it up into substeps, the damage will have been done because psychologically you'll feel like you're going backward instead of making progress. When I coach beginning programmers in a step-by-step approach, I sometimes have a student complain, "Hey, that step was too easy." To which I reply, "What are you complaining about?" If you've taken a problem that initially looked tough and broken it down into pieces so small that every piece is trivial to accomplish, I say: Congratulations! That's just what you should hope for.

Tracking State

The last problem we'll work through for this chapter is also the most difficult. This problem has a lot of different pieces and a complicated description, which will illustrate the importance of breaking down a complex problem.

PROBLEM: DECODE A MESSAGE

A message has been encoded as a text stream that is to be read character by character. The stream contains a series of comma-delimited integers, each a positive number capable of being represented by a C++ *int*. However, the character represented by a particular integer depends on the current *decoding mode*. There are three modes: *uppercase, lowercase,* and *punctuation.*

In *uppercase* mode, each integer represents an uppercase letter: The integer modulo 27 indicates the letter of the alphabet (where 1 = A and so on). So an input value of 143 in uppercase mode would yield the letter *H* because 143 modulo 27 is 8 and *H* is the eighth letter in the alphabet.

The *lowercase* mode works the same but with lowercase letters; the remainder of dividing the integer by 27 represents the lowercase letter (1 = a and so on). So an input value of 56 in lowercase mode would yield the letter *b* because 56 modulo 27 is 2 and *b* is the second letter in the alphabet.

In *punctuation* mode, the integer is instead considered modulo 9, with the interpretation given by Table 2-3 below. So 19 would yield an exclamation point because 19 modulo 9 is 1.

At the beginning of each message, the decoding mode is uppercase letters. Each time the modulo operation (by 27 or 9, depending on mode) results in 0, the decoding mode switches. If the current mode is uppercase, the mode switches to lowercase letters. If the current mode is lowercase, the mode switches to punctuation, and if it is punctuation, it switches back to uppercase.

Table 2-3: Punctuation Decoding Mode

Number	Symbol
1	!
2	?
3	,
4	.
5	(space)
6	;
7	"
8	'

As with the Luhn validation formula, we're going to walk through a concrete example to make sure we have all the steps straight. Figure 2-4 demonstrates a sample decoding. The original input stream is shown at the top. The processing steps proceed from the top down. Column (a) shows the current number in the input. Column (b) is the current mode, cycling from uppercase (U) to lowercase (L) to punctuation (P). Column (c) shows the divisor for the current mode. Column (d) is the remainder of dividing the current divisor in column (c) into the current input from column (a). The result is shown in column (e), either a character or, if the result in (d) is 0, a switch to the next mode in the cycle.

As with the previous problem, we can start by explicitly considering the skills we'll need to craft a solution. We need to read a string of characters until we reach an end-of-line. The characters represent a series of integers, so we need to read digit characters and convert them to integers for further processing. Once we have the integers, we need to convert the integer into a single character for output. Finally, we need some way to track the decoding mode so we know whether the current integer should be decoded into a lowercase letter, uppercase letter, or punctuation. Let's turn this into a formal list:

- Read character by character until we reach an end-of-line.
- Convert a series of characters representing a number to an integer.
- Convert an integer 1–26 into an uppercase letter.
- Convert an integer 1–26 into a lowercase letter.
- Convert an integer 1–8 into a punctuation symbol based on Table 2-3.
- Track a decoding mode.

The first item is something we already know how to do from the previous problem. Furthermore, although we only dealt with individual digits in the Luhn validation formula, I suspect some of what we did there will also be helpful on the second item of our list. The finished code for the Luhn algorithm is probably still fresh in your mind, but if you put the book down between that problem and this one, you'll want to go back and review that code. In general, when the description of a current problem "rings bells," you'll want to dig out any similar code from your archives for study.

Original input:
18,12312,171,763,98423,1208,216,11,500,18,241,0,32,20620,27,10

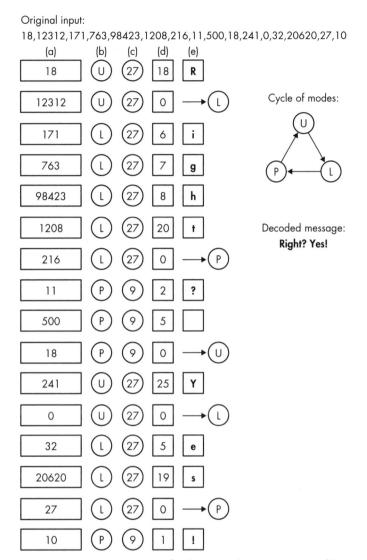

Figure 2-4: Sample processing for the "Decode a Message" problem

Let's get down to business on the items that remain. You may have noticed that I've made each of the conversions a separate item. I suspect that converting a number into a lowercase letter is going to be very similar to converting a number into an uppercase letter, but perhaps converting to a punctuation symbol will require something different. In any case, there's no real downside to chopping up the list too finely; it just means you'll be able to cross things off the list more often.

Let's start with those integer-to-character conversions. From the Luhn formula program, we know the code required to read a character digit 0–9 and convert it to an integer in the range 0–9. How can we extend this method to deal with multidigit numbers? Let's consider the simplest possibility: two-digit numbers. This looks straightforward. In a two-digit number, the first digit is the tens digit, so we should multiply this individual digit by 10, and then add the value of the second digit. For example, if the number were 35, after reading the individual digits as characters 3 and 5, and converting these to the integers 3 and 5, we would obtain the overall integer we need by the expression 3 * 10 + 5. Let's confirm this with code:

```
cout << "Enter a two-digit number: ";
char digitChar1 = cin.get();
char digitChar2 = cin.get();
int digit1 = digitChar1 - '0';
int digit2 = digitChar2 - '0';
int overallNumber = digit1 * 10 + digit2;
cout << "That number as an integer: " << overallNumber << "\n";
```

That works—the program outputs same two-digit number that we put in. We encounter a problem, however, when we try to extend this method. This program uses two different variables to hold the two character inputs, and while that causes no problems here, we certainly don't want to extend that as a general solution. If we did, we would need as many variables as we have digits. That would get messy, and it would be difficult to modify if the range of possible numbers in the input stream varied. We need a more general solution to this subproblem of converting characters to integers. The first step to finding that general solution is to reduce the previous code to just two variables—one char and one int:

```
cout << "Enter a two-digit number: ";
❶ char digitChar = cin.get();
❷ int overallNumber = (digitChar - '0') * 10;
```

```
❸  digitChar = cin.get();
❹  overallNumber += (digitChar - '0');
   cout << "That number as an integer: " << overallNumber << "\n";
```

We accomplish this by doing all the calculations on the first digit before reading the second digit. After reading the first character digit ❶ in one step, we convert to an integer, multiply by 10, and store the result ❷. After reading the second digit ❸, we add its integer value to the running total ❹. This is equivalent to the previous code while using only two variables, one for the last character read and one for the overall value of the integer. The next step is to consider extending this method to three-digit numbers. Once we do that, we're likely to see a pattern that will allow us to create a general solution for any number of digits.

When we try this, though, we encounter a problem. With the two-digit number, we multiplied the left digit by 10 because the left digit was in the tens position. The leftmost digit in a three-digit number would be in the hundreds position, so we would need to multiply that digit by 100. Then we could read in the middle digit, multiply it by 10, add it to the running total, and then read in the last digit and add it, as well. That should work, but it's not heading us in the direction of a general solution. Do you see the problem? Consider the previous statement: *The leftmost digit in a three-digit number would be in the hundreds position.* For a general solution, we won't know how many digits are in each number until we reach the next comma. The leftmost digit in a number with an unknown quantity of digits can't be labeled in the hundreds position or any other position. So how do we know what multiplier to use for each digit before adding to the running total? Or do we need another approach entirely?

As always, when stuck, it's a good idea to create a simplified problem to work on. The issue here is not knowing how many digits the number is going to have. The simplest problem that deals with this issue would be one that has just two possible digit counts.

PROBLEM: READING A NUMBER WITH THREE OR FOUR DIGITS

Write a program to read a number character by character and convert it to an integer, using just one char variable and one int variable. The number will have either three or four digits.

This issue of not knowing the count of characters until the end but needing the count right from the beginning is analogous to the issue in the Luhn formula. In the Luhn formula, we didn't know whether the identification number had an odd or even length. In that case, our solution was to calculate the results two different ways and choose the appropriate one at the end. Could we do something like that here? If the number is either three or four digits, there are only two possibilities. If the number has three digits, the leftmost digit is the hundreds digit. If the number has four digits, the leftmost digit is the thousands digit. We could compute as if we had a three-digit number and as if we had a four-digit number and then choose the right number at the end, but the problem description allows us to have only one numeric variable. Let's relax that restriction to make some progress.

PROBLEM: READING A NUMBER WITH THREE OR FOUR DIGITS, FURTHER SIMPLIFIED

Write a program to read a number character by character and convert it to an integer, using just one char variable and two int variables. The number will have either three or four digits.

Now we can put the "compute it both ways" method to work. We'll process the first three digits two different ways and then see whether there is a fourth digit:

```
cout << "Enter a three-digit or four-digit number: ";
char digitChar = cin.get();
❶ int threeDigitNumber = (digitChar - '0') * 100;
❷ int fourDigitNumber = (digitChar - '0') * 1000;
digitChar = cin.get();
threeDigitNumber += (digitChar - '0') * 10;
fourDigitNumber += (digitChar - '0') * 100;
digitChar = cin.get();
threeDigitNumber += (digitChar - '0');
fourDigitNumber += (digitChar - '0') * 10;
digitChar = cin.get();
if ❸(digitChar == 10) {
    cout << "Number entered: " << threeDigitNumber << "\n";
} else {
    ❹fourDigitNumber += (digitChar - '0');
    cout << "Number entered: " << fourDigitNumber << "\n";
}
```

After reading the leftmost digit, we multiply its integer value by 100, and store it in our three-digit variable ❶. We also multiply the integer value by 1,000, and store it in our four-digit variable ❷. This pattern continues for the next two digits. The second digit is treated both as a tens digit in a three-digit number and as a hundreds digit in a four-digit number. The third digit is treated as both a ones and a tens digit. After reading the fourth character, we check to see whether it's an end-of-line by comparing it to the number 10 ❸ (as in the previous problem, this value may vary per operating system). If it is an end-of-line, the input was a three-digit number. If not, we still need to add the ones digit to the total ❹.

Now we need to figure out how to get rid of one of the integer variables. Suppose we removed the variable fourDigitNumber entirely. The value of threeDigitNumber would still be correctly assigned, but when we reached a point where we needed fourDigitNumber, we wouldn't have it. Using the value in threeDigitNumber, is there some way to determine the value that would have been in `fourDigitNumber`? Suppose the original input was **1234**. After reading the first three digits, the value in `threeDigitNumber` would be 123; the value that would have been in `fourDigitNumber` is 1230. In general, since the multipliers for `fourDigitNumber` are 10 times those of `threeDigitNumber`, the former would always be 10 times the latter. Thus, only one integer variable is needed because the other variable can just be multiplied by 10 if necessary:

```
cout << "Enter a three-digit or four-digit number: ";
char digitChar = cin.get();
int number = (digitChar - '0') * 100;
digitChar = cin.get();
number += (digitChar - '0') * 10;
digitChar = cin.get();
number += (digitChar - '0');
digitChar = cin.get();
if (digitChar == 10) {
    cout << "Number entered: " << number << "\n";
} else {
    number = number * 10 + (digitChar - '0');
    cout << "Number entered: " << number << "\n";
}
```

Now we have an exploitable pattern. Consider expanding this code to handle five-digit numbers. After computing the right value for the first four digits, we would repeat the same process we followed for reading the fourth character instead of displaying the result immediately: Read a fifth character, check to see whether it's an end-of-line, display the previously computed number if it is—otherwise, multiply by 10, and add the digit value of the current character:

```
cout << "Enter a number with three, four, or five digits: ";
char digitChar = cin.get();
int number = (digitChar - '0') * 100;
digitChar = cin.get();
number += (digitChar - '0') * 10;
digitChar = cin.get();
number += (digitChar - '0');
digitChar = cin.get();
if (digitChar == 10) {
    cout << "Number entered: " << number << "\n";
} else {
    number = number * 10 + (digitChar - '0');
    digitChar = cin.get();
    if (digitChar == 10) {
        cout << "Number entered: " << number << "\n";
    } else {
        number = number * 10 + (digitChar - '0');
        cout << "Number entered: " << number << "\n";
    }
}
```

At this point, we could easily expand the code to handle six-digit numbers or numbers with fewer digits. The pattern is clear: If the next character is another digit, multiply the running total by 10 before adding the integer digit value of the character. With this understanding, we can write a loop to handle a number of any length:

```
     cout << "Enter a number with as many digits as you like: ";
❶ char digitChar = cin.get();
❷ int number = (digitChar - '0');
❸ digitChar = cin.get();
     while ❹(digitChar != 10) {
         ❺number = number * 10 + (digitChar - '0');
         ❻digitChar = cin.get();
     }
     ❼cout << "Number entered: " << number << "\n";
```

Here, we read the first character ❶, and determine its digit value ❷. Then we read the second character ❸ and reach the loop, where we check to see whether the most recently read character is an end-of-line ❹. If not, we multiply the running total in the loop by 10, and add the current character's digit value ❺ before reading the next character ❻. Once we reach the end-of-line, the running total variable number contains the integer value for us to output ❼.

That handles the conversion of one series of characters to its integer equivalent. In the final program, we'll be reading a series of numbers, separated by commas. Each number will have to be separately read and processed. As always, it's best to start by thinking about a simple situation that demonstrates the issue. Let's consider the input **101,22[EOL]**, where **[EOL]** is explicitly marking the end-of-line for clarity. It would be enough to modify the test condition of the loop to check for either the end-of-line character or a comma. Then we would need to place all the code that processes one number inside a larger loop that continues until all the numbers have been read. So the inner loop should stop for **[EOL]** or a comma, but the outer loop should stop only for **[EOL]**:

```
❶ char digitChar;
     do {
         digitChar = cin.get();
         int number = (digitChar - '0');
         digitChar = cin.get();
         while ((digitChar != 10) && (digitChar != ',')) {
             number = number * 10 + (digitChar - '0');
             digitChar = cin.get();
         }
         cout << "Number entered: " << number << "\n";
     } while ❷(digitChar != 10);
```

This is another great example of the importance of small steps. Although this is a short program, the wheels-within-wheels nature of the double loop would have made for tricky code if we had tried to write this from scratch. It's straightforward, though, when we arrive at this code by taking a step from the previous program. The declaration of `digitChar` ❶ is moved to a separate line so that the declaration is in scope throughout the code. The rest of the code is the same as the previous listing, except that it's placed inside a do-while loop that continues until we reach the end-of-line ❷.

With that part of the solution in place, we can focus on processing the individual numbers. The next item on our list is converting a number 1–26 to a letter A–Z. If you think about it, this is actually a reversal of the process we used to convert the individual digit characters to their integer equivalents. If we subtract the character code for 0 to translate from the 0–9 character code range to the 0–9 integer range, we should be able to add a character code to translate from 1–26 to A–Z. What if we added `'A'`? Here's an attempt along with a sample input and output:

```
cout << "Enter a number 1-26: ";
int number;
cin >> number;
char outputCharacter;
outputCharacter = ❶number + 'A';
cout << "Equivalent symbol: " << outputCharacter << "\n";

Enter a number 1-26: 5
Equivalent letter: F
```

That's not quite right. The fifth letter of the alphabet is E, not F. The problem occurs because we are adding a number in the range that starts from 1. When we were converting in the other direction, from a character digit to its integer equivalent, we were dealing with a range that started from 0. We can fix this problem by changing the computation ❶ from `number + 'A'` to `number + 'A' - 1`. Note that we could look up the character code value for the letter A (it's 65 in ASCII) and simply use one less than that value (for example, `number + 64` in ASCII). I prefer the first version, though, because it's more readable. In other words, if you come back to look at this code later, you can more quickly remember what `number + 'A' - 1` does than what `number + 64` does because the appearance of `'A'` in the former will remind you of converting to uppercase letters.

Having sorted that out, we can easily adapt this idea to convert to lowercase letters by changing the computation ❶ to `number + 'a' - 1`. The punctuation table conversion is not as concise because the punctuation symbols in the table do not appear in that order in ASCII or any other character code system. As such, we're going to have to handle this through brute force:

```
cout << "Enter a number 1-8: ";
int number;
cin >> number;
char outputCharacter;
❶ switch (number) {
    case 1: outputCharacter = '!'; break;
    case 2: outputCharacter = '?'; break;
    case 3: outputCharacter = ','; break;
```

```
    case 4: outputCharacter = '.'; break;
    case 5: outputCharacter = ' '; break;
    case 6: outputCharacter = ';'; break;
    case 7: outputCharacter = '"'; break;
    case 8: outputCharacter = ❷'\''; break;
}
cout << "Equivalent symbol: " << outputCharacter << "\n";
```

Here, we've used a switch statement ❶ to output the correct punctuation character. Note that a backslash has been employed as an "escape" in order to display the single quote ❷.

We have one last subproblem to tackle before putting everything together: switching from mode to mode whenever the most recent value decodes to 0. Remember that the problem description requires us to modulo each integer value by 27 (if we are currently in the uppercase mode or lowercase mode) or 9 (if we are in punctuation mode). When the result is 0, we switch to the next mode. What we need is a variable to store the current mode and logic inside our "read and process the next value" loop to switch modes if necessary. The variable tracking the current mode could be a simple integer, but it's more readable to use an enumeration. A good rule of thumb: If a variable is only tracking a state and there is no inherent meaning to any particular value, an enumeration is a good idea. In this case, we could have a variable int mode arbitrarily say that the value of 1 means uppercase, 2 means lowercase, and 3 means punctuation. There's no inherent reason, however, why those values are chosen. When we come back to look at the code later, we'll have to reacquaint ourselves with the system to make sense of a statement such as if (mode == 2). If we use an enumeration—as in the statement (mode == LOWERCASE)—there is nothing for us to remember because it's all spelled out. Here's the code that results from this idea, along with a sample interaction:

```
enum modeType {UPPERCASE, LOWERCASE, PUNCTUATION};
int number;
modeType mode = UPPERCASE;
cout << "Enter some numbers ending with -1: ";
do {
    cin >> number;
    cout << "Number read: " << number;
    switch (mode) {
        case UPPERCASE:
            number = number % 27;
            cout << ". Modulo 27: " << number << ". ";
            if (number == 0) {
                cout << "Switch to LOWERCASE";
                mode = LOWERCASE;
            }
            break;
        case LOWERCASE:
            number = number % 27;
            cout << ". Modulo 27: " << number << ". ";
            if (number == 0) {
```

```
            cout << "Switch to PUNCTUATION";
            mode = PUNCTUATION;
        }
        break;
    case PUNCTUATION:
        number = number % 9;
        cout << ". Modulo 9: " << number << ". ";
        if (number == 0) {
            cout << "Switch to UPPERCASE";
            mode = UPPERCASE;
        }
        break;
    }
    cout << "\n";
} while (number != -1);

Enter some numbers ending with -1: 2 1 0 52 53 54 55 6 7 8 9 10 -1
Number read: 2. Modulo 27: 2.
Number read: 1. Modulo 27: 1.
Number read: 0. Modulo 27: 0. Switch to LOWERCASE
Number read: 52. Modulo 27: 25.
Number read: 53. Modulo 27: 26.
Number read: 54. Modulo 27: 0. Switch to PUNCTUATION
Number read: 55. Modulo 9: 1.
Number read: 6. Modulo 9: 6.
Number read: 7. Modulo 9: 7.
Number read: 8. Modulo 9: 8.
Number read: 9. Modulo 9: 0. Switch to UPPERCASE
Number read: 10. Modulo 27: 10.
Number read: -1. Modulo 27: -1.
```

We have crossed off everything on our list, so now it's time to integrate these individual code listings to make a solution for the overall program. We could approach this integration in different ways. We might put just two pieces together and build up from there. For example, we could combine the code to read and convert the comma-separated numbers with the mode switching from the most recent listing. Then we could test that integration and add the code to convert each number to the appropriate letter or punctuation symbol. Or we could build up in the other direction, taking the number-to-character listing and turning it into a series of functions to be called from the main program. At this point, we've mostly moved beyond problem solving into software engineering, which is a different subject. We made a series of blocks—that was the hard part—and now we just have to assemble them, as shown in Figure 2-5.

Almost every line in this program was extracted from previous code in this section. The bulk of the code ❶ comes from the mode-switching program. The central processing loop ❷ comes from our code to read a series of comma-delimited numbers character by character. Finally, you'll recognize the code that converts the integers into uppercase letters, lowercase letters, and punctuation ❹. The small amount of new code is marked by ❸. The continue statements skip us to the next iteration of the loop when the last input was a mode-switch command, skipping the cout << outputCharacter at the end of the loop.

```
❶    char outputCharacter;
     enum modeType {UPPERCASE, LOWERCASE, PUNCTUATION};
     modeType mode = UPPERCASE;
❷  char digitChar;
   do {
       digitChar = cin.get();
       int number = (digitChar - '0');
       digitChar = cin.get();
       while ((digitChar != 10) && (digitChar != ',')) {
          number = number * 10 + (digitChar - '0');
          digitChar = cin.get();
       }
       switch (mode) {
           case UPPERCASE:
              number = number % 27;
              outputCharacter = number + 'A' - 1;
              if (number == 0) {
                 mode = LOWERCASE;
❸               continue;
              }
              break;
           case LOWERCASE:
              number = number % 27;
              outputCharacter = number + 'a' - 1;
              if (number == 0) {
                 mode = PUNCTUATION;
                 continue;
              }
              break;
           case PUNCTUATION:
              number = number % 9;
❹           switch (number) {
                 case 1: outputCharacter = '!'; break;
                 case 2: outputCharacter = '?'; break;
                 case 3: outputCharacter = ','; break;
                 case 4: outputCharacter = '.'; break;
                 case 5: outputCharacter = ' '; break;
                 case 6: outputCharacter = ';'; break;
                 case 7: outputCharacter = '"'; break;
                 case 8: outputCharacter = '\''; break;
              }
              if (number == 0) {
                 mode = UPPERCASE;
                 continue;
              }
              break;
       }
       cout << outputCharacter;
   } while (digitChar != 10);
   cout << "\n";
```

Figure 2-5: The assembled solution to the "Decode a Message" problem

While this is a cut-and-paste job, this is the *good* kind of cut-and-paste job, where you reuse the code you just wrote and therefore completely understand it. As before, think about how easy each step was in this process, versus trying to write the final listing from scratch. Undoubtedly, a good programmer could produce the final listing without going through the intermediate steps, but there would be false steps, times when the code looks ugly, and lines of code commented out and then put back again. By taking the smaller steps, all the dirty work gets done early, and the code never gets too ugly because the code we're currently working with never gets long or complicated.

Conclusion

In this chapter, we looked at three different problems. In one sense, we had to take three different paths to solve them. In another sense, we took the same route each time because we used the same basic technique of breaking up the problem into components; writing code to solve those components individually; and then using the knowledge gained from writing the programs, or even directly using lines of code from the programs, to solve the original problem. In the chapters that follow, we won't use this method explicitly for each problem, but the fundamental idea is always there: to chop up the problem into manageable pieces.

Depending on your background, these problems may have initially appeared to lie anywhere on the difficulty spectrum from fiendish to trivial. Regardless of how difficult a problem initially seems, I would recommend using this technique on each new problem you face. You don't want to wait until you reach a frustratingly difficult problem before trying out a new technique. Remember that one of the goals of this text is for you to develop confidence in your ability to solve problems. Practice using the techniques on "easy" problems and you'll have lots of momentum for when you hit the hard ones.

Exercises

As before, I urge you to try as many exercises as you can stand. Now that we are fully into the actual programming, working through exercises is essential for you to develop your problem-solving skills.

2-1.   Using only single-character output statements that output a hash mark, a space, or an end-of-line, write a program that produces the following shape:

```
########
 ######
  ####
   ##
```

2-2. Or how about:

```
   ##
  ####
 ######
########
########
 ######
  ####
   ##
```

2-3. Here's an especially tricky one:

```
#               #
 ##           ##
  ###       ###
   ########
   ########
  ###       ###
 ##           ##
#               #
```

2-4. Design your own: Think up your own symmetrical pattern of hash marks, and see whether you can write a program to produce it that follows the shapes rule.

2-5. If you like the Luhn formula problem, try writing a program for a different check-digit system, like the 13-digit ISBN system. The program could take an identification number and verify it or take a number without its check digit and generate the check digit.

2-6. If you've learned about binary numbers and how to convert from decimal to binary and the reverse, try writing programs to do those conversions with unlimited length numbers (but you can assume the numbers are small enough to be stored in a standard C++ int).

2-7. Have you learned about hexadecimal? Try writing a program that lets the user specify an input in binary, decimal, or hexadecimal, and output in any of the three.

2-8. Want an extra challenge? Generalize the code for the previous exercise to make a program that converts from any number base-16 or less to any other number base. So, for example, the program could convert from base-9 to base-4.

2-9. Write a program that reads a line of text, counting the number of words, identifying the length of the longest word, the greatest number of vowels in a word, and/or any other statistics you can think of.

3

SOLVING PROBLEMS WITH ARRAYS

In the previous chapter, we limited ourselves to *scalar variables*, that is, variables that can hold only one value at a time. In this chapter, we'll look at problems using the most common aggregate data structure, the array. Although arrays are simple structures with fundamental limitations, their use greatly magnifies the power of our programs.

In this chapter, we will primarily deal with actual arrays, that is, those declared with the built-in C++ syntax, such as:

```
int tenIntegerArray[10];
```

However, the techniques we discuss apply just as well to data structures with similar attributes. The most common of these structures is a vector. The term *vector* is often used as a synonym for any array of a single dimension, but we'll use it here in the more specific sense of a structure that has the attributes of an array without a specified maximum number of elements. So for our discussions, an array is of a fixed size, while a vector can grow or shrink automatically as needed. Each of the problems we discuss in this chapter includes some restriction that allows us to use a structure with a fixed number of elements. Problems without such restrictions, however, could be adapted to use a vector.

Moreover, the techniques used with arrays can often be used with data structures that do not have every attribute listed above. Some techniques, for example, don't require random access, so they can be used with structures like linked lists. Because arrays are so common in programming, and because array techniques are frequently used in non-array contexts, arrays are a great training ground for the study of problem solving with data structures.

Review of Array Fundamentals

You should already know what an array is, but let's go over some of the attributes of arrays for clarity. An *array* is a collection of variables of the same type organized under one name, where the individual variables are denoted by a number. We call the individual variables the *elements* of the array. In C++ and most other languages, the first element has number 0, but in some languages, this will vary.

The primary attributes of the array follow directly from the definition. Every value stored in an array is of the same type, whereas other aggregate data structures can store values of mixed types. An individual element is referenced by a number called a *subscript*; in other data structures, individual elements might be referenced by name or by a key value.

From these primary attributes, we can derive several secondary attributes. Because each of the elements is designated by a number in a sequence starting from 0, we can easily examine every value in an array. In other data structures, this may be difficult, inefficient, or even impossible. Also, whereas some data structures, such as linked lists, can be accessed only sequentially, an array offers *random access*, meaning we can access any element of the array at any time.

These primary and secondary attributes determine how we can use arrays. When dealing with any aggregate data structure, it's good to have a set of basic operations in mind as you consider problems. Think of these basic operations as common tools—the hammers, screwdrivers, and wrenches of the data structure. Not every mechanical problem can be solved with common tools, but you should always consider whether a problem can be solved with common tools before making a trip to the hardware store. Here's my list of basic operations for arrays.

Store

This is the most basic of operations. An array is a collection of variables, and we can assign a value to each of those variables. To assign the integer 5 to the first element (element 0) in the previously declared array, we just say:

```
tenIntegerArray[0] = 5;
```

As with any variable, the values of the elements inside our array will be random "garbage" until particular values are assigned, so arrays should be initialized before they are used. In some cases, especially for testing, we will want to assign a particular value to every element in the array. We can do that with an initializer when the array is declared.

```
int tenIntegerArray[10] = {4, 5, 9, 12, -4, 0, -57, 30987, -287, 1};
```

We'll see a good use of an array initializer shortly. Sometimes, instead of assigning a different value to each element, we just want every element in the array to be initialized to the same value. There are some shortcuts for assigning a zero to every element in the array, depending on the situation or the compiler used (the C++ compiler in Microsoft Visual Studio, for example, initializes every value in any array to zero unless otherwise specified). At this stage, however, I would always explicitly initialize an array wherever initialization is required in order to enhance readability, as in this code, which sets every element in a 10-element array to −1:

```
int tenIntegerArray[10];
for (int i = 0; i < 10; i++) tenIntegerArray[i] = -1;
```

Copy

We can make a copy of the array. There are two common situations in which this might be useful. First, we might want to heavily manipulate the array but still require the array in its original form for later processing. Putting the array back in its original form after manipulation may be difficult, or even impossible, if we've changed any of the values. By copying the entire array, we can manipulate the copy without disturbing the original. All we need to copy an entire array is a loop and an assignment statement, just like the code for initialization:

```
int tenIntegerArray[10] = {4, 5, 9, 12, -4, 0, -57, 30987, -287, 1};
int secondArray[10];
for (int i = 0; i < 10; i++) secondArray[i] = tenIntegerArray[i];
```

That operation is available to most aggregate data structures. The second situation is more specific to arrays. Sometimes we want to copy part of the data from one array to a second array, or we want to copy the elements from one array to a second array as a method of rearranging the order of the elements. If you have studied the merge-sort algorithm, you've seen this idea in action. We'll see examples of copying later in this chapter.

Retrieval and Search

With the ability to put values into the array, we also need the ability to get them out of the array. Retrieving the value from a particular location is straightforward:

```
int num = tenIntegerArray[0];
```

Searching for a Specific Value

Usually the situation isn't that simple. Often we don't know the location we need, and we instead have to *search* the array to find the location of a specific value. If the elements in the array are in no particular order, the best we can do is a sequential search, where we look at each element in the array from one end to the other until we find the desired value. Here's a basic version.

```
❶ const int ARRAY_SIZE = 10;
❷ int intArray[ARRAY_SIZE] = {4, 5, 9, 12, -4, 0, -57, 30987, -287, 1};
❸ int targetValue = 12;
❹ int targetPos = 0;
   while ((intArray[targetPos] != targetValue) && (targetPos < ❺ARRAY_SIZE))
       targetPos++;
```

In this code, we have a constant that stores the size of the array ❶, the array itself ❷, a variable to store the value we are looking for in the array ❸, and a variable to store the location where the value is found ❹. In this example, we use our ARRAY_SIZE constant to limit the number of iterations over our array ❺, so that we won't run past the end of the array when targetValue is not found among the array elements. You could "hard-wire" the number 10 in place of the constant, but using the constant makes the code more general, thus making it easy to modify and reuse. We'll use an ARRAY_SIZE constant in most of the code in this chapter. Note that if targetValue is not found in intArray, then targetPos will be equal to ARRAY_SIZE after the loop. This is enough to signify the event because ARRAY_SIZE is not a valid element number. It will be up to the code that follows, however, to check that. Also note that the code makes no effort to handle the possibility that the target value appears more than once. The first time the target value appears, the loop is over.

Criterion-Based Search

Sometimes the value we are looking for isn't a fixed value but a value based on the relationship with other values in the array. For example, we might want to find the highest value in the array. The mechanism to do that is what I call "King of the Hill," in reference to the playground game. Have a variable that represents the highest value seen *so far* in the array. Run through all the elements in the array with a loop, and each time you encounter a value higher than the previous highest value, the new value knocks the previous king off the hill, taking his place:

```
   const int ARRAY_SIZE = 10;
   int intArray[ARRAY_SIZE] = {4, 5, 9, 12, -4, 0, -57, 30987, -287, 1};
❶ int highestValue = intArray[0];
❷ for (int i = 1; i < ARRAY_SIZE; i++) {
       ❸if (intArray[i] ❹> highestValue) highestValue = intArray[i];
   }
```

The variable highestValue stores the largest value found in the array so far. At its declaration, it is assigned the value of the first element in the array ❶, which allows us to start the loop at the second element in the array (it allows us to start with i at 1 instead of 0) ❷. Inside the loop, we compare the value at the current position with highestValue, replacing highestValue if appropriate ❸. Note that finding the lowest value, instead of the highest, is just a matter of switching the "greater-than" comparison ❹ to a "less-than" comparison (and changing the name of the variable so we don't confuse ourselves). This basic structure can be applied to all sorts of situations in which we want to look at every element in the array to find the value that most exemplifies a particular quality.

Sort

Sorting means putting data in a specified order. You have probably already encountered sorting algorithms for arrays. This is a classic area for performance analysis because there are so many competing sorting algorithms, each with performance characteristics that vary depending on features of the underlying data. The study of different sorting algorithms could be the subject of an entire book by itself, so we're not going to explore this area in its full depth. Instead, we're going to focus on what is practical. For most situations, you can make do with two sorts in your toolbox: a fast, easy-to-use sort and a decent, easy-to-understand sort that you can modify with confidence when the situation arises. For fast and easy, we'll use the standard library function qsort, and when we need something to tweak, we'll use an insertion sort.

Fast-and-Easy Sorting with qsort

The default fast sort for C/C++ programmers is the qsort function in the standard library (the name suggests that the underlying sort employs a quicksort, but the implementer of the library is not required to use that algorithm). To use qsort, we have to write a comparator function. This function will be called by qsort whatever it needs to compare two elements in the array to see which should appear earlier in sorted order. The function is passed two void pointers. We haven't discussed pointers yet in this book, but all you need to know here is that you should cast those void pointers to pointers to the element type in your array. Then the function should return an int, either positive, negative, or zero, based on whether the first element is larger, smaller, or equal to the second element. The exact value returned doesn't matter, only whether it is positive, negative, or zero. Let's clear up this discussion with a quick example of sorting an array of 10 integers using qsort. Our comparator function:

```
int compareFunc(❶const void * voidA, const void * voidB) {
  ❷int * intA = (int *)(voidA);
    int * intB = (int *)(voidB);
  ❸return *intA - *intB;
}
```

The parameter list consists of two const void pointers ❶. Again, this is always the case for the comparator. The code inside the function begins by declaring two int pointers ❷ and casting the two void pointers to the int pointer type. We could write the function without the two temporary variables; I'm including them here for clarity. The point is, once we are done with those declarations, intA and intB will point at two elements in our array, and *intA and *intB will be two integers that must be compared. Finally, we return the result of subtracting the second integer from the first ❸. This produces the result we want. If *intA > *intB, for example, we want to return a positive number, and *intA − *intB will be positive if *intA > *intB. Likewise, *intA − *intB will be negative if *intB > *intA and will be zero when the two integers are equal.

With the comparator function in place, a sample use of qsort looks like this:

```
const int ARRAY_SIZE = 10;
int intArray[ARRAY_SIZE] = {87, 28, 100, 78, 84, 98, 75, 70, 81, 68};
qsort(❶intArray, ❷ARRAY_SIZE, ❸sizeof(int), ❹compareFunc);
```

As you can see, the call to qsort takes four parameters: the array to be sorted ❶; the number of elements in that array ❷; the size of one element in the array, usually determined, as it is here, by the sizeof operator ❸; and finally, the comparator function ❹. If you haven't had much experience passing functions as parameters to other functions, note the syntax used for the last parameter. We are passing the function itself, not calling the function and passing the result of the call. Therefore, we simply state the name of the function, with no parameter list or parentheses.

Easy-to-Modify Sorting with Insertion Sort

In some cases, you will need to write your own sorting code. Sometimes the built-in sort just won't work for your situation. For example, suppose you had an array of data that you wanted to order based on the data in *another* array. When you have to write your own sort, you will want a straightforward sorting routine that you believe in and can crank out on demand. A reasonable suggestion for a go-to sort is an *insertion sort*. The insertion sort works the way many people would sort cards when playing bridge: They pick up the cards one at a time and insert them in the appropriate place in their hands to maintain the overall order, moving the other cards down to make room. Here's a basic implementation for our integer array:

```
❶ int start = 0;
❷ int end = ARRAY_SIZE - 1;
❸ for (int i = start + 1; i <= end; i++) {
        for (❹int j = i; ❺j > start && ❻intArray[j-1] > intArray[j]; j--) {
            ❼int temp = intArray[j-1];
            intArray[j-1] = intArray[j];
            intArray[j] = temp;
        }
    }
```

We start by declaring two variables, start ❶ and end ❷, indicating the subscript of the first and last elements in the array. This improves the readability of the code and also allows the code to be easily modified to sort just a portion of the array, if desired. The outer loop selects the next "card" to be

inserted into our ever-increasing sorted hand ❸. Notice that the loop initializes i to start + 1. Remember in the "find the largest value" code, we initialized our highest-value variable to the first element in the array and started
our loop with the second element in the array. This is the same idea. If we
have only one value (or "card"), then by definition it is "in order" and we can
begin by considering whether the second value should come before or after
the first. The inner loop puts the current value in its correct position by
repeatedly swapping the current value with its predecessor until it reaches
the correct location. The loop counter j starts at i ❹, and the loop decre-
ments j so long as we haven't reached the lower end of the array ❺ and
haven't yet found the right stopping point for this new value ❻. Until then,
we use three assignment statements to swap the current value down one position in the array ❼. In other words, if you had a hand of 13 playing cards and
had already sorted the leftmost 4 cards, you could put the 5th card from the
left in the correct position by repeatedly moving it down one card until it was
no longer of a lower value than the card to its left. That's what the inner loop
does. The outer loop does this for every card starting from the leftmost. So
when we're done, the entire array is sorted.

An insertion sort is not the most efficient sort for most circumstances,
and to tell the truth, the previous code is not even the most efficient way to
perform an insertion sort. It is reasonably efficient for small to moderately
sized arrays, however, and it is simple enough that it can be memorized—
think of it as a mental macro. Whether you choose this sort or another, you
should have one decent or better sorting routine that you can code yourself
with confidence. It's not enough to have access to someone else's sorting code
that you don't fully understand. You don't want to tinker with the machinery
if you're not sure how everything works.

Compute Statistics

The final operation is similar to the retrieval operation, in that we need to
look at every element in the array before returning a value. It is different
from the retrieval operation, in that the value is not simply one of the elements
in the array but some statistic computed from all the values in the array. For
example, we might compute the average, median, or mode, and we will perform all of these computations later in this chapter. A basic statistic we might
compute could be the average of a set of student grades:

```
const int ARRAY_SIZE = 10;
int gradeArray[ARRAY_SIZE] = {87, 76, 100, 97, 64, 83, 88, 92, 74, 95};
double sum = 0;
for (int i = 0; i < ARRAY_SIZE; i++) {
    sum += gradeArray[i];
}
double average = sum / ARRAY_SIZE;
```

As another simple example, consider data validation. Suppose an array
of double values called vendorPayments represents payments to vendors. Only
positive values are valid, and therefore negative values indicate data integrity

problems. As part of a validation report, we might write a loop to count the number of negative values in the array:

```
const int ARRAY_SIZE = 10;
int countNegative = 0;
for (int i = 0; i < ARRAY_SIZE; i++) {
    if (vendorPayments[i] < 0) countNegative++;
}
```

Solving Problems with Arrays

Once you have the common operations understood, solving an array problem is not much different than solving problems with simple data, as we did in the previous chapter. Let's take one example and run all the way through it using the techniques of the previous chapter and any of the common operations for arrays that we might need.

PROBLEM: FINDING THE MODE

In statistics, the mode of a set of values is the value that appears most often. Write code that processes an array of survey data, where survey takers have responded to a question with a number in the range 1–10, to determine the mode of the data set. For our purpose, if multiple modes exist, any may be chosen.

In this problem, we're asked to retrieve one of the values from an array. Using the techniques of searching for analogies and starting with what we know, we might hope that we can apply some variation of the retrieval technique we have already seen: finding the largest value in an array. That code works by storing the largest value seen thus far in a variable. The code then compares each subsequent value to this variable, replacing it if necessary. The analogous method here would be to say we'd store the most frequently seen value thus far in a variable and then replace the value in the variable whenever we discovered a more common value in the array. When we say it like that, in English, it almost sounds as if it could work, but when we think about the actual code, we discover the problem. Let's take a look at a sample array and size constant for this problem:

```
const int ARRAY_SIZE = 12;
int surveyData[ARRAY_SIZE] = {4, 7, 3, 8, 9, 7, 3, 9, 9, 3, 3, 10};
```

The mode of this data is 3 because 3 appears four times, which is more often than any other value. But if we're processing this array sequentially, as we do for the "highest value" problem, at what point do we decide that 3 is our mode? How do we know, when we have encountered the fourth and final appearance of 3 in the array, that it is indeed the fourth and final appearance? There doesn't seem to be any way to discover this information with a single, sequential processing of the array data.

So let's turn to one of our other techniques: simplifying the problem. What if we made things easier on ourselves by putting all occurrences of the same number together? So, for example, what if our sample array survey data looked like this:

```
int surveyData[ARRAY_SIZE] = {4, 7, 7, 9, 9, 9, 8, 3, 3, 3, 3, 10};
```

Now both of the 7s are together, the 9s are together, and the 3s are together. With the data grouped in this manner, it seems that we should be able to sequentially process the array to find the mode. Processing the array by hand, it's easy to count the occurrences of each value, because you just keep counting down the array until you find the first number that's different. Converting what we can do in our head into programming statements, however, can be tricky. So before we try writing the code for this simplified problem, let's write some *pseudocode*, which is programming-like statements that are not entirely English or C++ but something in between. This will remind us what we're trying to do with each statement we need to write.

```
int mostFrequent = ❶?;
int highestFrequency = ❶?;
int currentFrequency = 0;
❷ for (int i = 0; i < ARRAY_SIZE; i++) {
    ❸currentFrequency++;
    ❹if (surveyData[i] IS LAST OCCURRENCE OF A VALUE) {
        ❺if (currentFrequency > highestFrequency) {
            highestFrequency = currentFrequency;
            mostFrequent = surveyData[i];
        }
        ❻currentFrequency = 0;
    }
}
```

There is no right or wrong way to write pseudocode, and if you use this technique, you should adopt your own style. When I write pseudocode, I tend to write legal C++ for any statement I'm already confident about and then spell out in English the places where I still have thinking to do. Here, we know that we will need a variable (mostFrequent) to hold the most frequently found value so far, which at the end of the loop will be the mode once we've written everything correctly. We also need a variable to store how often that value occurs (highestFrequency) so we have something to compare against. Finally, we need a variable we can use to count the number of occurrences of the value we're currently tracking as we sequentially process the array (currentFrequency). We know we need to initialize our variables. For currentFrequency, it logically has to start at 0, but it's not clear how we need to initialize the other variables yet, without the other code in place. So let's just drop in question marks ❶ to remind us to look at that again later.

The loop itself is the same array-processing loop we've already seen, so that's already in final form ❷. Inside the loop, we increment the variable that counts the occurrences of the current value ❸, and then we reach the pivotal statement. We know we need to check to see whether we've reached the last occurrence of a particular value ❹. The pseudocode allows us to skip figuring out the logic for now and sketch out the rest of the code. If this *is* the last occurrence of the value, though, we know what to do because this is like the "highest value" code: We need to see whether this value's count is higher than the highest seen so far. If it is, this value becomes the new most frequent value ❺. Then, because the next value read will be the first occurrence of a new value, we reset our counter ❻.

Let's return to the if statement logic we skipped. How do we know whether this is the last occurrence of a value in the array? Because the values in the array are grouped, we know whether a value is the last occurrence when the next value in the array is something different: in C++ terms, when surveyData[i] and surveyData[i + 1] are not equal. Furthermore, the last value in the array is also the last occurrence of some value, even though there's not a next value. We can check for this by checking to see whether i == ARRAY_SIZE - 1, in which case this is the last value in the array.

With all of that figured out, let's think about those initial values for our variables. Remember with the "highest value" array-processing code, we initialized our "highest so far" variable to the first value in the array. Here, the "most frequently seen" value is represented by two variables, mostFrequent for the value itself and highestFrequency for the number of occurrences. It would be great if we could initialize mostFrequent to the first value that appears in the array and highestFrequency to its frequency count, but there's no way to determine the first value's frequency until we get into the loop and start counting. At this point, it might occur to us that the first value's frequency, whatever it is, would be greater than zero. Therefore, if we set highestFrequency to zero, once we reach the last occurrence of the first value, our code will replace mostFrequent and highestFrequency with the numbers for the first value anyway. The completed code looks like this:

```
int mostFrequent;
int highestFrequency = 0;
int currentFrequency = 0;
for (int i = 0; i < ARRAY_SIZE; i++) {
    currentFrequency++;
  ❶// if (surveyData[i] IS LAST OCCURENCE OF A VALUE)
  ❷if (i == ARRAY_SIZE - 1 || surveyData[i] != surveyData[i + 1]) {
        if (currentFrequency > highestFrequency) {
            highestFrequency = currentFrequency;
            mostFrequent = surveyData[i];
        }
        currentFrequency = 0;
    }
}
```

In this book, we won't talk much about pure style issues, such as documentation (commenting) style, but since we are using pseudocode on this problem, I want to mention a tip. I've noticed that the lines I leave as "plain English" in the pseudocode are the lines that benefit most from a comment in the final code, and the plain English itself makes a great comment. I've demonstrated that in the code here. You might forget the exact meaning behind the conditional expression in the `if` statement ❷, but the comment on the preceding line ❶ clears things up nicely.

As for the code itself, it does the job, but remember that it requires our survey data to be grouped. Grouping the data might be a job in itself, except—what if we *sorted* the array? We don't actually need the data to be sorted, but sorting will accomplish the grouping we need. Because we don't intend to do any special kind of sorting, let's just add this call to qsort to the beginning of our code:

```
qsort(surveyData, ARRAY_SIZE, sizeof(int), compareFunc);
```

Note that we're using the same `compareFunc` we wrote earlier for use with qsort. With the sorting step in place, we have a complete solution to the original problem. So our work is done. Or is it?

Refactoring

Some programmers talk about code that gives off "bad smells." They are talking about working code that is free of bugs but still problematic in some way. Sometimes this means code that is too complicated or has too many special cases, making the program difficult for a programmer to modify and maintain. In other cases, the code isn't as efficient as it could be, and while it works for test cases, the programmer worries that performance will break down with larger cases. That's my concern here. The sorting step is nearly instantaneous for our tiny test case, but what if the array is huge? Also, I know that the quicksort algorithm, which qsort may be using, has its lowest performance when there are lots of duplicate values in the array, and the whole point of this problem is that all of our values are in the range 1–10. I therefore propose to *refactor* the code. *Refactoring* means improving working code, not changing what it does but how it does it. I want a solution that is highly efficient for even huge arrays, assuming that the values are in the range of 1–10.

Let's think again about the operations we know how to do with arrays. We've already explored several versions of the "find the highest" code. We know that applying the "find the highest" code directly to our surveyData array won't produce useful results. Is there an array to which we could apply the "stock" version of "find the highest" and get the mode of the survey data? The answer is yes. The array we need is the histogram of the surveyData array. A histogram is a graph showing how often different values appear in an underlying dataset; our array will be the data for such a histogram. In other words, we'll store, in a 10-element array, how often each of the values 1 through 10 appears in surveyData. Here's the code to create our histogram:

```
const int MAX_RESPONSE = 10;
❶ int histogram[MAX_RESPONSE];
```

```
❷ for (int i = 0; i < MAX_RESPONSE; i++) {
      histogram[i] = 0;
  }
❸ for (int i = 0; i < ARRAY_SIZE; i++) {
      ❹histogram[surveyData[i] - 1]++;
  }
```

On the first line, we declare the array to hold our histogram data ❶.
You'll note we declare the array with 10 elements, but the range of our survey responses is 1–10, and the range of subscripts for this array is 0–9. Thus,
we'll have to make adjustments, putting the count of 1s in histogram[0] and so
on. (Some programmers would choose to declare the array with 11 elements,
leaving location [0] unused, to allow each count to go into its natural position.)
We explicitly initialize the array values to zero with a loop ❷, and then we are
ready to count the occurrences of each value in surveyData with another loop ❸.
The statement inside the loop ❹ has to be read carefully; we are using the
value in the current location of surveyData to tell us which position in histogram
to increment. To make this clear, let's take an example. Suppose i is 42. We
inspect surveyData[42] and find (let's say) the value 7. So we need to increment our 7 counter. We subtract 1 from 7 to get 6 because the counter for 7s
is in position [6] in histogram, and histogram[6] is incremented.

With the histogram data in place, we can write the rest of the code. Note
that the histogram code was written separately so that it could be tested separately. No time is saved by writing all of the code at once in a situation where
the problem is easily separated into parts that can be individually written and
tested. Having tested the above code, we now search for the largest value in
the histogram array:

```
❶ int mostFrequent = 0;
  for (int i = 1; i < MAX_RESPONSE; i++) {
      if (histogram[i] > ❷histogram[mostFrequent]) ❸mostFrequent = i;
  }
❹ mostFrequent++;
```

Although this is an adaptation of the "find the highest" code, there is a
difference. Although we are searching for the highest value in the histogram
array, ultimately, we don't want the value itself, but the position. In other
words, with our sample array, we want to know that 3 occurs more often than
any other value in the survey data, but the actual number of times 3 occurs
isn't important. So mostFrequent will be the position of the highest value in
histogram, not the highest value itself. Therefore, we initialize it to 0 ❶ and
not the value in location [0]. This also means that in the if statement, we
compare against histogram[mostFrequent] ❷ and not mostFrequent itself, and
we assign i, not histogram[i], to mostFrequent ❸ when a larger value is found.
Finally, we increment mostFrequent ❹. This is the reverse of what we did in the
earlier loop, subtracting 1 to get the right array position. If mostFrequent is telling us that the highest array position is 5, for example, it means that the most
frequent entry in the survey data was 6.

The histogram solution scales linearly with the number of elements in our surveyData array, which is as good as we could hope for. Therefore, it's a better solution than our original approach. This doesn't mean that the first approach was a mistake or a waste of time. It's possible, of course, to have written this code without going through the previous version, and we can be forgiven for wishing that we had driven directly to our destination instead of taking the longer route. However, I would caution against slapping yourself on the forehead on those occasions when the first solution turns out not to be the final solution. Writing an original program (and remember this means *original for the programmer writing it*) is a learning process and can't be expected to always progress in a straight line. Also, it's often the case that taking a longer path on one problem helps us take a shorter path on a later problem. In this particular case, note that our original solution (while it doesn't scale well for our particular problem) could be the right solution if the survey responses weren't strictly limited to the small range of 1–10. Or suppose that you are later asked to write code that finds the *median* of a set of integer values (the median is the value in the middle, such that half of the other values in the set are higher and half of the other values are lower). The histogram approach doesn't get you anywhere with the median, but our first approach for the mode does.

The lesson here is that a long journey is not a waste of time if you learned something from it that you wouldn't have learned by going the short way. This is another reason why it's helpful to methodically store all of the code that you write so that you can easily find and reuse it later. Even the code that turns out to be a "dead end" can become a valuable resource.

Arrays of Fixed Data

In most array problems, the array is a repository for data external to the program, such as user-entered data, data on a local disk, or data from a server. To get the most out of the array tool, however, you need to recognize other situations in which an array can be used. It's often useful to create an array where the values never change after the initialization. Such an array can allow a simple loop or even a direct array lookup to replace a whole block of control statements.

In the final code for the "Decode a Message" problem on page 52, we used a switch statement to translate the decoded input number (in the range 1–8) to the appropriate character when in "punctuation mode" because the connection between the number and the character was arbitrary. Although this worked fine, it made that section of code longer than the equivalent code for the uppercase and lowercase modes, and the code would not scale well if the number of punctuation symbols increased. We can use an array to solve this problem instead of the switch statement. First, we need to permanently assign the punctuation symbols to an array in the same order they appear in the coding scheme:

```
const char punctuation[8] = {'!', '?', ',', '.', ' ', ';', '"', '\''};
```

Notice that this array has been declared `const` because the values inside will never change. With that declaration in place, we can replace the entire switch statement with a single assignment statement that references the array:

```
outputCharacter = punctuation[number - 1];
```

Because the input number is in the range 1–8, but array elements are numbered starting from 0, we have to subtract 1 from the input number before referencing the array; this is the same adjustment we made in the histogram version of the "Finding the Mode" program. You can use the same array to go in the other direction. Suppose instead of decoding the message, we had to encode a message—that is, we were given a series of characters to convert into numbers that could be decoded using the rules of the original problem. To convert a punctuation symbol into its number, we have to locate the symbol in the array. This is a retrieval, performed using the sequential search technique. Assuming the character is to be converted and stored in the char variable `targetValue`, we could adapt the sequential search code as follows:

```
const int ARRAY_SIZE = 8;
int targetPos = 0;
while (punctuation[targetPos] != targetValue && targetPos < ARRAY_SIZE)
    targetPos++;
int punctuationCode = targetPos + 1;
```

Note that just as we had to subtract 1 from `number` in the previous example to get the right array position, we have to add 1 to the array position in this example to get our punctuation code, converting from the array's range of 0–7 to our punctuation code range of 1–8. Although this code is not as simple as a single line, it's still much simpler than a series of `switch` statements, and it scales well. If we were to double the number of punctuation symbols in our coding scheme, it would double the number of elements in the array, but the length of the code would stay the same.

In general, then, `const` arrays can be used as lookup tables, replacing a burdensome series of control statements. Suppose you are writing a program to compute the cost of a business license in a state where the license cost varies as the gross sales figures of the business vary.

Table 3-1: Business License Costs

Business category	Sales threshold	License cost
I	$0	$25
II	$50,000	$200
III	$150,000	$1,000
IV	$500,000	$5,000

With this problem, we could use arrays both to determine the business category based on the company's gross sales and to assign the license cost based on the business category. Suppose a `double` variable, `grossSales`, stores the gross sales of a business, and based on the sales figure, we want to assign the proper values to `int category` and `double cost`:

```
   const int NUM_CATEGORIES = 4;
❶ const double categoryThresholds[NUM_CATEGORIES ] =
       {0.0, 50000.0, 150000.0, 500000.0};
❷ const double licenseCost[NUM_CATEGORIES ] =
       {50.0, 200.0, 1000.0, 5000.0};
❸ category = 0;
❹ while (category < NUM_CATEGORIES &&
       categoryThresholds[category] <= grossSales) {
           category++;
   }
❺ cost = licenseCost[category - 1];
```

This code uses two arrays of fixed values. The first array stores the gross sales threshold for each business category ❶. For example, a business with $65,000 in yearly gross sales is in category II because this amount exceeds the $50,000 threshold of category II but is less than the $150,000 threshold of category III. The second array stores the cost of a business license for each category ❷. With the arrays in place, we initialize `category` to 0 ❸ and search through the `categoryThresholds` array, stopping when the threshold exceeds the gross sales or when we run out of categories ❹. In either case, when the loop is done, `category` will be correctly assigned 1–4 based on the gross sales. The last step is to use `category` to reference the license cost from the `licenseCost` array ❺. As before, we have to make a small adjustment from the 1–4 range of the business categories to the 0–3 range of our array.

Non-scalar Arrays

So far, we've just worked with arrays of simple data types, such as `int` and `double`. Often, however, programmers must deal with arrays of compound data, either structures or objects (`struct` or `class`). Although the use of compound data types necessarily complicates the code somewhat, it doesn't have to complicate our thinking about array processing. Usually the array processing just involves one data member of the `struct` or `class`, and we can ignore the other parts of the data structure. Sometimes, though, the use of compound data types requires us to make some changes to our approach.

For example, consider the problem of finding the highest of a set of student grades. Suppose that instead of an array of `int`, we have an array of data structures, each representing a student's record:

```
struct student {
    int grade;
    int studentID;
    string name;
};
```

One nice thing about working with arrays is that it is easy to initialize a whole array with literal values for easy testing, even with an array of struct:

```
const int ARRAY_SIZE = 10;
student studentArray[ARRAY_SIZE] = {
    {87, 10001, "Fred"},
    {28, 10002, "Tom"},
    {100, 10003, "Alistair"},
    {78, 10004, "Sasha"},
    {84, 10005, "Erin"},
    {98, 10006, "Belinda"},
    {75, 10007, "Leslie"},
    {70, 10008, "Candy"},
    {81, 10009, "Aretha"},
    {68, 10010, "Veronica"}
};
```

This declaration means that studentArray[0] has an 87 for its grade, 10001 for its studentID, and "Fred" for a name, and so on for the other nine elements in the array. As for the rest of the code, it could be as simple as copying the code from the beginning of this chapter, and then replacing every reference of the form intArray[subscript] with studentArray[subscript].grade. That would result in the following:

```
int highest = studentArray[0].grade;
for (int i = 1; i < ARRAY_SIZE; i++) {
    if (studentArray[i].grade > highest) highest = studentArray[i].grade;
}
```

Suppose instead that because we now have additional information for each student, we want to find the name of the student with the best grade, not the grade itself. This would require additional modification. When our loop is over, the only statistic we have is the best grade, and that does not allow us to directly determine the student to which it belongs. We'd have to run through the array again, searching for the struct with the matching grade, which seems like extra work we shouldn't have to do. To avoid this issue, we should either additionally track the name of the student that matches the current value in highest, or, instead of tracking the highest grade, track the location in the array where the highest grade is found, much as we did with histogram earlier. The latter approach is the most general because tracking the array position allows us to retrieve *any* of the data for that student later:

```
❶ int highPosition = 0;
  for (int i = 1; i < ARRAY_SIZE; i++) {
      if (studentArray[i].grade > ❷studentArray[highPosition].grade) {
          ❸highPosition = i;
      }
  }
```

Here, the variable `highPosition` ❶ takes the place of `highest`. Because we aren't directly tracking the highest grade, when it's time to compare the highest grade against the current grade, we use `highPosition` as a reference into `studentArray` ❷. If the grade in the current array position is higher, the current position in our processing loop is assigned to `highPosition` ❸. Once the loop is over, we can access the name of the student with the highest grade using `studentArray[highPosition].name`, and we can also access any other data related to that student record.

Multidimensional Arrays

So far, we've only discussed one-dimensional arrays because they are the most common. Two-dimensional arrays are uncommon, and arrays with three or more dimensions are rare. That's because most data is one-dimensional by nature. Furthermore, data that is inherently multidimensional can be represented as multiple single-dimension arrays, so using a multidimensional array is always the choice of the programmer. Consider the business license data of Table 3-1. That's clearly multidimensional data. I mean, look at it—it's a grid! I represented this multidimensional data, however, as two one-dimensional arrays, `categoryThresholds` and `licenseCost`. I could have represented the data table as a two-dimensional array, like this:

```
const double licenseData[2][numberCategories] = {
    {0.0, 50000.0, 150000.0, 500000.0},
    {50.0, 200.0, 1000.0, 5000.0}
};
```

It's difficult to discern any advantage from combining the two arrays into one. None of our code is simplified because there is no reason to process all of the data in the table at once. What is clear, though, is that we have lowered the readability and ease of use for our table data. In the original version, the names of the two separate arrays make it clear what data is stored in each. With the combined array, we programmers will have to remember that references of the form `licenseData[0][]` refer to the gross sales thresholds of the different business categories, while references of the form `licenseData[1][]` refer to business license costs.

Sometimes it does make sense to use a multidimensional array, though. Suppose we are processing the monthly sales data for three sales agents, and one of the tasks is finding the highest monthly sales, from any agent. Having all of the data in one 3 x 12 array means we can process the entire array at once, using nested loops:

```
  const int NUM_AGENTS = 3;
  const int NUM_MONTHS = 12;
❶ int sales[NUM_AGENTS][NUM_MONTHS] = {
      {1856, 498, 30924, 87478, 328, 2653, 387, 3754, 387587, 2873, 276, 32},
      {5865, 5456, 3983, 6464, 9957, 4785, 3875, 3838, 4959, 1122, 7766, 2534},
      {23, 55, 67, 99, 265, 376, 232, 223, 4546, 564, 4544, 3434}
  };
```

```
❷ int highestSales = sales[0][0];
  for (❸int agent = 0; agent < NUM_AGENTS; agent++) {
      for (❹int month = 0; month < NUM_MONTHS; month++) {
          if (sales[agent][month] > highestSales)
              highestSales = sales[agent][month];
      }
  }
```

Although this is a straightforward adaptation of the basic "find the largest number" code, there are a few wrinkles. When we declare our two-dimensional array, notice that the initializer is organized by agent, that is, as 3 groups of 12, not 12 groups of 3 ❶. As you'll see in the next problem, this decision can have consequences. We initialize highestSales to the first element in the array, as usual ❷. It may occur to you that the first time through the nested loops, both of our loop counters will be 0, so we will be comparing this initial value of highestSales to itself. This doesn't affect the outcome, but sometimes novice programmers will attempt to avoid this tiny inefficiency by putting in a second if statement in the inner loop body:

```
if (agent != 0 || month != 0)
    if (sales[agent][month] > highestSales)
        highestSales = sales[agent][month];
```

This, however, is considerably *less* efficient than the previous version because we would be performing 50 extra comparisons while avoiding only one.

Notice also that I have used meaningful names for the loop variables: agent for the outside loop ❸ and month for the inside loop ❹. In a single loop that processes a one-dimensional array, little is gained by a descriptive identifier. In a double loop that processes a two-dimensional array, however, the meaningful identifiers help me keep my dimensions and subscripts straight because I can look up and see that I am using agent in the same dimension where I used NUM_AGENTS in the array declaration.

Even when we have a multidimensional array, sometimes the best approach is to deal with just one dimension at a time. Suppose, using the same sales array as the previous code, we wanted to display the highest agent monthly sales average. We could do this using a double loop, as we have previously, but the code would be clearer to read and easier to write if we treated the whole array as three individual arrays and processed them separately.

Remember the code we've been repeatedly using to compute the average of an array of integers? Let's make that into a function:

```
double arrayAverage(int intArray[], int ARRAY_SIZE) {
    double sum = 0;
    for (int i = 0; i < ARRAY_SIZE; i++) {
        sum += intArray[i];
    }
    double average = sum / ARRAY_SIZE;
    return average;
}
```

With the function in place, we can modify the basic "find the largest number" again to find the agent with the highest monthly sales average:

```
double highestAverage = ❶arrayAverage(sales[0], 12);
for (int agent = 1; agent < NUM_AGENTS; agent++) {
    double agentAverage = ❷arrayAverage(sales[agent], 12);
    if (agentAverage > highestAverage)
        highestAverage = agentAverage;
}
cout << "Highest monthly average: " << highestAverage << "\n";
```

The big new idea here is shown in the two calls to arrayAverage. The first parameter accepted by this function is a one-dimensional array of int. In the first call, we pass sales[0] for the first argument ❶, and in the second call, we pass sales[agent] ❷. So in both cases, we specify a subscript for the first dimension of our two-dimensional array sales, but not for the second dimension. Because of the direct relationship between arrays and addresses in C++, this reference indicates the address of the first element of the specified row, which can then be used by our function as the base address of a one-dimensional array consisting of just that row.

If that sounds confusing, look again at the declaration of the sales array, and in particular, the initializer. The values are laid out in the initializer in the same order they will be laid out in memory when the program is executing. So sales[0][0], which is 1856, will come first, followed by sales[0][1], 498, and so on through the last month for the first agent, sales[0][11], 32. Then the values for the second agent will begin, starting with sales[1][0], 5865. Therefore, even though the array is conceptually 3 rows of 12 values, it's laid out in memory as one big sequence of 36 values.

It's important to note that this technique works because of the order we've placed the data into the array. If the array were organized along the other axis, that is, by month instead of by agent, we couldn't do what we are doing here. The good news is that there is an easy way to make sure you have set up the array appropriately—just check the initializer. If the data you want to individually process isn't contiguous in the array initializer, you've organized the data the wrong way.

The last thing to note about this code is the use of the temporary variable, agentAverage. Because the average monthly sales for the current agent is potentially referenced twice, once in the conditional expression of the if statement and then again in the assignment statement in the body, the temporary variable eliminates the possibility of calling arrayAverage twice for the same agent's data.

This technique of considering a multidimensional array as an array of arrays follows directly from our core principle of breaking problems up into simpler components and in general makes multidimensional array problems a lot easier to conceptualize. Even so, you may be thinking that the technique looks a little tricky to employ, and if you're like most new C++ programmers, you are probably a little wary of addresses and behind-the-scenes address arithmetic. The best way around those feelings, I think, is to make the separation between the dimensions even stronger, by placing one level of array inside a struct or class. Suppose we made an agentStruct:

```
struct agentStruct {
    int monthlySales[12];
};
```

Having gone to the trouble of making a struct, we might think about adding other data, like an agent identification number, but this will get the job done in terms of simplifying our thought processes. With the struct in place, instead of creating a two-dimensional array of sales, we create a one-dimensional array of agents:

```
agentStruct agents[3];
```

Now when we make our call to the array-averaging function, we aren't employing a C++ specific trick; we're just passing a one-dimensional array. For example:

```
int highestAverage = arrayAverage(agents[1].monthlySales, 12);
```

Deciding When to Use Arrays

An array is just a tool. As with any tool, an important part of learning *how* to use an array is learning *when* to use it—and when not to use it. The sample problems discussed so far assumed the use of arrays in their descriptions. In most situations, though, we won't have this detail spelled out for us, and we must instead make our own determination on array use. The most common situations in which we must make this decision are those in which we are given aggregate data but not told how it must be stored internally. For example, in the problem where we found the mode, suppose the line that began *Write code that processes an array of survey data . . .*, had read *Write code that processes a collection of survey data . . . .* Now the choice of using an array or not would be ours. How would we make this decision?

Remember that we cannot change the size of an array after it has been created. If we ran out of space, our program would fail. So the first consideration is whether we will know, at the place in our program where we need an aggregate data structure, how many values we will store or at least a reliable estimate on the maximum size. This doesn't mean we have to know the size of the array when we write the program. C++, as well as most other languages, allows us to create an array that is sized at runtime. Suppose the mode problem was modified so that we didn't know ahead of time how many survey responses we would have, but that number came to the program as user input. Then we could dynamically declare an array to store the survey data.

```
int ARRAY_SIZE;
cout << "Number of survey responses: ";
cin >> ARRAY_SIZE;
❶ int *surveyData = new int[ARRAY_SIZE];
for(int i = 0; i < ARRAY_SIZE; i++) {
    cout << "Survey response " << i + 1 << ": ";
  ❷cin >> surveyData[i];
}
```

We declare the array using pointer notation, initializing it through an invocation of the new operator ❶. Because of the fluidity between pointer and array types in C++, the elements can then be accessed using array notation ❷, even though surveyData is declared as a pointer. Note that because this array is dynamically allocated, at the end of the program when we no longer need the array, we have to make sure to deallocate it:

```
delete[] surveyData;
```

The delete[] operator, rather than the usual delete operator, is used for arrays. Although it won't make any difference with an array of integers, if you create an array of objects, the delete[] operator ensures that the individual objects in the array are deleted before the array itself is deleted. So you should adopt the habit of always using delete[] with dynamically allocated arrays.

Having the responsibility of cleaning up dynamic memory is the bane of the C++ programmer, but if you program in the language, it is something you simply must do. Beginning programmers often shirk this responsibility because their programs are so small and execute for such short periods of time that they never see the harmful effects of memory leaks (memory that is no longer used by the program but never deallocated and therefore unavailable to the rest of the system). Don't develop this bad habit.

Note that we can use the dynamic array only because the user tells us the number of survey responses beforehand. Consider another variant where the user begins by entering survey responses without telling us the number of responses, indicating that there are no more responses by entering a –1 (a data entry method known as a *sentinel*). Can we still use an array to solve this problem?

This is a gray area. We could still use an array if we had a guaranteed maximum number of responses. In such a case, we could declare an array of that size and assume that we are safe. We might still have concerns over the long term, though. What if the size of the survey pool increases in the future? What if we want to use the same program with a different survey taker? More generally, why build a program with a known limitation if we can avoid it?

Better, then, to use a data collection without a fixed size. As discussed earlier, the vector class from the C++ standard template library acts like an array but grows as necessary. Once declared and initialized, the vector can be processed exactly the same way as an array. We can assign a value to a vector element or retrieve a value using standard array notation. If the vector has filled its initial size and we need to add another element, we can do so using the push_back method. Solving the modified problem with a vector looks like this:

```
❶ vector<int> surveyData;
❷ surveyData.reserve(30);
   int surveyResponse;
   cout << "Enter next survey response or -1 to end: ";
❸ cin >> surveyResponse;
   while (surveyResponse != -1) {
      ❹surveyData.push_back(surveyResponse);
      cout << "Enter next survey response or -1 to end: ";
      cin >> surveyResponse;
   }
❺ int vectorSize = surveyData.size();
   const int MAX_RESPONSE = 10;
   int histogram[MAX_RESPONSE];
   for (int i = 0; i < MAX_RESPONSE; i++) {
      histogram[i] = 0;
   }
   for (int i = 0; i < vectorSize; i++) {
      histogram[surveyData[i] - 1]++;
   }
   int mostFrequent = 0;
   for (int i = 1; i < MAX_RESPONSE; i++) {
      if (histogram[i] > histogram[mostFrequent]) mostFrequent = i;
   }
   mostFrequent++;
```

In this code, we first declare the vector ❶ and then reserve space for 30 survey responses ❷. The second step is not strictly necessary, but reserving a small amount of space that is in excess of the likely number of elements prevents the vector from resizing itself frequently as we add values to it. We read the first grade before the data entry loop ❸, a technique we first used in the previous chapter that allows us to check each entered value before processing. In this case, we want to avoid adding the sentinel value, −1, to our vector. The survey results are added to the vector using the push_back method ❹. After the data entry loop is completed, we retrieve the size of the vector using the size method ❺. We could also have counted the number of elements ourselves in the data entry loop, but since the vector is already tracking its size, this avoids duplicate effort. The rest of the code is the same as the previous version with the array and the fixed number of responses, except that we have changed the names of the variables.

All this discussion of vectors, though, overlooks an important point. If we are reading the data directly from the user, rather than being told that we are starting with an array or other data collection, we may not need an array for the survey data, only one for the histogram. Instead, we can process the survey values as we read them. We need a data structure only when we need to read in all the values before processing or need to process the values more than once. In this case, we don't need to do either:

```
const int MAX_RESPONSE = 10;
int histogram[MAX_RESPONSE];
for (int i = 0; i < MAX_RESPONSE; i++) {
    histogram[i] = 0;
}
int surveyResponse;
cout << "Enter next survey response or -1 to end: ";
cin >> surveyResponse;
while (surveyResponse != -1) {
    histogram[surveyResponse - 1]++;
    cout << "Enter next survey response or -1 to end: ";
    cin >> surveyResponse;
}
int mostFrequent = 0;
for (int i = 1; i < MAX_RESPONSE; i++) {
    if (histogram[i] > histogram[mostFrequent]) mostFrequent = i;
}
mostFrequent++;
```

Although this code was easy to write, given the previous versions as a guide, it would have been even easier just to read the user data into an array and use the previous processing loop verbatim. The benefit to this process-as-you-go approach is efficiency. We avoid unnecessarily storing each of the survey responses, when we need to store just one response at a time. Our vector-based solution was *inefficient in space*: It took more space than required without providing a corresponding benefit. Furthermore, reading all of the survey responses into the vector required a loop on its own, separate from the loops to process all of the survey responses and find the highest value in the histogram. That means the vector version does more work than the version above. Therefore, the vector version is also *inefficient in time*: It does more work than required without providing a corresponding benefit. In some cases, different solutions offer trade-offs, and programmers must decide between space efficiency and time efficiency. In this case, however, the use of the vector makes the program inefficient all around.

In this book, we won't spend a lot of time tracking down every inefficiency. Programmers must sometimes engage in *performance tuning*, which is the systematic analysis and improvement of a program's efficiency in time and space. Performance tuning a program is a lot like performance tuning a race car: an exacting job, where small adjustments can have large effects and expert knowledge of how mechanisms work "under the hood" is required. Even if we don't have the time, desire, or knowledge to fully tune a program's performance, though, we should still avoid decisions that lead to gross inefficiencies. Using a vector or an array unnecessarily is not like an engine with a fuel-to-air mix that is too lean; it's like driving a bus to the beach for vacation when you could have fit everything you were taking into a Honda Civic.

If we're sure we need to process the data multiple times, and we have a good handle on the maximum size of the data set, the last criterion for deciding whether to use an array is random access. Later on, we'll discuss alternate data structures, such as lists, which like vectors can grow as needed but unlike vectors and arrays the elements can be accessed only sequentially. That is, if we want to access the 10th element in a list, we have to run through the first 9 items to get to it. By contrast, *random access* means that we can access any element in an array or vector at any time. So the last rule is that we should use an array when we need random access. If we need only sequential access, we might consider a different structure.

You might notice that many of the programs in this chapter fail on this last criterion; we access the data sequentially, not randomly, and yet we are using an array. This leads to the great, common-sense exception to all of these rules. If an array is small, then none of the previous objections holds much weight. What constitutes "small" may vary based on the platform or application. The point is, if your program needs a collection of as few as 1 or as many as 10 items, each of which requires 10 bytes, you have to consider whether the potential waste of 90 bytes that could result from allocating an array of the maximum required size is worth searching for a better solution. Use arrays wisely, but don't let the perfect be the enemy of the good.

Exercises

As always, I urge you to try as many exercises as you can stand.

3-1. Are you disappointed we didn't do more with sorting? I'm here to help. To make sure you are comfortable with qsort, write code that uses the function to sort an array of our student struct. First have it sort by grade, and then try it again using the student ID.

3-2. Rewrite the code that finds the agent with the best monthly sales average so that it finds the agent with the highest *median* sales. As stated earlier, the median of a set of values is the "one in the middle," such that half of the other values are higher and half of the other values are lower. If there is an even number of values, the median is the simple average of the two values in the middle. For example, in the set 10, 6, 2, 14, 7, 9, the values in the middle are 7 and 9. The average of 7 and 9 is 8, so 8 is the median.

3-3. Write a bool function that is passed an array and the number of elements in that array and determines whether the data in the array is sorted. This should require only one pass!

3-4. Here's a variation on the array of const values. Write a program for creating a substitution cipher problem. In a substitution cipher problem, all messages are made of uppercase letters and punctuation. The original message is called the plaintext, and you create the ciphertext by substituting each letter with another letter (for example, each C could become an X). For this problem, hard-code a const array of 26 char elements for the cipher, and have your program read a plaintext message and output the equivalent ciphertext.

3-5. Have the previous program convert the ciphertext back to the plaintext to verify the encoding and decoding.

3-6. To make the ciphertext problem even more challenging, have your program randomly generate the cipher array instead of a hard-coded const array. Effectively, this means placing a random character in each element of the array, but remember that you can't substitute a letter for itself. So the first element can't be A, and you can't use the same letter for two substitutions—that is, if the first element is S, no other element can be S.

3-7. Write a program that is given an array of integers and determines the *mode,* which is the number that appears most frequently in the array.

3-8. Write a program that processes an array of student objects and determines the grade quartiles—that is, the grade one would need to score as well as or better than 25% of the students, 50% of the students, and 75% of the students.

3-9. Consider this modification of the sales array: Because salespeople come and go throughout the year, we are now marking months prior to a sales agent's hiring, or after a sales agent's last month, with a –1. Rewrite your highest sales average, or highest sales median, code to compensate.

4

SOLVING PROBLEMS
WITH POINTERS AND
DYNAMIC MEMORY

In this chapter, we'll learn to solve problems using pointers and dynamic memory, which will allow us to write flexible programs that can accommodate data sizes that are unknown until the program runs. Pointers and dynamic memory allocation are "hard-core" programming. When you can write programs that grab blocks of memory on the fly, link them into useful structures, and clean up everything at the end so there is no residue, you're not just someone who can do a little coding—you're a programmer.

Because pointers are tricky, and because many popular languages, such as Java, appear to forgo the use of pointers, some fledgling programmers will convince themselves that they can skip this subject entirely. This is a mistake. Pointers and indirect memory access will always be used in advanced programming, even though they may be hidden by the mechanisms of a high-level language. Therefore, to truly think like a programmer, you have to be able to think your way through pointers and pointer-based problems.

Before we get down to solving pointer problems, though, we're going to carefully examine all aspects of how pointers work, both on the surface and behind the scenes. This study provides two benefits. First, this knowledge will allow us to make the most effective use of pointers. Second, by dispelling the mysteries of pointers, we can employ them with confidence.

Review of Pointer Fundamentals

As with topics covered in previous chapters, you should have had some exposure to basic pointer use, but to make sure we're on the same page, here's a quick review.

Pointers in C++ are indicated with an asterisk (*). Depending on the context, the asterisk indicates either that a pointer is being declared or that we mean the pointed-to memory, not the pointer itself. To declare a pointer, we place the asterisk between the type name and the identifier:

```
int * intPointer;
```

This declares the variable intPointer as a pointer to an int. Note that the asterisk binds with the identifier, not the type. In the following, variable1 is a pointer to an int, but variable2 is just an int:

```
int * variable1, variable2;
```

An ampersand in front of a variable acts as the *address-of* operator. So we could assign the address of variable2 to variable1 with:

```
variable1 = &variable2;
```

We can also assign the value of one pointer variable to another directly:

```
intPointer = variable1;
```

Perhaps most importantly, we can allocate memory during runtime that can be accessed only through a pointer. This is accomplished with the new operator:

```
double * doublePointer = new double;
```

Accessing the memory at the other end of the pointer is known as *dereferencing* and is accomplished with an asterisk to the left of a pointer identifier. Again, this is the same placement we would use for a pointer declaration. The context makes the meaning different. Here's an example:

```
❶ *doublePointer = 35.4;
❷ double localDouble = *doublePointer;
```

We assign a value to the double allocated by the previous code ❶ before copying the value from this memory location to the variable localDouble ❷.

To deallocate memory allocated with new, once we no longer need it, we use the keyword delete:

```
delete doublePointer;
```

The mechanics of this process are described in detail in "Memory Matters" on page 85.

Benefits of Pointers

Pointers give us abilities not available with static memory allocation and also provide new opportunities for efficient use of memory. The three main benefits of using pointers are:

- Runtime-sized data structures
- Resizable data structures
- Memory sharing

Let's take a look at each of these in a bit more detail.

Runtime-Sized Data Structures

By using pointers, we can make an array with a size determined at runtime, rather than having to choose the size before building our application. This saves us from having to choose between potentially running out of space in the array and making the array as large as could possibly be needed, thereby wasting much of the array space in the average case. We first saw runtime data sizing in "Deciding When to Use Arrays" on page 74. We'll use this concept later in this chapter, in "Variable-Length Strings" on page 91.

Resizable Data Structures

We can also make pointer-based data structures that grow or shrink during runtime as needed. The most basic resizable data structure is the linked list, which you may have already seen. Although the data in the structure can be accessed only in sequential order, the linked list always has just as many places for data as it has data itself, with no wasted space. Other, more elaborate pointer-based data structures, as you will see later, have orderings and "shapes" that can reflect the relationship of the underlying data better than an array can. Because of this, even though an array offers full random-access that no pointer-based structure offers, the *retrieval* operation (where we find the element in the structure that best meets a certain criterion) can be much faster with a pointer-based structure. We'll use this benefit later in this chapter to create a data structure for student records that grows as needed.

Memory Sharing

Pointers can improve program efficiency by allowing memory blocks to be shared. For example, when we call a function, we can pass a pointer to a block of memory instead of passing a copy of the block using *reference parameters*. You've most likely seen these before; they are parameters in which an ampersand (&) appears between the type and the name in the formal parameter list:

```
void refParamFunction (int ❶& x) {
    ❷x = 10;
}

int number = 5;
refParamFunction(❸number);
cout << ❹number << "\n";
```

NOTE   *The spaces shown before and after the ampersand symbol are not required—I just include them here for aesthetic reasons. In other developers' code, you may see* int& x, *int* &x, *or perhaps even* int&x.

In this code, the formal parameter x ❶ is not a copy of the argument number ❸; rather, it is a reference to the memory where number is stored. Therefore, when x is changed ❷, the memory space for number is changed, and the output at the end of the code snippet is 10 ❹. Reference parameters can be used as a mechanism to send values out of a function, as shown in this example. More broadly, reference parameters allow the called function and the calling function to share the same memory, thus lowering overhead. If a variable being passed as a parameter occupies a kilobyte of memory, passing the variable as a reference means copying a 32- or 64-bit pointer instead of the kilobyte. We can signal that we are using a reference parameter for performance, not its output, by using the const keyword:

```
int anotherFunction(const int & x);
```

By prefixing the word const in the declaration of the reference parameter x, anotherFunction will receive a reference to the argument passed in the call but will be unable to modify the value in that argument, just like any other const parameter.

In general, we can use pointers in this way to allow different parts of a program, or different data structures within the program, to have access to the same data without the overhead of copying.

When to Use Pointers

As we discussed with arrays, pointers have potential drawbacks and should be used only when appropriate. How do we know when pointer use is appropriate? Having just listed the benefits of pointers, we can say that pointers should be used only when we require one or more of their benefits. If your program needs a structure to hold an aggregate of data, but you can't accurately estimate how much data ahead of runtime; if you need a structure that can grow and shrink during execution; or if you have large objects or other blocks of data being passed around your program, pointers may be the way to go. In the absence of any of these situations, though, you should be wary of pointers and dynamic memory allocation.

Given pointers' notorious reputation as one of the most difficult C++ features, you might think that no programmer would ever try to use a pointer when it isn't necessary. I have been surprised many times, however, to find otherwise. Sometimes programmers simply trick themselves into thinking a pointer is required. Suppose you are making a call to a function written by someone else, from a library or application programming interface, perhaps, with the following prototype:

```
void compute(int input, int* output);
```

We might imagine that this function is written in C, not C++, and that is why it uses a pointer rather than a reference (&) to make an "outgoing" parameter. In calling this function, a programmer might carelessly do something like this:

```
int num1 = 10;
int* num2 = new int;
compute(num1, num2);
```

This code is inefficient in space because it creates a pointer where none is needed. Instead of the space for two integers, it uses the space for two integers and a pointer. The code is also inefficient in time because the unnecessary memory allocation takes time (as explained in the next section). Lastly, the programmer now has to remember to delete the allocated memory. All of this could've been avoided by using the other aspect of the & operator, which allows you to get the address of a statically allocated variable, like this:

```
int num1 = 10;
int num2;
compute(num1, &num2);
```

Strictly speaking, we're still using a pointer in the second version, but we're using it implicitly, without a pointer variable or dynamic memory allocation.

Memory Matters

To understand how dynamic memory allocation gives us runtime sizing and memory sharing, we have to understand a little bit about how memory allocation works in general. This is one of the areas where I think it benefits new programmers to learn C++. All programmers must eventually understand how memory systems work in a modern computer, and C++ forces you to face this issue head-on. Other languages hide enough of the dirty details of memory systems that new programmers convince themselves that these details are of no concern, which is simply not the case. Rather, the details are of no concern so long as everything is working. As soon as there is a problem, however, ignorance of the underlying memory models creates an insurmountable obstacle between the programmer and the solution.

The Stack and the Heap

C++ allocates memory in two places: the *stack* and the *heap*. As the names imply, the stack is organized and neat, and the heap is disjointed and messy. The name *stack* is especially descriptive because it helps you visualize the contiguous nature of the memory allocation. Think of a stack of crates, as in Figure 4-1 (a). When you have a crate to store, you place it on the top of the stack. To remove a particular crate from the stack, you have to first remove all the crates that are on top of it. In practical programming terms, this means that once you have allocated a block of memory (a crate) on the stack, there's no way to resize it because at any time you may have other memory blocks immediately following it (other crates on top of it).

In C++, you might explicitly create your own stack for use in a particular algorithm, but regardless, there is one stack your program will always be using, known as the program's *runtime stack*. Every time a function is called (and this includes the main function), a block of memory is allocated on the top of the runtime stack. This block of memory is called an *activation record*. A full discussion of its contents is beyond the scope of this text, but for your understanding as a problem-solver, the main content of the activation record is the storage space for variables. Memory for all the local variables, including the function's parameters, is allocated within the activation record. Let's take a look at an example:

```
int functionB(int inputValue) {
  ❶return inputValue - 10;
}
int functionA(int num) {
    int localVariable = functionB(num * 10);
    return localVariable;
}
int main()
{
    int x = 12;
    int y = functionA(x);
    return 0;
}
```

In this code, the main function calls functionA, which in turn calls functionB. Figure 4-1 (b) shows a simplified version of how the runtime stack would be arranged at the point right before we execute the return statement of functionB ❶. The activation records for all three functions would be arranged in a stack of contiguous memory, with the main function at the bottom of the stack. (Just to make things extra confusing, it's possible that the stack begins at the highest possible point in memory and is built downward to lower memory addresses rather than upward to higher memory addresses. You do yourself no harm, though, by ignoring the possibility.) Logically, the main function activation record is on the bottom of the stack, with the functionA activation record on top of it and the functionB activation record on top of functionA. Neither of the lower two activation records can be removed before functionB's activation record is removed.

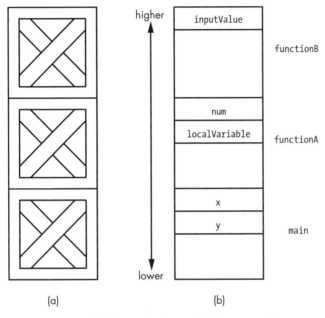

Figure 4-1: A stack of crates and a stack of function calls

While a stack is highly organized, a heap, by contrast, has little organization. Suppose you're storing things in crates again, but these crates are fragile and you can't stack them on top of each other. You've got a big, initially empty room to store the crates, and you can put them anywhere you want on the floor. The crates are heavy, however, so once you put one down, you'd rather just leave it where it is until you're ready to take it out of the room. This system has advantages and disadvantages compared to the stack. On the one hand, this storage system is flexible and allows you to get to the contents of any crate at any time. On the other hand, the room is going to quickly become a mess. If the crates are all different sizes, it's going to be especially difficult to make use of all of the available space on the floor. You'll end up with a lot of gaps between crates that are too small to fill with another crate. Because the crates can't be easily moved, removing several crates just creates several hard-to-fill gaps rather than providing the wide-open storage of our original empty floor. In practical programming terms, our heap is like the floor of that room. A block of memory is a contiguous series of addresses; thus, over the lifetime of a program with many memory allocations and deallocations, we'll end up with lots of gaps between the remaining allocated memory blocks. This problem is known as *memory fragmentation*.

Every program has its own heap, from which memory is dynamically allocated. In C++, this usually means an invocation of the new keyword, but you will also see calls to the old C functions for memory allocation, such as malloc. Each call to new (or malloc) sets aside a chunk of memory in the heap and returns a pointer to the chunk, while each call to delete (or free if the memory was allocated with malloc) returns the chunk to the pool of available heap memory. Because of fragmentation, not all of the memory in the pool is equally useful. If our program begins by allocating variables A, B, and C in heap memory, we might expect those blocks to be contiguous. If we deallocate B, the gap it leaves behind can be filled only by another request that is of B's size or smaller, until either A or C is also deallocated.

Figure 4-2 clarifies the situation. In part (a), we see the floor of our room littered with crates. At one point the room was probably well organized, but over time, the arrangement became haphazard. Now there is a small crate (b) that cannot fit in any open space on the floor, even though the overall unused floor area greatly exceeds the footprint of the crate. In part (c), we represent a small heap. The dashed-line squares are the smallest (indivisible) chunks of memory, which might be a single byte, a memory word, or something larger, depending on the heap manager. The shaded areas represent allocations of contiguous memory; for clarity, one allocation has some of its chunks numbered. As with the fragmented floor, the fragmented heap has the unallocated memory chunks separated, which reduces their usability. There are a total of 85 unused chunks of memory, but the largest contiguous range of unused memory, as indicated by the arrow, is only 17 chunks long. In other words, if each chunk were a byte, this heap could not fulfill any request from an invocation of new for more than 17 bytes, even though the heap has 85 bytes free.

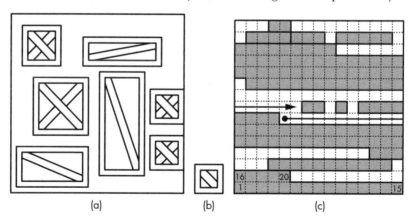

Figure 4-2: A fragmented floor, a crate that cannot be placed, and fragmented memory

Memory Size

The first practical issue with memory is limiting its use to what is necessary. Modern computer systems have so much memory that it's easy to think of it as an infinite resource, but in fact each program has a limited amount of memory. Also, programs need to use memory efficiently to avoid overall system slowdown. In a multitasking operating system (which means just about every modern operating system), every byte of memory wasted by one program pushes the system as a whole toward the point where the set of currently running programs doesn't have enough memory to run. At that point, the operating system constantly swaps out chunks of one program for another and thus grinds to a crawl. This condition is known as *thrashing*.

Note that, beyond the desire to keep the overall program memory footprint as small as possible, the stack and the heap have maximum sizes. To prove this, let's allocate memory from the heap a kilobyte at a time, until something blows up:

```
const int intsPerKilobyte = 1024 / sizeof(int);
while (true) {
    int *oneKilobyteArray = new int[intsPerKilobyte];
}
```

Let me emphasize that this is horrible code written purely to demonstrate a point. If you try this code out on your system, you should save all of your work first, just to be safe. What should happen is that the program halts and your operating system complains that the code generated but did not handle a bad_alloc exception. This exception is thrown by new when no block of unallocated memory in the heap is large enough to fulfill the request. Running out of heap memory is called a *heap overflow*. On some systems, a heap overflow can be common, while on other systems, a program will cause thrashing long before it produces a bad_alloc (on my system, the new call didn't fail until I had allocated two gigabytes in previous calls).

A similar situation exists with the runtime stack. Each function call allocates space on the stack, and there is some fixed overhead for each activation record, even for a function with no parameters or local variables. The easiest way to demonstrate this is with a runaway recursive function:

```
❶ int count = 0;
void stackOverflow() {
    ❷count++;
    ❸stackOverflow();
}
int main()
{
    ❹stackOverflow();
    return 0;
}
```

This code has a global variable ❶, which in most cases is bad style, but here I need a value that persists throughout all of the recursive calls. As this variable is declared outside of the function, no memory is allocated for it in the function's activation record, nor are there any other local variables or parameters. All the function does is increment count ❷ and make a recursive call ❸. Recursion is discussed extensively in Chapter 6 but is used here simply to make the chain of function calls as long as possible. The activation record of a function remains on the stack until that function ends. So when the first call is made to stackOverflow from main ❹, an activation record is placed on the runtime stack that cannot be removed until that first function call ends. This will never happen because the function makes a second call to stackOverflow, placing another activation record on the stack, which then makes a third call, and so on. These activation records stack up until the stack runs out of room. On my system, count is around 4,900 when the program bombs. My development environment, Visual Studio, defaults to a 1MB stack allocation, which means that each of these function calls, even without any local variables or parameters, creates an activation record of over 200 bytes.

Lifetime

The *lifetime* of a variable is the time span between allocation and deallocation. With a stack-based variable, meaning either a local variable or a parameter, the lifetime is handled implicitly. The variable is allocated when the function is called and deallocated when the function ends. With a heap-based variable, meaning a variable dynamically allocated using new, the lifetime is in our hands. Managing the lifetime of dynamically allocated variables is the bane of every C++ programmer. The most obvious issue is the dreaded *memory leak*, a situation in which memory is allocated from the heap but never deallocated and not referenced by any pointer. Here's a simple example:

```
❶ int *intPtr = new int;
❷ intPtr = NULL;
```

In this code, we declare a pointer to an integer ❶, initializing it by allocating an integer from the heap. Then in the second line, we set our integer pointer to NULL ❷ (which is simply an alias for the number zero). The integer we allocated with new still exists, however. It sits, lonely and forlorn, in its place in the heap, awaiting a deallocation that can never come. We cannot deallocate the integer because to deallocate a block of memory, we use delete followed by a pointer to the block, and we no longer have a pointer to the block. If we tried to follow the code above with delete intPtr, we would get an error because intPtr is zero.

Sometimes, instead of memory that never gets deallocated, we have the opposite problem, attempting to deallocate the same memory twice, which produces a runtime error. This might seem like an easy problem to avoid: Just don't call delete twice on the same variable. What makes this situation tricky is that we may have multiple variables pointing to the same memory. If multiple variables point to the same memory and we call delete on any of those variables, we have effectively deallocated the memory for all of the variables. If we don't explicitly clear the variables to NULL, they will be known as *dangling references*, and calling delete on any of them will produce a runtime error.

Solving Pointer Problems

By this point, you're probably ready for some problems, so let's look at a couple and see how we can use pointers and dynamic memory allocation to solve them. First we'll work with some dynamically allocated arrays, which will demonstrate how to keep track of heap memory through all of our manipulations. Then we'll get our feet wet with a truly dynamic structure.

Variable-Length Strings

In this first problem, we're going to create functions to manipulate strings. Here, we're using the term in its most general sense: a sequence of characters, regardless of how those characters are stored. Suppose we need to support three functions on our string type.

PROBLEM: VARIABLE-LENGTH STRING MANIPULATION

Write heap-based implementations for three required string functions:

append   This function takes a string and a character and appends the character to the end of the string.

concatenate   This function takes two strings and appends the characters of the second string onto the first.

characterAt   This function takes a string and a number and returns the character at that position in the string (with the first character in the string numbered zero).

Write the code with the assumption that characterAt will be called frequently, while the other two functions will be called relatively seldom. The relative efficiency of the operations should reflect the calling frequency.

In this case, we want to choose a representation for our string that allows for a fast characterAt function, which means we need a fast way to locate a particular character. As you probably recall from the previous chapter, this is what an array does best: random access. So let's solve this problem using arrays of char. The append and concatenate functions change the size of the string, which means we run into all the array problems we discussed earlier. Because there's no built-in limitation to the size of the string in this problem, we can't pick a large initial size for our arrays and hope for the best. Instead, we'll need to resize our arrays during runtime.

To start off, let's create a typedef for our string type. We know we're going to be dynamically creating our arrays, so we need to make our string type a pointer to char.

```
typedef char * arrayString;
```

With that in place, let's start on the functions. Using the principle of starting with what we already know how to do, we can quickly write the characterAt function.

```
char characterAt(arrayString s, int position) {
    ❶return s[position];
}
```

Recall from Chapter 3 that if a pointer is assigned the address of an array, we can access elements in the array using normal array notation ❶. Note, however, that bad things can happen if position is not actually a valid element number for the array s, and this code places the responsibility of validating the second parameter on the caller. We'll consider alternatives to this situation in the exercises. For now, let's move onto the append function. We can imagine what this function will do generally, but to get the specifics right, we should consider an example. This is a technique I call *solving by sample case*.

Start with a nontrivial sample input for the function or program. Write down all the details of that input along with all the details of the output. Then when you write your code, you'll be writing for the general case while also double-checking how each step transforms your sample to make sure that you reach the desired output state. This technique is especially helpful when dealing with pointers and dynamically allocated memory, because so much of what happens in the program is outside of direct view. Following through a case on paper forces you to track all the changing values in memory—not just those directly represented by variables but also those in the heap.

Suppose we start with the string test, which is to say we have an array of characters in the heap with t, e, s, and t, in that order, and we want to append, using our function, an exclamation point. Figure 4-3 shows the state of memory before (a) and after (b) this operation. In these diagrams, anything to the left of the dashed vertical line is stack memory (local variables or parameters) and anything to the right is heap memory, dynamically allocated using new.

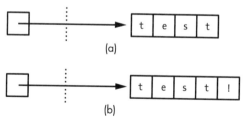

Figure 4-3: Proposed "before" (a) and "after" (b) states for append function

Looking at this figure, right away I'm seeing a potential issue for our function. Based on our implementation approach for the strings, the function is going to create a new array that is one element larger than the original array and copy all the characters from the first array to the second. But how are we to know how large the first array is? From the previous chapter, we know that we have to track the size of our arrays ourselves. So something is missing.

If we've had experience working with strings in the standard C/C++ library, we will already know the missing ingredient, but if we don't, we can quickly reason it out. Remember that one of our problem-solving techniques is *looking for analogies*. Perhaps we should think about other problems in which the length of something was unknown. Back in Chapter 2, we processed identification codes with an arbitrary number of digits for the "Luhn Checksum Validation" problem. In that problem, we didn't know how many digits the user would enter. In the end, we wrote a while loop that continued until the last character read was the end-of-line.

Unfortunately, there is no end-of-line character waiting for us at the end of our arrays. But what if we *put* an end-of-line character in the last element of all our string arrays? Then we could discover the length of our arrays the same way we discovered how many digits were in the identification codes. The only downside to this approach is that we could no longer use the end-of-line character in our strings, except as the string terminator. That's not necessarily a huge restriction, depending on how the strings will be used, but for maximum flexibility, it would be best to choose a value that cannot be confused with any character anyone might actually want to use. Therefore, we'll use a zero to terminate our arrays because a zero represents a null character in ASCII and other character code systems. This is exactly the method used by the standard C/C++ library.

With that issue cleared up, let's get more specific about what append will do with our sample data. We know our function is going to have two parameters, the first being an arrayString, a pointer to an array of characters in the heap, and the second being the char to be appended. To keep things straight, let's go ahead and write the outline of the append function and the code to test it.

```
void append(❶arrayString& s, char c) {
}
void appendTester() {
    ❷arrayString a = new char[5];
    ❸a[0] = 't'; a[1] = 'e'; a[2] = 's'; a[3] = 't'; a[4] = 0;
    ❹append(a, '!');
    ❺cout << a << "\n";
}
```

The appendTester function allocates our string in the heap ❷. Note that the size of the array is five, which is necessary so that we can assign all four letters of the word test along with our terminating null character ❸. Then we call append ❹, which at this point is just an empty shell. When I wrote the shell, I realized that the arrayString parameter had to be a reference (&) ❶ because the function is going to create a new array in the heap. That's the whole point, after all, of using dynamic memory here: to create a new array whenever the string is resized. Therefore, the value that the variable a has when passed to append is not the same value it should have when the function is through, because it needs to point to a new array. Note that because our arrays use the null-character termination expected by the standard libraries, we can send the array referenced by the pointer a directly to the output stream to check the value ❺.

Figure 4-4 shows our new understanding of what the function will do with our test case. The array terminators are in place, shown as NULL for clarity. In the after (b) state, it's clear that s is pointing at a new allocation of memory. The previous array is now in a shaded box; in these diagrams, I'm using shaded boxes to indicate memory that has been deallocated. Including the deallocated memory in our diagrams helps remind us to actually perform the deallocation.

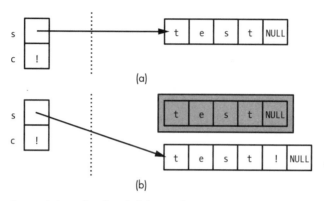

Figure 4-4: Updated and elaborated memory states before (a) and after (b) the append function

With everything properly visualized, we can write this function:

```
void append(arrayString& s, char c) {
    int oldLength = 0;
❶  while (s[oldLength] != 0) {
        oldLength++;
    }
❷  arrayString newS = new char[oldLength + 2];
❸  for (int i = 0; i < oldLength; i++) {
        newS[i] = s[i];
    }
❹  newS[oldLength] = c;
❺  newS[oldLength + 1] = 0;
❻  delete[] s;
❼  s = newS;
}
```

There's a lot going on in this code, so let's check it out piece by piece. At the beginning of the function, we have a loop to locate the null character that terminates our array ❶. When the loop completes, oldLength will be the number of legitimate characters in the array (that is, not including the terminating null character). We allocate the new array from the heap with a size of oldLength + 2 ❷. This is one of those details that is tricky to keep straight if you're figuring it all out in your head but easy to get right if you have a diagram. Following the code through our example in Figure 4-5, we see that oldLength would be four in this case. We know that oldLength would be four because test has four characters and that the new array in part (b) requires six characters because we need space for the appended character and the null terminator.

With the new array allocated, we copy all of the legitimate characters from the old array to the new ❸, and we then assign the appended character ❹ and the null character terminator ❺ to their appropriate locations in the new array. Again, our diagram helps us keep things straight. To make things even clearer, Figure 4-5 shows how the value of oldLength was computed and what position that value would indicate in the new array. With that visual reminder, it's easy to get the subscripts correct in those two assignment statements.

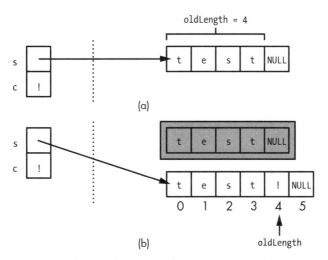

Figure 4-5: Showing the relationship of a local variable, parameters, and allocated memory before and after the append function

The last three lines in the append function are all about that shaded box in part (b) of the figure. To avoid a memory leak, we have to deallocate the array in the heap that our parameter s originally pointed to ❻. Finally, we leave our function with s pointing to the new, longer array ❼. Unfortunately, one of the reasons memory leaks are so common in C++ programming is that until the total amount of memory leaks is large, the program and overall system will display no ill effects. Thus, the leaks can go totally unnoticed by programmers during testing. As programmers, therefore, we must be diligent and always consider the lifetime of our heap memory allocations. Every time you use the keyword new, think about where and when the corresponding delete will occur.

Notice how everything in this function follows directly from our diagrams. Tricky programming becomes so much less tricky with good diagrams, and I wish more new programmers would take the time to draw before they code. This goes back to our most fundamental problem-solving principle: Always have a plan. A well-drawn diagram for a problem example is like having a mapped-out route to your destination before starting on a long vacation drive. It's a little bit of extra effort at the start to potentially avoid much more effort and frustration at the end.

CREATING DIAGRAMS

All you need to draw a diagram is a pencil and paper. If you've got the time, though, I would recommend using a drawing program. There are drawing tools with templates specifically for programming problems, but any general vector-based drawing program will get you started (the term *vector* here means the program works with lines and curves and isn't a paintbox program like Photoshop). I made the original illustrations for this book using a program called Inkscape, which is freely available. Creating the diagrams on your computer allows you to keep them organized in the same place where you store the code that the diagrams illustrate. The diagrams are also likely to be neater and therefore more easily understood if you come back to them after an absence. Finally, it's easy to copy and modify a computer-created diagram, as I did when I created Figure 4-5 from Figure 4-4, and if you want to make some quick temporary notations, you can always print out a copy to doodle on.

Getting back to our append function, the code looks solid, but remember that we based this code on a particular sample case. Thus, we shouldn't get cocky and assume that the code will work for all valid cases. In particular, we need to check for special cases. In programming, a *special case* is a situation in which valid data will cause the normal flow of code to produce erroneous results.

Note that this problem is distinct from that of bad data, such as out-of-range data. In the code for this book, we've made the assumption of good input data for programs and individual functions. For example, if the program is expecting a series of integers separated by commas, we've assumed that's what the program is getting, not extraneous characters, nonnumbers, and so on. Such an assumption is necessary to keep code length reasonable and to avoid repeating the same data-checking code over and over. In the real world, however, we should take reasonable precautions against bad input. This is known as robustness. A *robust* program performs well even with bad input. For example, such a program could display an error message to the user instead of crashing.

Checking for Special Cases

Let's look at append again, checking for special cases—in other words, making sure we don't have any oddball situations among the possible good input values. The most common culprits for special cases are at the extremes, such as the smallest or largest possible input. With append, there's no maximum size for our string array, but there is a minimum size. If the string has no legitimate characters, it would actually correspond to an array of one character (the one character being the null terminating character). As before, let's make a diagram to keep things straight. Suppose we appended the exclamation point to a null string, as shown in Figure 4-6.

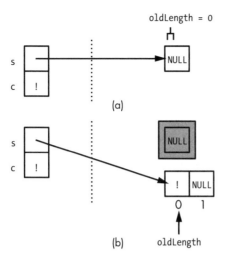

Figure 4-6: Testing the smallest case for the append function

When we look at the diagram, this doesn't appear to be a special case, but we should run the case through our function to check. Let's add the following to our appendTester code:

```
arrayString b = new char[1];
b[0] = 0;
append(b, '!');
cout << b << "\n";
```

That works, too. Now that we're reasonably sure that the append function is correct, do we like it? The code seemed straightforward, and I'm not getting any "bad smells," but it does seem a little long for a simple operation. As I think ahead to the concatenate function, it occurs to me that, like append, the concatenate function will need to determine the length of a string array—or maybe the lengths of two string arrays. Because both operations will need a loop that finds the null character that terminates the string, we could put that code in its own function, which is then called from append and concatenate as needed. Let's go ahead and do that and modify append accordingly.

```
int length(arrayString s) {
  ❶int count = 0;
    while (s[count] != 0) {
        count++;
    }
    return count;
}
void append(arrayString& s, char c) {
  ❷int oldLength = length(s);
    arrayString newS = new char[oldLength + 2];
    for (int i = 0; i < oldLength; i++) {
        newS[i] = s[i];
    }
```

```
    newS[oldLength] = c;
    newS[oldLength + 1] = 0;
    delete[] s;
    s = newS;
}
```

The code in the length function ❶ is essentially the same code that previously began the append function. In the append function itself, we've replaced that code with a call to length ❷. The length function is what's known as a *helper function*, a function that encapsulates an operation common to several other functions. Besides reducing the length of our code, the elimination of redundant code means our code is more reliable and easier to modify. It also helps our problem solving because helper functions divide our code into smaller chunks, making it easier for us to recognize opportunities for code reuse.

Copying Dynamically Allocated Strings

Now it's time to tackle that concatenate function. We'll take the same approach we did with append. First, we'll write an empty shell version of the function to get the parameters and their types straight in our heads. Then, we'll make a diagram of a test case, and finally, we'll write code to match our diagram. Here is the shell of the function, along with additional testing code:

```
void concatenate(❶arrayString& s1, ❷arrayString s2) {
}
void concatenateTester() {
    arrayString a = new char[5];
    a[0] = 't'; a[1] = 'e'; a[2] = 's'; a[3] = 't'; a[4] = 0;
    arrayString b = new char[4];
    b[0] = 'b'; b[1] = 'e'; b[2] = 'd'; b[3] = 0;
    concatenate(a, b);
}
```

Remember that the description of this function says that the characters in the second string (the second parameter) are appended to the end of the first string. Therefore, the first parameter to concatenate will be a reference parameter ❶, for the same reason as the first parameter of append. The second parameter ❷, though, should not be changed by the function, so it will be a value parameter. Now for our sample case: We're concatenating the strings test and bed. The before-and-after diagram is shown in Figure 4-7.

The details of the diagram should be familiar from the append function. Here, for concatenate, we start with two dynamically allocated arrays in the heap, pointed to by our two parameters, s1 and s2. When the function is complete, s1 will point to a new array in the heap that's nine characters long. The array that s1 previously pointed to has been deallocated; s2 and its array are unchanged. While it might seem pointless to include s2 and the bed array on our diagram, when trying to avoid coding errors, keeping track of what doesn't change is as important as keeping track of what does. I've also numbered the elements of the old and new arrays, as that came in handy with the append function. Everything is in place now, so let's write this function.

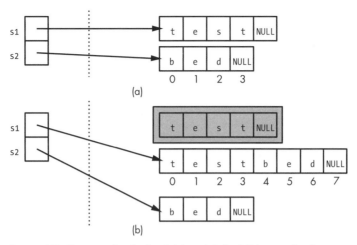

Figure 4-7: Showing the "before" (a) and "after" (b) states for the concatenate method

```
void concatenate(arrayString& s1, arrayString s2) {
  ❶int s1_OldLength = length(s1);
   int s2_Length = length(s2);
   int s1_NewLength = s1_OldLength + s2_Length;
  ❷arrayString newS = new char[s1_NewLength + 1];
  ❸for(int i = 0; i < s1_OldLength; i++) {
       newS[i] = s1[i];
   }
   for(int i = 0; i < s2_Length; i++) {
       newS[❹s1_OldLength + i] = s2[i];
   }
  ❺newS[s1_NewLength] = 0;
  ❻delete[] s1;
  ❼s1 = newS;
}
```

First, we determine the lengths of both of the strings we're concatenating ❶, and then we sum those values to get the length the concatenated string will have when we are done. Remember that all of these lengths are for the number of legitimate characters, not including the null terminator. Thus, when we create the array in the heap to store the new string ❷, we allocate one more than the combined length to have a space for the terminator. Then we copy the characters from the two original strings to the new string ❸. The first loop is straightforward, but notice the computation of the subscript in the second loop ❹. We're copying from the beginning of s2 into the middle of newS; this is yet another example of translating from one range of values to another range of values, which we've been doing in this text since Chapter 2. By looking at the element numbers on my diagram, I'm able to see what variables I need to put together to compute the right destination subscript. The remainder of the function puts the null terminator in place at the end of the new string ❺. As with append, we deallocate the original heap memory pointed to by our first parameter ❻ and repoint the first parameter at the newly allocated string ❼.

This code appears to work, but as before, we want to make sure that we haven't inadvertently made a function that succeeds for our test case but not all cases. The most likely trouble cases would be when either or both of the parameters are zero-length strings (just the null terminator). We should check these cases explicitly before moving on. Note that when you are checking for correctness in code that uses pointers, you should take care to look at the pointers themselves and not just the values in the heap that they reference. Here is one test case:

```
arrayString a = new char[5];
a[0] = 't'; a[1] = 'e'; a[2] = 's'; a[3] = 't'; a[4] = 0;
arrayString c = new char[1];
c[0] = 0;
concatenate(c, a);
cout << a << "\n" << c << "\n";
❶ cout << (void *) a << "\n" << (void *) c << "\n";
```

I wanted to be sure that the call to concatenate results in a and c both pointing to the string test—that is, that they point to arrays with identical values. Equally important, though, is that they point to *different* strings, as shown in Figure 4-8 (a). I check this in the second output statement by changing the types of the variables to void *, which forces the output stream to display the raw value of the pointers ❶. If the pointers themselves had the same value, then we would say that the pointers had become *cross-linked*, as shown in Figure 4-8 (b). When pointers have unknowingly become cross-linked, subtle problems occur because changing the contents of one variable in the heap mysteriously changes another variable—really the same variable, but in a large program, that can be hard to see. Also, remember that if two pointers are cross-linked, when one of them is deallocated via delete, the remaining pointer becomes a dangling reference. Therefore, we have to be diligent when we review our code and always check potential cross-linking.

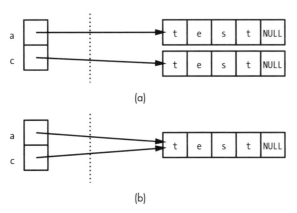

(a)

(b)

Figure 4-8: concatenate should result in two distinct strings (a), not two cross-linked pointers (b).

With all three functions implemented—characterAt, append, and concatenate—we've completed the problem.

Linked Lists

Now we're going to try something trickier. The pointer manipulations will be more complicated, but we'll keep everything straight now that we know how to crank out the diagrams.

PROBLEM: TRACKING AN UNKNOWN QUANTITY OF STUDENT RECORDS

In this problem, you will write functions to store and manipulate a collection of student records. A student record contains a student number and a grade, both integers. The following functions are to be implemented:

addRecord   This function takes a pointer to a collection of student records, a student number, and a grade, and it adds a new record with this data to the collection.

averageRecord   This function takes a pointer to a collection of student records and returns the simple average of student grades in the collection as a double.

The collection can be of any size. The addRecord operation is expected to be called frequently, so it must be implemented efficiently.

A number of approaches would meet the specifications, but we're going to choose a method that helps us practice our pointer-based problem-solving techniques: linked lists. You may have already seen a linked list before, but if not, know that the introduction of linked lists represents a kind of sea change from what we have discussed so far in this text. A good problem-solver could have developed any of the previous solutions given enough time and careful thought. Most programmers, however, wouldn't come up with the linked list concept without help. Once you see it and master the basics, though, other linked structures will come to mind, and then you are off and running. A linked list is truly a dynamic structure. Our string arrays were stored in dynamically allocated memory, but once created, they were static structures, never getting any larger or smaller, just being replaced. A linked list, in contrast, grows piece by piece over time like a daisy chain.

Building a List of Nodes

Let's construct a sample linked list of student records. To make a linked list, you need a struct that contains a pointer to the same struct, in addition to whatever data you want to store in the collection represented by the linked list. For our problem, the struct will contain a student number and grade.

```
struct ❶listNode {
  ❷int studentNum;
    int grade;
  ❸listNode * next;
};
❹ typedef listNode * studentCollection;
```

The name of our struct is listNode ❶. A struct used to create a linked list is always referred to as a *node*. Presumably the name is an analogy to the botanical term, meaning a point on a stem from which a new branch grows. The node contains the student number ❷ and grade that make up the real "payload" of the node. The node also contains a pointer to the very type of struct we are defining ❸. The first time most programmers see this, it looks confusing and perhaps even a syntactical impossibility: How can we define a structure in terms of itself? But this is legal, and the meaning will become clear shortly. Note that the self-referring pointer in a node is typically given a name like *next, nextPtr,* or the like. Lastly, this code declares a typedef for a pointer to our node type ❹. This will help the readability of our functions. Now let's build our sample linked list using these types:

```
❶ studentCollection sc;
❷ listNode * node1 = new listNode;
❸ node1->studentNum = 1001; node1->grade = 78;
  listNode * node2 = new listNode;
  node2->studentNum = 1012; node2->grade = 93;
  listNode * node3 = new listNode;
❹ node3->studentNum = 1076; node3->grade = 85;
❺ sc = node1;
❻ node1->next = node2;
❼ node2->next = node3;
❽ node3->next = NULL;
❾ node1 = node2 = node3 = NULL;
```

We begin by declaring a studentCollection, sc ❶, which will eventually become the name for our linked list. Then we declare node1 ❷, a pointer to a listNode. Again, studentCollection is synonymous with listNode *, but for readability I'm using the studentCollection type only for variables that will refer to the whole list structure. After declaring node1 and pointing it to a newly allocated listNode in the heap ❷, we assign values to the studentNum and grade fields in that node ❸. At this point, the next field is unassigned. This is not a book on syntax, but if you haven't seen the -> notation before, it's used to indicate the field of a pointed-to struct (or class). So node1->studentNum means "the studentNum field in the struct pointed to by node1" and is equivalent to (*node1).studentNum. We then repeat the same process for node2 and node3. After assigning the field values to the last node, the state of memory is as shown in Figure 4-9. In these diagrams, we'll use the divided-box notation we previously used for arrays to show the node struct.

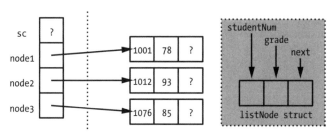

Figure 4-9: Halfway through building a sample linked list

Now that we have all of our nodes, we can string them together to form a linked list. That's what the rest of the previous code listing does. First, we point our studentCollection variable to the first node ❺, then we point the next field of the first node to the second node ❻, and then we point the next field of the second node to the third node ❼. In the next step, we assign NULL (again, this is just a synonym for zero) to the next field of the third node ❽. We do this for the same reason we put a null character at the end of our arrays in the previous problem: to terminate the structure. Just as we needed a special character to show us the end of the array, we need a zero in the next field of the last node in our linked list so that we know it *is* the last node. Finally, to clean things up and avoid potential cross-linking problems, we assign NULL to each of the individual node pointers ❾. The resulting state of memory is shown in Figure 4-10.

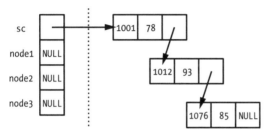

Figure 4-10: The completed sample linked list

With this visual in front of us, it's clear why the structure is called a linked list: Each node in the list is linked to the next. You'll often see linked lists drawn linearly, but I actually prefer the scattered-in-memory look of this diagram because it emphasizes that these nodes have no relationship to each other besides the links; each of them could be anywhere inside the heap. Make sure you trace through the code until you are confident you agree with the diagram.

Notice that, in the concluding state, only one stack-based pointer remains in use, our studentCollection variable sc, which points to the first node. A pointer external to the list (that is, not the next field of a node in the list) that points to the first node in a linked list is known as a *head pointer*. On a symbolic level, this variable represents the list as a whole, but of course it directly references only the first node. To get to the second node, we have to go through the first, and to get to the third node, we have to go through the first two, and so on. This means that linked lists offer only sequential access, as opposed to the random access provided by arrays. Sequential access is the weakness of linked-list structures. The strength of linked-list structures, as previously alluded to, is our ability to grow or shrink the size of the structure by adding or removing nodes, without having to create an entirely new structure and copy the data over, as we've done with arrays.

Adding Nodes to a List

Now let's implement the addRecord function. This function is going to create a new node and connect it into an existing linked list. We'll use the same techniques we used in the previous problem. First up: a function shell and a sample call. For testing, we'll add code to the previous listing, so sc already exists as the head pointer to the list of three nodes.

```
void addRecord(studentCollection& sc, int stuNum, int gr) {
}
❶ addRecord(sc, 1274, 91);
```

Again, the ❶ call would come at the end of the previous listing. With the function shell outlining the parameters, we can diagram the "before" state of this call, as shown in Figure 4-11.

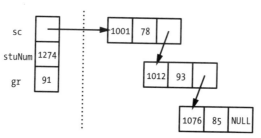

Figure 4-11: The "before" state for the addRecord function

Regarding the "after" state, though, we have a choice. We can guess that we're going to create a new node in the heap and copy the values from the parameters stuNum and gr into the studentNum and grade fields of the new node. The question is where this node is going to go, logically, in our linked list. The most obvious choice would be at the end; there's a NULL value in a next field just asking to be pointed to a new node. That would correspond to Figure 4-12.

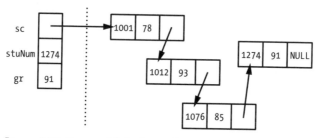

Figure 4-12: Proposed "after" state for addRecord function

But if we can assume that the order of the records doesn't matter (that we don't need to keep the records in the same order they were added to the collection), then this is the wrong choice. To see why, consider a collection, not of three student records, but of 3,000. To reach the last record in our linked list in order to modify its next field would require traveling through all 3,000 nodes. That's unacceptably inefficient because we can get the new node into the list without traveling through *any* of the existing nodes.

Figure 4-13 shows how. After the new node is created, it is linked into the list at the *beginning*, not at the end. In the "after" state, our head pointer sc points to the new node, while the next field of the new node points to what was previously the first node in the list, the one with student number 1001. Note that while we assign a value to that next field of the new node, the only existing pointer that changes is sc, and none of the values in the existing nodes are altered or even inspected. Working from our diagram, here's the code:

```
void addRecord(studentCollection& sc, int stuNum, int gr) {
  ❶listNode * newNode = new listNode;
  ❷newNode->studentNum = stuNum;
    newNode->grade = gr;
  ❸newNode->next = sc;
  ❹sc = newNode;
}
```

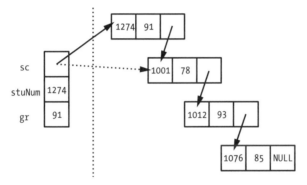

Figure 4-13: Acceptable "after" state for addRecord function. The dashed arrow indicates the previous value of the pointer stored in sc.

Again, let me emphasize that translating a diagram and that code is a lot easier than trying to keep things straight in your head. The code comes directly from the illustration. We create a new node ❶ and assign the student number and grade from the parameters ❷. Then we link the new node into the list, first by pointing the next field of the new node to the former first node (by assigning it the value of sc) ❸ and then by pointing sc itself at the new node ❹. Note that the last two steps have to happen in that order; we need to use the original value of sc before we change it. Also note that because we change sc, it must be a reference parameter.

As always, when we build code from a sample case, we have to check potential special cases. Here, that means checking to see that the function works with an empty list. With our string arrays, an empty string was still a valid pointer because we still had an array to point to, an array with just the null terminating character. Here, though, the number of nodes is the same as the number of records, and an empty list would be a NULL head pointer. Will our code still hold up if we try to insert our sample data when the incoming head pointer is NULL? Figure 4-14 shows the "before" state and the desired "after" state.

Walking this example through our code, we see that it handles this case fine. The new node is created just as before. Because sc is NULL in the "before" state, when ❸ this value is copied into the next field of our new node, that's exactly what we want, and our one-node list is properly terminated. Note that if we had continued with the other implementation idea—adding the new node at the end of the linked list rather than at the beginning—an initially empty list *would* be a special case because it would then be the only case in which sc is modified.

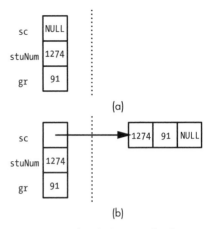

Figure 4-14: The "before" and "after" states for the smallest addRecord case

List Traversal

Now it's time to figure out the averageRecord function. As before, we'll start with a shell and a diagram. Here's the function shell and sample call. Assume the sample call ❶ occurs after the creation of our original sample list, as shown in Figure 4-10.

```
double averageRecord(studentCollection sc) {
}
❶ int avg = averageRecord(sc);
```

As you can see, I've chosen to compute the average as an int, as we did with arrays in the previous chapter. Depending on the problem, however, it might be better to compute it as a floating point value. Now we need a diagram, but we pretty much already have a "before" state with Figure 4-9. We don't need a diagram for the "after" state because this function isn't going to change our dynamic structure, just report on it. We just need to know the expected result, which in this case is about 85.3333.

So how do we actually compute the average? From our experience computing the average of all values in an array, we know the general concept. We need to add up every value in the collection and then divide that sum by the number of values. With our array averaging code, we inspected every value using a for loop from 0 to one less than the size of the array, using the loop counter as the array subscript. We can't use a for loop here because we don't know ahead of time how many numbers are in the linked list; we have to keep going until we reach the NULL value in a node's next field indicating list termination. This suggests a while loop, something like what we used earlier in this chapter to process our arrays of unknown length. Running through a linked list like this, from beginning to terminus, is known as a *list traversal*. This is one of the basic operations on a linked list. Let's put the traversal idea to work to solve this problem:

```
double averageRecord(studentCollection sc) {
  ❶int count = 0;
  ❷double sum = 0;
  ❸listNode * loopPtr = sc;
  ❹while (loopPtr != NULL) {
        ❺sum += loopPtr->grade;
        ❻count++;
        ❼loopPtr = loopPtr->next;
    }
  ❽double average = sum / count;
    return average;
}
```

We start by declaring a variable count to store the number of nodes we encounter in the list ❶; this will also be the number of values in the collection, which we'll use to compute the average. Next we declare a variable sum to store the running total of grade values in the list ❷. Then we declare a listNode * called loopPtr, which we'll use to traverse the list ❸. This is the equivalent of our integer loop variable in an array-processing for loop; it keeps track of where we are in the linked list, not with the position number but by storing a pointer to the node we are processing currently.

At this point, the traversal itself begins. The traversal loop continues until our loop-tracking pointer reaches our terminating NULL ❹. Inside the loop, we add the value of the grade field in the currently referenced node to sum ❺. We increment the count ❻, and then we assign the next field of the current node to our loop-tracking pointer ❼. This has the effect of moving our traversal one node ahead. This is the tricky part of the code, so let's make sure we have this straight. In Figure 4-15, I'm showing how the node variable changes over time. The letters (a) through (d) mark different points during the execution of the code on our sample data, showing different points during the lifetime of loopPtr and the locations from which loopPtr's value has been obtained. Point (a) is just as the loop begins; loopPtr has just been initialized with the value of sc. Therefore, loopPtr points to the first node in the list, just as sc does. During the first iteration of the loop, then, the first node's grade value of 78 is added to sum. The first node's next value is copied to loopPtr so that now loopPtr points to the second node of the list; this is point (b). During the second iteration, we add 93 to sum and copy the next field of the second node to loopPtr; this is point (c). Finally, during the third and last iteration of the loop, we add 85 to sum and assign the NULL of the next field in the third node to loopPtr; this is point (d). When we reach the top of the while loop again, the loop ends because loopPtr is NULL. Because we incremented count each time we iterated, count is three.

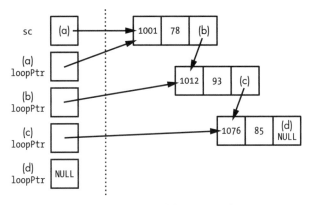

Figure 4-15: How the local variable `loopPtr` *changes during loop iterations in the* `averageRecord` *function*

Once the loop is all done, we just divide the sum by the count and return the result ❽.

The code works on our sample case, but as always, we need to check for potential special cases. Again, with lists, the most obvious special case is an empty list. What happens with our code if sc is NULL when the function begins?

Guess what? The code blows up. (I had to make one of these special cases turn out badly; otherwise, you wouldn't take me seriously.) There's nothing wrong with the loop for the processing of the linked list itself. If sc is NULL, then loopPtr is initialized to NULL, the loop ends as soon as it begins, and sum is left at zero, which seems reasonable enough. The problem is when we perform the division to compute the average ❽, count is also zero, which means we are dividing by zero and which will result in either a program crash or a garbage result. To handle this special case, we could check count against zero at the end of the function, but why not handle the situation up front and check sc? Let's add the following as the new first line in our averageRecord function:

```
if (sc == NULL) return 0;
```

As this example shows, handling special cases is usually pretty simple. We just have to make sure we take the time to identify them.

Conclusion and Next Steps

This chapter has just scratched the surface of problem solving using pointers and dynamic memory. You'll see pointers and heap allocations throughout the rest of this text. For example, object-oriented programming techniques, which we'll discuss in Chapter 5, are especially helpful when dealing with pointers. They allow us to encapsulate pointers in such a way that we don't have to worry about memory leaks, dangling pointers, or any of the other common pointer pitfalls.

Even though there is much more to learn about problem solving in this area, you'll be able to develop your skills with pointer-based structures of increasing complexity if you follow the basic ideas in this chapter: First, apply the general rules of problem solving. Then, apply specific rules for pointers, and use a diagram or similar tool to visualize each solution before you start coding.

Exercises

I'm not kidding about doing the exercises. You're not just reading the chapters and moving on, are you?

4-1. Design your own: Take a problem that you already know how to solve using an array but that is limited by the size of the array. Rewrite the code to remove that limitation using a dynamically allocated array.

4-2. For our dynamically allocated strings, create a function `substring` that takes three parameters: an `arrayString`, a starting position integer, and an integer length of characters. The function returns a pointer to a new dynamically allocated string array. This string array contains the characters in the original string, starting at the specified position for the specified length. The original string is unaffected by the operation. So if the original string was `abcdefg`, the position was 3, and the length was 4, then the new string would contain `cdef`.

4-3. For our dynamically allocated strings, create a function `replaceString` that takes three parameters, each of type `arrayString`: `source`, `target`, and `replaceText`. The function replaces every occurrence of `target` in `source` with `replaceText`. For example, if `source` points to an array containing `abcdabee`, `target` points to `ab`, and `replaceText` points to `xyz`, then when the function ends, `source` should point to an array containing `xyzcdxyzee`.

4-4. Change the implementation of our strings such that `location[0]` in the array stores the size of the array (and therefore `location[1]` stores the first actual character in the string), rather than using a null-character terminator. Implement each of the three functions, `append`, `concatenate`, and `charactertAt`, taking advantage of the stored size information whenever possible. Because we'll no longer be using the null-termination convention expected by the standard output stream, you'll need to write your own `output` function that loops through its string parameter, displaying the characters.

4-5. Write a function `removeRecord` that takes a pointer to a `studentCollection` and a student number and that removes the record with that student number from the collection.

4-6. Let's create an implementation for strings that uses a linked list of characters instead of dynamically allocated arrays. So we'll have a linked list where the data payload is a single char; this will allow strings to grow without having to re-create the entire string. We'll start by implementing the `append` and `characterAt` functions.

4-7. Following up on the previous exercise, implement the concatenate function. Note that if we make a call concatenate(s1, s2), where both parameters are pointers to the first nodes of their respective linked lists, the function should create a copy of each of the nodes in s2 and append them to the end of s1. That is, the function should not simply point the next field of the last node in s1's list to the first node of s2's list.

4-8. Add a function to the linked-list string implementation called removeChars to remove a section of characters from a string based on the position and length. For example, removeChars(s1, 5, 3) would remove the three characters starting at the fifth character in the string. Make sure the removed nodes are properly deallocated.

4-9. Imagine a linked list where instead of the node storing a character, the node stores a digit: an int in the range 0–9. We could represent positive numbers of any size using such a linked list; the number 149, for example, would be a linked list in which the first node stores a 1, the second a 4, and the third and last a 9. Write a function intToList that takes an integer value and produces a linked list of this sort. Hint: You may find it easier to build the linked list backward, so if the value were 149, you would create the 9 node first.

4-10. For the digit list of the previous exercise, write a function that takes two such lists and produces a new list representing their sum.

5

SOLVING PROBLEMS
WITH CLASSES

In this chapter, we're going to discuss classes and object-oriented programming. As before, the assumption is that you've seen the class declaration in C++ and understand the basic syntax of creating a class, invoking the methods of a class, and so on. We'll have a quick review in the next section, but we'll mostly discuss the problem-solving aspects of classes.

This is another situation in which I think C++ has an advantage over other languages. Because C++ is a hybrid language, the C++ programmer can create classes where appropriate but never has to. By contrast, in a language like Java or C#, all code must appear within the confines of a class declaration. In the hands of expert programmers, this causes no undue harm, but in the hands of novices, it can lead to bad habits. To a Java or C# programmer, everything is an object. While all the code written in these languages must be encapsulated into objects, the result doesn't always reflect sensible object-oriented design. An object should be a meaningful, closely knit collection of data and code that operates on that data. It shouldn't be an arbitrary grab bag of leftovers.

Because we are programming in C++ and therefore have the choice between procedural and object-oriented programming, we'll talk about good class design, as well as when classes should and should not be used. Recognizing a situation in which a class would be useful is essential to reaching the higher levels of programming style, but it's equally important to recognize situations in which a class is going to make things worse.

Review of Class Fundamentals

As always, this book assumes you have previous contact with fundamentals and references for C++ syntax, but let's review the fundamentals of class syntax so we are on the same page with terminology. A *class* is a blueprint for constructing a particular package of code and data; each variable created according to a class's blueprint is known as an *object* of that class. Code outside of a class that creates and uses an object of that class is known as a *client* of the class. A *class declaration* names the class and lists all of the *members*, or items inside that class. Each item is either a *data member*—a variable declared within the class—or a *method* (also known as a *member function*), which is a function declared within the class. Member functions can include a special type called a *constructor*, which has the same name as the class and is invoked implicitly when an object of the class is declared. In addition to the normal attributes of a variable or function declaration (such as type, and for functions, the parameter list), each member also has an *access specifier*, which indicates what functions can access the member. A *public member* can be accessed by any code using the object: code inside the class, a client of the class, or code in a *subclass*, which is a class that "inherits" all the code and data of an existing class. A *private member* can be accessed only by the code inside the class. *Protected members*, which we'll see briefly in this chapter, are similar to private members, except that methods in subclasses can also reference them. Both private and protected members, though, are inaccessible from client code.

Unlike attributes such as the return type, the access specifier inside the class declaration holds until replaced by a different specifier. Thus, each specifier usually appears only once, with the members grouped together by access. This leads programmers to refer to "the public section" or "the private section" of a class, as in, "We should put this method in the private section."

Let's look at a tiny example class declaration:

```
class ❶sample {
❷ public:
    ❸sample();
    ❹sample(int num);
    ❺int doesSomething(double param);
private:
    ❻int intData;
}❼;
```

This declaration starts by naming the class ❶, so afterward `sample` becomes a type name. The declaration begins with a `public` access specifier ❷, so until we reach the private specifier ❻, everything that follows is public. Many programmers include the public declarations first, expecting the public interface to be of most interest to other readers. The public declarations here are two constructors (❸ and ❹) named sample and another method, doesSomething ❺. The constructors are implicitly invoked when objects of this class are declared.

```
sample object1;
sample object2(15);
```

Here, object1 would invoke the first constructor ❸, known as the *default constructor*, which has no parameters, while object2 would invoke the second constructor ❹ because it specifies a single integer value and thus matches the parameter signature of the second constructor.

The declaration concludes with a private data member, intData ❻. Remember that a class declaration ends with a closing brace and a semicolon ❼. This semicolon may look a little mysterious because we don't conclude functions, if statement blocks, or any other closing braces with semicolons. The semicolon's presence actually indicates that class declarations are also, optionally, object declarations; we could put identifiers in between the closing brace and semicolon and make objects as we make our classes. This isn't too common in C++, though, especially considering that many programmers put their class definitions in separate files from the programs that use them. The mysterious semicolon appears after the closing brace of a struct, as well.

Speaking of struct, you should know that in C++, struct and class denote nearly the same thing. The only difference between the two involves members (data or methods) declared before the first access specifier. In a struct, these members would be public, while in a class, they would be private. Good programmers, though, use the two structures in different ways. This is analogous to how any for loop could be written as a while loop, but a good programmer can make code more readable by using for loops in more straightforward counting loops. Most programmers reserve struct for simpler structures, either those with no data members beyond constructors or those intended for use as parameters to methods of a larger class.

Goals of Class Use

In order to recognize the right and wrong situations for class use and the right and wrong way to build a class, we have to decide what our goals are for using classes in the first place. In considering this, we should remember that classes are always optional. That is, classes do not give us new capabilities in the way that an array or a pointer-based structure does. If you take a program that uses an array to sort 10,000 records, it won't be possible to write that same program without the array. If you have a program that depends on a linked list's ability to grow and shrink over time, you won't be able to create the same effects with the same efficiency without using a linked list or similar pointer-based structure. If you take away the classes from an object-oriented program, though, and rewrite it, the program will look different, but the capabilities and efficiency of the program will not be diminished. Indeed, early C++ compilers worked as preprocessors. The C++ compiler would read C++ source code and output new source on the fly that was legal C syntax. This modified source code would then be sent to a C compiler. What this tells us is that the major additions that C++ made to the C language were not about the functional capabilities of the language but about how the source code reads to the programmer.

Therefore, in choosing our general class design goals, we are choosing goals to help us, as programmers, accomplish our tasks. In particular, because this book is about problem solving, we should think about how classes help us solve problems.

Encapsulation

The word *encapsulation* is a fancy way of saying that classes put multiple pieces of data and code together into a single package. If you've ever seen a gelatin medicine capsule filled with little spheres, that's a good analogy: The patient takes one capsule and swallows all the individual ingredient spheres inside.

Encapsulation is the mechanism that allows many of the other goals we list below to succeed, but it is also a benefit in itself because it organizes our code. In a long program listing of purely procedural code (in C++, this would mean code with functions but no classes), it can be difficult to find a good order for our functions and compiler directives that allows us to easily remember their locations. Instead, we're forced to rely on our development environment to find our functions for us. Encapsulation keeps stuff together that goes together. If you're working on a class method and you realize you need to look at or modify other code, it's likely that other code appears in another method of the same class and is therefore nearby.

Code Reuse

From a problem-solving standpoint, encapsulation allows us to more easily reuse the code from previous problems to solve current problems. Often, even though we have worked on a problem similar to our current project, reusing what we learned before still takes a lot of work. A fully encapsulated class can work like an external USB drive; you just plug it in and it works. For this to happen, though, we must design the class correctly to make sure that the code and data is truly encapsulated and as independent as possible from anything outside of the class. For example, a class that references a global variable can't be copied into a new project without copying the global variable, as well.

Beyond reusing classes from one program to the next, classes offer the potential for a more immediate form of code reuse: inheritance. Recall that, back in Chapter 4, we talked about using helper functions to "factor out" the code common to two or more functions. Inheritance takes this idea to a larger scale. Using inheritance, we create parent classes with methods common to two or more child classes, thereby "factoring out" not just a few lines of code but whole methods. Inheritance is a large subject unto itself, and we'll explore this form of code reuse later in the chapter.

Dividing the Problem

One technique we've returned to again and again is dividing a complex problem into smaller, more manageable pieces. Classes are great at dividing programs up into functional units. Encapsulation not only holds data and code together in a reusable package; it also cordons off that data and code from the rest of the program, allowing us to work on that class, and everything else separately. The more classes we make in a program, the greater the problem-dividing effect.

So, where possible, we should let the class be our method of dividing complex problems. If the classes are well designed, this will enforce functional separation, and the problem will be easier to solve. As a secondary effect, we may find that classes we created for one problem are reusable in other problems, even if we didn't fully consider that possibility when we created them.

Information Hiding

Some people use the terms *information hiding* and *encapsulation* interchangeably, but we'll separate the ideas here. As described previously in this chapter, encapsulation is packaging data and code together. Information hiding means separating the interface of a data structure—the definition of the operations and their parameters—from the implementation of a data structure, or the code inside the functions. If a class has been written with information hiding as a goal, then it's possible to change the implementation of the methods without requiring any changes in the client code (the code that uses the class). Again, we have to be clear on the term *interface*; this means not only the name of the methods and their parameter list but also the explanation (perhaps expressed in code documentation) of what the different methods do. When we talk about changing the implementation without changing the interface, we mean that we change *how* the class methods work but not *what* they do. Some programming authors have referred to this as a kind of implicit contract between the class and the client: The class agrees never to change the effects of existing operations, and the client agrees to use the class strictly on the basis of its interface and to ignore any implementation details. Think of having a universal remote that can control any television, whether that's an old tube model or one that uses an LCD or plasma screen. You press 2, then 5, then Enter, and any of the screens will display channel 25, even though the mechanism to make that happen is vastly different depending on the underlying technology.

There is no way to have information hiding without encapsulation, but as we have defined the terms, it's possible to have encapsulation without information hiding. The most obvious way this can happen is if a class's data members are declared `public`. In such a case, the class is still an encapsulation, in that it's a package of code and data that belong together. However, the client code now has access to an important class implementation detail: the variables and types the class uses to store its data. Even if the client code doesn't modify the class data directly and only inspects it, the client code then requires that particular class implementation. Any change to the class that changes the name or type of any of the variables accessed by the client code requires changes to the client code, as well.

Your first thought might be that information hiding is assured so long as all data is made private and we spend enough time designing the list of member functions and their parameter lists so that they never need to change. While all of that is required for information hiding, it's not sufficient because information-hiding problems can be more subtle. Remember that the class is agreeing not to change what any of the methods do, regardless of the situation. In previous chapters, we've had to decide the smallest case a function will handle or what to do with an anomalous case, like finding the average of an array when the parameter that stores the size of the array is zero. Changing the result of a method even for an oddball case represents a change of the interface and should be avoided. This is another reason why explicitly considering special cases is so important in programming. Many a program has blown up when its underlying technology or application programming interface (API) has been updated, and some system call that used to reliably return a −1 when one of the parameters was erroneous now returns a seemingly random, but still negative, number. One of the best ways to avoid this problem is to state special case results in the class or method documentation. If your own documentation says that you return a −1 error code when a certain situation occurs, you'll think twice about having your method return anything else.

So how does information hiding affect problem solving? The principle of information hiding tells the programmer to put aside class implementation details when working on the client code, or more broadly, to be concerned about a particular class's implementation only when working inside that class. When you can put implementation details out of your mind, you can eliminate distracting thoughts and concentrate on solving the problem at hand.

We should be aware, however, of the limitations of information hiding as it relates to problem solving. Sometimes implementation details do matter to the client. In previous chapters, we've seen the strengths and weaknesses of some array-based and pointer-based data structures. Array-based structures allow random access but cannot easily grow or shrink, while pointer-based structures offer only sequential access but can have pieces added or removed without having to re-create the entire structure. Therefore, a class built with an array-based structure as a foundation will have qualities different from one based on a pointer-based structure.

In computer science, we often talk about the concept of an *abstract data type*, which is information hiding in its purest form: a data type defined only by its operations. In Chapter 4, we discussed the concept of a stack and described how a program's stack is a contiguous block of memory. But as an abstract data type, a stack is any data type where you can add and remove individual items, and the items are removed in the opposite order that they were added. This is known as last-in first-out ordering, or LIFO. Nothing requires a stack to be a contiguous block of memory, and we could make a stack using a linked list. Because a contiguous block of memory and a linked list have different properties, a stack that uses one implementation or the other will also have different properties, and these may make a big difference to the client using the stack.

The point of all this is that information hiding will be a useful goal for us as problem solvers, to the extent it allows us to divide problems and work on different parts of a program separately. We cannot, however, allow ourselves to ignore implementation details entirely.

Readability

A good class enhances the readability of the program in which it appears. Objects can correspond to how we look at the real world, and therefore method calls often have an English-like readability. Also, the relationship between objects is often clearer than the relationship between simple variables. Enhancing readability enhances our ability to solve problems, because we can understand our own code more easily while it is in development and because reuse is enhanced when old code is easy to follow.

To maximize the readability benefit of classes, we need to think about how the methods of our class will be used in practice. Method names should be chosen with care to reflect the most specific meaning of the method's effects. For example, consider a class representing a financial investment that contains a method for computing the future value. The name compute doesn't convey nearly as much information as computeFutureValue. Even choosing the right part of speech for the name can be helpful. The name computeFutureValue is a verb, while futureValue is a noun. Look at how the names are used in the code samples that follow:

```
  double FV;
❶ investment.computeFutureValue(FV, 2050);

❷ if (investment.futureValue(2050) > 10000) { ...
```

If you think about it, the former makes more sense for a call that would stand alone, that is, a void function in which the future value is sent back to the caller via a reference parameter ❶. The latter makes better sense for a call that would be used in an expression, that is, the future value comes back as the value of the function ❷.

We'll see specific examples later in the chapter, but the guiding principle for maximizing readability is to always think about the client code when you are writing any part of the class interface.

Expressiveness

A final goal of a well-designed class is expressiveness, or what might be broadly called writability—the ease with which code can be written. A good class, once written, makes the rest of the code simpler to write in the same way that a good function makes code simpler to write. Classes effectively extend the language, becoming high-level counterparts to basic low-level features such as loops, if statements, and so forth. In C++, even central functionality like input and output is not an inherent part of the language syntax but is provided as a set of classes that must be explicitly included in the program that uses it. With classes, programming actions that previously took many steps can be done in just a few steps or just one. As problem solvers, we should make this goal a special priority. We should always be thinking, "How is this class going to make the rest of this program, and future programs that may use this class, easier to write?"

Building a Simple Class

Now that we know what goals our classes should aim for, it's time to put theory into practice and build some classes. First, we'll develop our class in stages for use in the following problem.

PROBLEM: CLASS ROSTER

Design a class or set of classes for use in a program that maintains a class roster. For each student, store the student's name, ID, and final grade score in the range 0–100. The program will allow student records to be added or removed; display the record of a particular student, identified by ID, with the grade displayed as a number and as a letter; and display the average score for the class. The appropriate letter grade for a particular score is shown in Table 5-1.

Table 5-1: Letter Grades

Score Range	Letter Grade
93–100	A
90–92	A–
87–89	B+
83–86	B
80–82	B–
77–79	C+
73–76	C
70–72	C–
67–69	D+
60–66	D
0–59	F

We'll start by looking at a basic class framework that forms the foundation of the majority of classes. Then we'll look at ways in which the basic framework is expanded.

The Basic Class Framework

The best way to explore the basic class framework is through a sample class. For this example, we're going to start from the student struct from Chapter 3 and build it into a full class. For ease of reference, here's the original struct:

```
struct student {
    int grade;
    int studentID;
    string name;
};
```

Even with a simple struct in this form, we at least get encapsulation. Remember that in Chapter 3 we built an array of student data with this struct, and without using the struct, we would have had to build three parallel arrays, one each for the grades, IDs, and names—ugly! What we definitely don't get with this struct, though, is information hiding. The basic class framework gives us information hiding by declaring all the data as private and then adding public methods to allow client code to indirectly access, or change, this data.

```
  class studentRecord {
❶ public:
    ❷studentRecord();
      studentRecord(int newGrade, int newID, string newName);
    ❸int grade();
    ❹void setGrade(int newGrade);
      int studentID();
      void setStudentID(int newID);
      string name();
      void setName(string newName);
❺ private:
    ❻int _grade;
      int _studentID;
      string _name;
};
```

As promised, this class declaration is separated into a public section with member functions ❶ and a private section ❺, which contains the same data as the original struct ❻. There are eight member functions: two constructors ❷ and then a pair of member functions for each data member. For example, the _grade data member has two associated member functions, grade ❸ and setGrade ❹. The first of these methods will be used by client code to retrieve the grade of a particular studentRecord, while the second of these methods is used to store a new grade for this particular studentRecord.

Retrieval and store methods associated with a data member are so common that they are typically referred to by the shorthand terms *get* and *set*. As you can see, I incorporated the word *set* into the methods that store new values into the data members. Many programmers would have also incorporated *get* into the other names, for example, getGrade instead of grade. Why didn't I do this? Because then I would have been using a verb name for a function that is used as a noun. Some would argue, though, that the *get* term is so universally understood, and its meaning therefore so clear, that its use overrides the other concern. Ultimately, that's a matter of personal style.

Although I've been quick in this book to point out the advantages C++ has over other languages, I must admit that more recent languages, like C#, have C++ beat when it comes to *get* and *set* methods. C# has a built-in mechanism called a property that acts as both a *get* and *set* method. Once defined, the client code can access the property as though it were a data member rather than a function call. This is a great enhancement to readability and expressiveness. In C++, without a built-in mechanism, it's important that we decide on some naming convention for our methods and use it consistently.

Note that my naming convention extends to the data members, which, unlike the original struct, all begin with underscores. This allows me to name the *get* functions with (almost) the same name as the data members they retrieve. This also allows easy recognition of data member references in code, enhancing readability. Some programmers use the keyword this for all data member references instead of using an underscore prefix. So instead of a statement such as:

```
return _grade;
```

they would have:

```
return this.grade;
```

If you haven't seen the keyword this before, it's a reference to the object in which it appears. So if the statement above appeared in a class method and that method also declared a local variable with the name grade, the expression this.grade would refer to the data member grade, not the local variable with the same name. Employing the keyword in this way has an advantage in a development environment with automatic syntax completion: The programmer can just type **this**, press the period key, and select the data member from a list, avoiding extra typing and potential misspellings. Either technique highlights data member references, though, which is what's important.

Now that we've seen the class declaration, let's look at the implementation of the methods. We'll start with the first *get/set* pair.

```
int studentRecord::grade() {
   ❶return _grade;
}
void studentRecord::setGrade(int newGrade) {
   ❷_grade = newGrade;
}
```

This is the most basic form of the *get/set* pair. The first method, grade, returns the current value of the associated data member, _grade ❶. The second method, setGrade, assigns the value of the parameter newGrade to the data member _grade ❷. If this were all we did with our class, however, we wouldn't have accomplished anything. Although this code provides information hiding because it passes data in both directions without any consideration or modification, it's only better than having _grade declared public because it reserves us the right to change the data member's name or type. The setGrade method should at least perform some rudimentary validation; it should prevent values of newGrade that don't make sense as a grade from being assigned to the _grade data member. We have to be careful to follow problem specifications, though, and not to make assumptions about data based on our own experiences, without consideration of the user. It might be reasonable to limit grades to the range 0–100, but it might not, for example, if a school allows extra credit to push a score above 100 or uses a grade of –1 as a code for a class withdrawal. In this case, because we are given some guidance by the problem description, we can incorporate that knowledge into validation.

```
void studentRecord::setGrade(int newGrade) {
    if ((newGrade >= 0) && (newGrade <= 100))
        _grade = newGrade;
}
```

Here, the validation is just a gatekeeper. Depending upon the definition of the problem, however, it might make sense for the method to produce an error message, write to an error log, or otherwise handle the error.

The other *get/set* pairs would work exactly the same way. There are undoubtedly rules about the construction of student ID numbers at a particular school that could be used for validation. With a student name, however, the best we can do is reject strings with oddball characters, like % or @, and these days perhaps even that wouldn't be possible.

The last step in completing our class is writing the constructors. In the basic framework, we include two constructors: a default constructor, which has no parameters and sets the data members to reasonable default values, and a constructor with parameters for every data member. The second constructor form is important for our *expressiveness* goal, as it allows us to create an object of our class and initialize the values inside in one step. Once you have written the code for the other methods, this second constructor almost writes itself.

```
studentRecord::studentRecord(int newGrade, int newID, string newName) {
    setGrade(newGrade);
    setStudentID(newID);
    setName(newName);
}
```

As you can see, the constructor merely calls the appropriate *set* methods for each of the parameters. In most cases, this is the correct approach because it avoids duplicating code and ensures that the constructor will take advantage of any validation code in the *set* methods.

The default constructor is sometimes a little tricky, not because the code is complicated but because there is not always an obvious default value. When choosing default values for data members, keep in mind the situations in which an object created with the default constructor would be used and, in particular, whether there is a legitimate default object for that class. This will tell you whether you should fill the data members with useful default values or with values that signal that the object is not properly initialized. For example, consider a class representing a collection of values that encapsulates a linked list. There *is* a meaningful default linked list, and that's an empty linked list, so we would set our data members to create a legitimate, but conceptually empty, list. But with our sample basic class, there's no meaningful definition of a default student; we wouldn't want to give a valid ID number to a default studentRecord object because that could potentially cause confusion with a legitimate studentRecord. Therefore, we should choose a default value for the _studentID field that is obviously illegitimate, such as −1:

```
studentRecord::studentRecord() {
    setGrade(0);
    setStudentID(-1);
    setName("");
}
```

We assign the grade with setGrade, which validates its parameter. This means we have to assign a valid grade, in this case, 0. Because the ID is set to an invalid value, the record as a whole can be easily identified as illegitimate. Therefore, the valid grade shouldn't be an issue. If that were a concern, we could assign an invalid value directly to the _grade data member.

This completes the basic class framework. We have a group of private data members that reference attributes of the same logical object, in this case, a student's class record; we have member functions to retrieve or alter the object's data, with validation as appropriate; and we have a useful set of constructors. We have a good class foundation. The question is, do we need to do more?

Support Methods

A *support method* is a method in a class that does not merely retrieve or store data. Some programmers may refer to these as helper methods, auxiliary methods, or something else, but whatever they are called, they are what take a class beyond the basic class framework. A well-designed set of support methods is often what makes a class truly useful.

To determine possible support methods, consider how the class will be used. Are there common activities we would expect client code to perform on our class's data? In this case, we're told that the program for which we are initially designing our class will display students' grades not only as numerical scores but also as letters. So let's create a support method that returns a student's grade as a letter. First, we'll add the method declaration to the public section of our class declaration.

```
string letterGrade();
```

Now we need to implement this method. The function will convert the numerical value stored in _grade to the appropriate string based on the grade table shown in the problem. We could accomplish this with a series of if statements, but is there a cleaner, more elegant way? If you just thought, "Hey, this sounds a lot like how we converted incomes into business license categories back in Chapter 3," congratulations—you've spotted an apt programming analogy. We can adapt that code, with parallel const arrays to store the letter grades and the lowest numerical scores associated with those grades, to convert the numerical score with a loop.

```
string studentRecord::letterGrade() {
    const int NUMBER_CATEGORIES = 11;
    const string GRADE_LETTER[] = {"F", "D", "D+", "C-", "C", "C+", "B-", "B", "B+", "A-", "A"};
    const int LOWEST_GRADE_SCORE[] = {0, 60, 67, 70, 73, 77, 80, 83, 87, 90, 93};
    int category = 0;
    while (category < NUMBER_CATEGORIES && LOWEST_GRADE_SCORE[category] <= _grade)
        category++;
    return GRADE_LETTER[category - 1];
}
```

This method is a direct adaptation of the function from Chapter 3, so there's nothing new to explain about how the code works. However, its adaptation for a class method does introduce some design decisions. The first thing to note is that we have not created a new data member to store the letter grade but instead to compute the appropriate letter grade on the fly for every request. The alternative approach would be to have a _letterGrade data member and rewrite the setGrade method to update _letterGrade alongside _grade. Then this letterGrade method would become a simple *get* method, returning the value of the already-computed data member.

The issue with this approach is *data redundancy*, a term describing a situation in which data is stored that is either a literal duplicate of other data or can be directly determined from other data. This issue is most commonly seen with databases, and database designers follow elaborate processes to avoid creating redundant data in their tables. Data redundancy can occur in any program, however, if we are unwary. To see the danger, consider a medical records program that stores age and date of birth for each of a set of patients. The date of birth gives us information the age does not. The two data items are therefore not equal, but the age does not tell us anything we can't already tell from the birth date. And what if the two values are not in agreement (which will happen eventually, unless the age is automatically updated)? Which value do we trust? I'm reminded of the famous (though possibly apocryphal) proclamation of the Caliph Omar when he ordered the burning of the Library of Alexandria. He proclaimed that if the books in the library agreed with the Koran, they were redundant and need not be preserved, but if they disagreed with the Koran, they were pernicious and should be destroyed. Redundant data is trouble waiting to happen. The only justification would be performance, if we thought updates to _grade would be seldom and calls to letterGrade would be frequent, but it's hard to imagine a significant overall performance boost to the program.

However, this method could be improved. In testing this method, I noticed a problem. Although the method produces correct results for valid values of _grade, the method crashes when _grade is a negative value. When the while loop is reached, the negative value of _grade causes the loop test to immediately fail; therefore, category remains zero and the return statement attempts to reference GRADE_LETTER[-1]. We could avoid this problem by initializing category to one instead of zero, but that would mean that a negative grade would be assigned "F" when it really shouldn't be assigned any string at all because, as an invalid grade value, it doesn't fit into any category.

Instead, we could validate _grade before converting it to a letter grade. We're already validating grade values in the setGrade method, so instead of adding new validation code to the letterGrade method, we should "factor out" what would be the common code in these methods to make a third method. (You might wonder how, if we're validating grades as they are assigned, we could ever have an invalid grade, but we might decide to assign an invalid grade in the constructor to signal that no legitimate grade has been assigned yet.) This is another kind of support method, which is the class equivalent of the general helper function concept introduced in previous chapters. Let's implement this method and modify our other methods to use it:

```
❶ bool studentRecord::❷isValidGrade(❸int grade) {
       if ((grade >= 0) && (grade <= 100))
           return true;
       else
           return false;
   }
   void studentRecord::setGrade(int newGrade) {
       if (❹isValidGrade(newGrade))
           _grade = newGrade;
   }
   string studentRecord::letterGrade() {
       if (❺!isValidGrade(_grade)) return "ERROR";
       const int NUMBER_CATEGORIES = 11;
       const string GRADE_LETTER[] = {"F", "D", "D+", "C-", "C", "C+", "B-", "B", "B+", "A-", "A"};
       const int LOWEST_GRADE_SCORE[] = {0, 60, 67, 70, 73, 77, 80, 83, 87, 90, 93};
       int category = 0;
       while (category < NUMBER_CATEGORIES && LOWEST_GRADE_SCORE[category] <= _grade)
           category++;
       return GRADE_LETTER[category - 1];
   }
```

The new grade validation method is of type bool ❶, and since this is a yes-or-no issue I've chosen the name isValidGrade ❷. This gives the most English-like reading to calls to this method, such as those in the setGrade ❹ and letterGrade ❺ methods. Also, note that the method takes the grade to validate as a parameter ❸. Although letterGrade is validating the value already in the _grade data member, setGrade is validating the value that we may or may not assign the data member. So isValidGrade needs to take the grade as a parameter to be useful to both of the other methods.

Although the isValidGrade method is implemented, one decision regarding it remains: What access level should we assign to it? That is, should we place it in the public section of the class or the private section? Unlike the *get* and *set* methods of the basic class framework, which always go in the public section, support methods may be public or private depending on their use. What are the effects of making isValidGrade public? Most obviously, client code can access the method. Because having more public methods appears to make a class more useful, many novice programmers make every method public that could possibly be used by the client. This, however, ignores the other effect of the public access designation. Remember that the public section defines the interface of our class, and we should be reluctant to change the method once our class is integrated into one or more programs because such a change is likely to cascade and require changes in all the client code. Placing a method in the public section, therefore, locks the method's interface and its effects. In this case, suppose that some client code, based on the original formulation of isValidGrade, relies upon it as a 0–100 range checker, but later, the rules for acceptable grades get more complicated. The client code could fail. To avoid that, we might have to instead create a second grade validation method inside the class and leave the first one alone.

Let's suppose that we expect isValidGrade to be of limited use to the client and have decided not to make it public. We could make the method private, but that's not the only choice. Because the function does not directly reference any data member or any other method of the class, we could declare the function outside of the class altogether. This, however, not only creates the same problem public access has on modifiability but also lowers encapsulation because now this function, which is required by the class, is no longer part of it. We could also leave the method in the class but make it *protected* instead of private. The difference would be seen in any subclasses. If isValidGrade is protected, the method can be called by methods in subclasses; if isValidGrade is private, it can be used only by other methods in the studentRecord class. This is the same quandary as public versus private on a smaller scale. Do we expect methods in subclasses to get much use from our method, and do we expect that the method's effect or its interface could change in the future? In many cases, the safest thing to do is make all helper methods private and make public only those support methods that were written to benefit the client.

Classes with Dynamic Data

One of the best reasons to create a class is to encapsulate dynamic data structures. As we discussed back in Chapter 4, programmers face a real chore keeping track of dynamic allocations, pointer assignments, and deallocations so that we avoid memory leaks, dangling references, and illegal memory references. Putting all of the pointer references into a class doesn't eliminate the difficult work, but it does mean that once we've got it right, we can safely drop that code into other projects. It also means that any problems with our dynamic data structure are isolated to the code within the class itself, simplifying debugging.

Let's build a class with dynamic data to see how this works. For our sample problem, we're going to use a modified version of the major problem from Chapter 4.

PROBLEM: TRACKING AN UNKNOWN QUANTITY OF STUDENT RECORDS

In this problem, you will write a class with methods to store and manipulate a collection of student records. A student record contains a student number and a grade, both integers, and a string for the student name. The following functions are to be implemented:

addRecord This method takes a student number, name, and grade and adds a new record with this data to the collection.

recordWithNumber This function takes a student number and retrieves the record with that student number from the collection.

removeRecord This function takes a student number and removes the record with that student number from the collection.

The collection can be of any size. The *addRecord* operation is expected to be called frequently, so it must be implemented efficiently.

The main differences between this description and the original version are that we've added a new operation, recordWithNumber, and also that none of the operations make any reference to a pointer parameter. This is the key benefit of using a class to encapsulate a linked list. The client may be aware that the class implements the student record collection as a linked list and may even be counting on that (remember our prior discussion about the limitations of information hiding). The client code, however, will have no direct interaction with the linked list or any pointer in the class.

Because this problem is storing the same information per student as the previous problem, we have an opportunity for class reuse here. In our linked list node type, instead of separate fields for each of the three pieces of student data, we'll have one studentRecord object. Using an object of one class as a data type in a second class is known as *composition*.

We have enough information now to make a preliminary class declaration:

```
class studentCollection {
private:
  ❶struct studentNode {
    ❷studentRecord studentData;
      studentNode * next;
  };
```

```
❸ public:
      studentCollection();
      void addRecord(studentRecord newStudent);
      studentRecord recordWithNumber(int idNum);
      void removeRecord(int idNum);
   private:
      ❹typedef studentNode * studentList;
      ❺studentList _listHead;
};
```

Previously, I said programmers tend to start classes with public declarations, but here we have to make an exception. We begin with a private declaration of the node struct, studentNode ❶, which we'll use to make our linked list. This declaration has to come before the public section because several of our public member functions reference this type. Unlike our node type in Chapter 4, this node doesn't have individual fields for the payload data but rather includes a member of the studentRecord class ❷. The public member functions ❸ follow directly from the problem description; plus, as always, we have a constructor. In the second private section, we declare a typedef ❹ for a pointer to our node type for clarity, just as we did in Chapter 4. Then we declare our list head pointer, cleverly called _listHead ❺.

This class declares two private types. Classes can declare types as well as member functions and data members. As with other members, types appearing in the class can be declared with any access specifier. As with data members, though, you should think of type definitions as private by default, and only make them less restrictive if you have a clear reason to do so. Type declarations are typically at the heart of how a class operates behind the scenes, and as such, they are critical to information hiding. Furthermore, in most cases, client code has no use for the types you will declare in your class. An exception occurs when a type defined in the class is used as the return type of a public method or as the type of a parameter to a public method. In this case, the type has to be public or the public method can't be used by client code. Class studentCollection assumes that the struct type studentRecord will be separately declared, but we could make it part of the class as well. If we did, we would have to declare it in the public section.

Now we are ready to implement our class methods, starting with the constructor. Unlike our previous example, we have only the default constructor here, not a constructor that takes a parameter to initialize our data member. The whole point of our class is to hide the details of our linked list, so we don't want the client even thinking about our _listHead, let alone manipulating it. All we need to do in our default constructor is set the head pointer to NULL:

```
studentCollection::studentCollection() {
    _listHead = NULL;
}
```

Adding a Node

We move on to addRecord. Because nothing in the problem description requires us to keep student records in any particular order, we can directly adapt the addRecord function from Chapter 4 for use here.

```
void studentCollection::addRecord(❶studentRecord newStudent) {
    ❷studentNode * newNode = new studentNode;
    ❸newNode->studentData = newStudent;
    ❹newNode->next = _listHead;
    ❺_listHead = newNode;
}
```

There are only two differences between this code and our blueprint function. Here, we need only one parameter in our parameter list ❶, which is the studentRecord object we're going to add to our collection. This encapsulates all of the data for a student, which reduces the number of parameters needed. We also don't need to pass a list head pointer because that is already stored in our class as _listHead and is referenced directly when needed. As with the addRecord function from Chapter 4, we create a new node ❷, copy the new student data into the new node ❸, point the next field of the new node at the previous first node in the list ❹, and finally point _listHead at the new node ❺. Normally I recommend drawing a diagram for all pointer manipulations, but since this is the same manipulation we were already doing, we can reference our previously drawn diagram.

Now we can turn our attention to the second member function in the list, recordWithNumber. That name is a bit of a mouthful, and some programmers might have chosen *retrieveRecord* or something similar. Following my previously stated naming rules, however, I decided to use a noun because this method returns a value. This method will be similar to averageRecord in that it needs to traverse the list; the difference in this case is that we can stop once we find the matching student record.

```
studentRecord studentCollection::recordWithNumber(int idNum) {
    ❶studentNode * loopPtr = _listHead;
    ❷while (loopPtr->studentData.studentID() != idNum) {
        loopPtr = loopPtr->next;
    }
    ❸return loopPtr->studentData;
}
```

In this function, we initialize our loop pointer to the head of the list ❶ and traverse the list as long as we haven't seen the desired ID number ❷. Finally, arriving at the desired node, we return the entire matching record as the value of the function ❸. This code looks good, but as always, we have to consider potential special cases. The case we always consider when dealing with linked lists is an initially NULL head pointer. Here, that definitely causes a problem, as we are not checking for that and the code will blow up when we try to dereference `loopPtr` upon first entering the loop. More generally, though, we have to consider the possibility that the ID number provided by the client code doesn't actually match any of the records in our collection. In that case, even if `_listHead` is not `NULL`, `loopPtr` will eventually become `NULL` when we reach the end of the list.

So the general issue is that we need to stop the loop if `loopPtr` becomes `NULL`. That's not difficult, but then, what do we return in this situation? We certainly can't return `loopPtr->studentData` because `loopPtr` will be `NULL`. Instead, we can build and return a dummy `studentRecord` with obvious invalid values inside.

```
studentRecord studentCollection::recordWithNumber(int idNum) {
    studentNode * loopPtr = _listHead;
    while (❶loopPtr != NULL && loopPtr->studentData.studentID() != idNum) {
        loopPtr = loopPtr->next;
    }
    if (❷loopPtr == NULL) {
        ❸studentRecord dummyRecord(-1, -1, "");
        return dummyRecord;
    } else {
        return loopPtr->studentData;
    }
}
```

In this version of the method, if our loop pointer is `NULL` when the loop is over ❷, we create a dummy record with a null string for a name and −1 values for the grade and student ID ❸ and return that. Back in the loop, we are checking for that `NULL` `loopPtr` condition, which again can happen either because there is no list to traverse or because we have traversed it with no success. One key point here is that the loop's conditional expression ❶ is a compound expression with `loopPtr != NULL` first. This is absolutely required. C++ uses a mechanism for evaluating compound Boolean expressions known as *short-circuit evaluation*; put simply, it doesn't evaluate the right half of a compound Boolean expression when the overall value of the expression is already known. Because `&&` represents a logical Boolean *and*, if the left side of an `&&` expression evaluates to false, the overall expression must also be false, regardless of the right-side evaluation. For efficiency, C++ takes advantage of this fact, skipping the evaluation of the right side of an `&&` expression when the left side is false (for an `||`, logical *or*, the right side is not evaluated when the left side is true, for the same reason). Therefore, when `loopPtr` is `NULL`, the expression `loopPtr != NULL` evaluates to false, and the right side of the `&&` is never evaluated. Without short-circuit evaluation, the right side *would* be evaluated, and we would be dereferencing a `NULL` pointer, crashing the program.

The implementation avoids the potential crash of the first version, but we need to be aware that it places a good deal of trust in the client code. That is, the function that calls this method is responsible for checking the `studentRecord` that comes back and making sure it's not the dummy record before further processing. If you're like me, this makes you a little uneasy.

Rearranging the List

The removeRecord method is similar to recordWithNumber in that we must traverse the list to find the node we're going to remove from the list, but there's a lot more to it. Removing a node from a list requires care to keep the remaining nodes in the list linked. The simplest way to sew up the hole we will have created is to link the node that came before the removed node to the node that came after. We don't need a function outline because we already have a function prototype in the class declaration, so we just need a test case:

```
studentCollection s;
studentRecord stu3(84, 1152, "Sue");
studentRecord stu2(75, 4875, "Ed");
studentRecord stu1(98, 2938, "Todd");
s.addRecord(stu3);
s.addRecord(stu2);
s.addRecord(stu1);
❶ s.removeRecord(4875);
```

Here we've created a studentCollection object s, as well as three studentRecord objects, each of which is added to our collection. Note that we could reuse the same record, changing the values between the calls to addRecord, but doing it this way simplifies our test code. The last line in the test is the call to removeRecord ❶, which in this case is going to remove the second record, the one for the student named "Ed." Using the same style of pointer diagrams used in Chapter 4, Figure 5-1 shows the state of memory before and after this call.

In Figure 5-1 (a), we see the linked list that was created by our test code. Note that because we're using a class, our diagram conventions are a little skewed. On the left side of our stack/heap division, we have _listHead, which is the private data member inside our studentCollection object s, and idNum, which is the parameter to removeRecord. On the right side is the list itself, out in the heap. Remember that addRecord puts the new record at the beginning of the list, so the records are in the opposite order from how they were added in the test code. The middle node, "Ed", has the ID number that matches the parameter, 4875, so it will be removed from the list. Figure 5-1 (b) shows the result of the call. The first node in the list, that of "Todd", now points to what was the third node in the list, that of "Sue". The "Ed" node is no longer linked into the larger list and has been deleted.

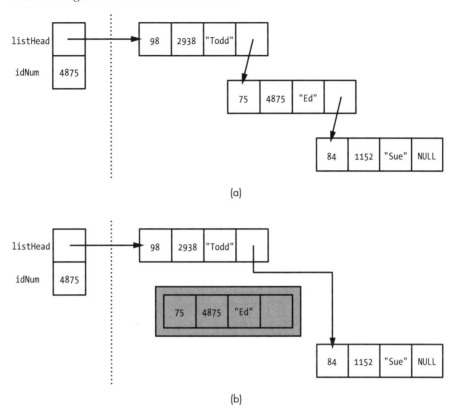

Figure 5-1: "Before" and "after" states for the removeRecord test case

Now that we know what effect the code should have, we can start to write it. Since we know we need to find the node with the matching ID number, we could start with the while loop from recordWithNumber. When that loop is complete, we would have a pointer to the node we needed to remove. Unfortunately, we need more than that to complete the removal. Look at Figure 5-1; in order to close the hole and maintain the linked list, we need to change the next field of the "Todd" node. If all we have is a pointer to the "Ed" node, there is no way to reference the "Todd" node because each node in the linked list references its successor, not its predecessor. (Because of situations like this, some linked lists link in both directions; these are known as *doubly linked lists*, but they are rarely needed.) So in addition to a pointer to the node to be removed (which will be called loopPtr if we adapt the code from the previous function), we need a pointer to the node immediately previous: Let's call this pointer trailing. Figure 5-2 shows this concept applied to our sample case.

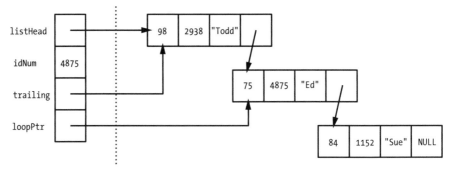

Figure 5-2: The pointers required to remove the node specified by idNum

With `loopPtr` referencing the node we're removing and `trailing` referencing the previous node, we can remove the desired node and keep the list together.

```
void studentCollection::removeRecord(int idNum) {
    studentNode * loopPtr = _listHead;
❶ studentNode * trailing = NULL;
    while (loopPtr != NULL && loopPtr->studentData.studentID() != idNum) {
❷     trailing = loopPtr;
        loopPtr = loopPtr->next;
    }
❸ if (loopPtr == NULL) return;
❹ trailing->next = loopPtr->next;
❺ delete loopPtr;
}
```

The first part of this function is like that of `recordWithNumber`, except that we declare our trailing pointer ❶ and, inside the loop, we assign the old value of `loopPtr` to `trailing` ❷ before advancing `loopPtr` to the next node. In this way, `trailing` is always one node behind `loopPtr`. Because of our work with the previous function, we are already on guard against one special case. Therefore, when the loop is over, we check to see whether `loopPtr` is `NULL`. If so, it means we never found a node with the desired ID number, and we immediately return ❸. I call a return statement that appears in the middle of a function "getting out of Dodge." Some programmers object to this because functions with multiple exit points can be more difficult to read. The alternative in this case, though, is another level of nesting for the `if` statements that follow, and I would rather just get out of Dodge.

Having determined that there is a node to remove, it's time to remove it. From our diagram, we see that we need to set the `next` field of the trailing node to point to the node currently pointed to by the `next` field of the `loopPtr` node ❹. Then we can safely `delete` the node pointed to by `loopPtr` ❺.

That works for our test case, but as always, we need to check for potential special cases. We've already handled the possibility that `idNum` doesn't appear in any of the records in our collection, but is there another possible issue? Looking at our test case, would anything change if we tried to delete the first or third node rather than the middle node? Testing and hand-checking shows no issues with the third (last) node. The first node, however, does cause trouble because in this situation, there is no previous node for trailing to point to. Instead, we must manipulate _listHead itself. Figure 5-3 shows the situation after the while loop ends.

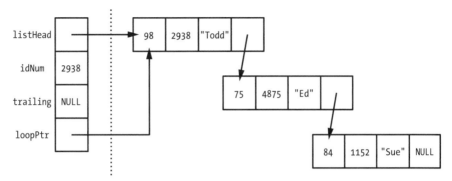

Figure 5-3: The situation prior to removing the first node in the list

In this situation, we need to repoint _listHead to the former second node in the list, the one for "Ed". Let's rewrite our method to handle the special case.

```
void studentCollection::removeRecord(int idNum) {
    studentNode * loopPtr = _listHead;
    studentNode * trailing = NULL;
    while (loopPtr != NULL && loopPtr->studentData.studentID() != idNum) {
        trailing = loopPtr;
        loopPtr = loopPtr->next;
    }
    if (loopPtr == NULL) return;
  ❶if (trailing == NULL) {
      ❷_listHead = _listHead->next;
    } else {
        trailing->next = loopPtr->next;
    }
    delete loopPtr;
}
```

As you can see, both the conditional test ❶ and the code to handle the special case ❷ are straightforward because we have carefully analyzed the situation before writing the code.

Destructor

With the three methods specified by the problem implemented, we might think that our studentCollection class is complete. However, as it stands, it has serious problems. The first is that the class lacks a *destructor*. This is a special method that is called when the object goes out of scope (when the function that declared the object completes). When a class has no dynamic data, it typically doesn't need a destructor, but if you have the former, you definitely need the latter. Remember that we have to delete everything we have allocated with new to avoid memory leaks. If an object of our studentCollection class has three nodes, each of those nodes needs to be deallocated. Fortunately, this is not too difficult. We just need to traverse our linked list, deleting as we go. Instead of doing this directly, though, let's write a helper method that deletes all the nodes in a studentList. In the private section of our class, we add the declaration:

```
void deleteList(studentList &listPtr);
```

The code for the method itself would be:

```
void studentCollection::deleteList(studentList &listPtr) {
    while (listPtr != NULL) {
        ❶studentNode * temp = listPtr;
        ❷listPtr = listPtr->next;
        ❸delete temp;
    }
}
```

The traversal copies the pointer to the current node to a temporary variable ❶, advances the current node pointer ❷, and then deletes the node pointed to by the temporary variable ❸. With this code in place, we can code the destructor very simply. First, we add the destructor to the public section of our class declaration:

```
~studentCollection();
```

Note that like a constructor, the destructor is specified using the name of the class, and there is no return type. The tilde before the name distinguishes the destructor from the constructors. The implementation is as follows:

```
studentCollection::~studentCollection() {
    deleteList(_listHead);
}
```

The code in these methods is straightforward, but it's important to test the destructor. Although a poorly written destructor could crash your program, many destructor problems don't result in crashes, only memory leaks, or worse, inexplicable program behavior. Therefore, it's important to test the destructor using your development environment's debugger so that you can see that the destructor is actually calling delete on each node.

Deep Copy

Another serious problem remains. Back in Chapter 4, we briefly discussed the concept of cross-linking, where two pointer variables had the same value. Even though the variables themselves were distinct, they pointed to the same data structure; therefore, modifying the structure of one variable modified them both. This problem can easily occur with classes that incorporate dynamically allocated memory. To see why this can be such a problem, consider the following elementary C++ code sequence:

```
int x = 10;
int y = 15;
x = y;
❶ x = 5;
```

Suppose I asked you what effect the last statement ❶ had on the value of the variable y. You would probably wonder whether I had misspoken. The last statement wouldn't have any effect on y at all, only x. But now consider this:

```
studentCollection s1;
studentCollection s2;
studentRecord r1(85, 99837, "John");
s2.addRecord(r1);
studentRecord r2(77, 4765, "Elsie");
s2.addRecord(r2);
❶ s1 = s2;
❷ s2.removeRecord(99837);
```

Suppose I ask you what effect the last statement ❷ had on s1. Unfortunately, it does have an effect. Although s1 and s2 are two different objects, they are no longer entirely separate objects. By default, when one object is assigned to another, as we assign s2 to s1 here ❶, C++ performs what is known as a *shallow copy*. In a shallow copy, each data member of one object is directly assigned to the other. So if _listHead, our only data member, were public, s1 = s2 would be the same as s1._listHead = s2._listHead. This leaves the _listHead data member of both objects pointing at the same place in memory: the node for "Elsie", which points at the other node, the one for "John". Therefore, when the node for "John" is removed, it's apparently removed from two lists because there is actually only one list. Figure 5-4 shows the situation at the end of the code.

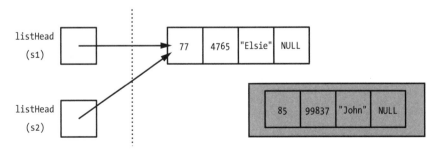

Figure 5-4: Shallow copy results in cross-linking; deleting "John" node from one list deletes from both.

As quirky as that is, though, it could actually have been much worse. What if the last line of the code had removed the first record, the "Elsie" node? In that case, the _listHead inside s2 would have been updated to point to "John", and the "Elsie" node would have been deleted. The _listHead inside s1, however, would still point to the deleted "Elsie" node, a dangerous dangling reference, as shown in Figure 5-5.

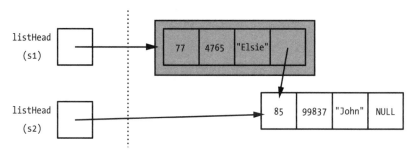

Figure 5-5: Removal from s2 causing a dangling reference in s1

The solution to this issue is a *deep copy*, which means we don't just copy the pointer to the structure but rather make copies of everything in the structure. In this case, it means copying all of the nodes in the list to make a true list copy. As before, let's start by making a private helper method, in this case, one that copies a studentList. The declaration in the class's private section looks like this:

```
studentList copiedList(const studentList original);
```

As before, I've chosen a noun for a method that returns a value. The implementation for the method is as follows:

```
❶ studentCollection::studentList studentCollection::copiedList(const studentList original) {
    ❷if (original == NULL) {
        return NULL;
    }
    studentList newList = new studentNode;
  ❸newList->studentData = original->studentData;
  ❹studentNode * oldLoopPtr = original->next;
  ❺studentNode * newLoopPtr = newList;
    while (oldLoopPtr != NULL) {
        ❻newLoopPtr->next = new studentNode;
        newLoopPtr = newLoopPtr->next;
        newLoopPtr->studentData = oldLoopPtr->studentData;
        oldLoopPtr = oldLoopPtr->next;
    }
  ❼newLoopPtr->next = NULL;
  ❽return newList;
}
```

There's a lot going on in this method, so let's take it step by step. On a syntax note, when specifying the return type in the implementation, we have to prefix the name of the class ❶. Otherwise, the compiler won't know what type we are talking about. (Inside the method, that's not necessary because the compiler already knows what class the method is a part of—a bit confusing!) We check to see whether the incoming list is empty. If so, we get out of Dodge ❷. Once we know there is a list to be copied, we copy the first node's data prior to the loop ❸ because for that node we have to modify our new list's head pointer.

We then set up two pointers for tracking through the two lists. The oldLoopPtr ❹ traverses the incoming list; it's always going to point to the node we are about to copy. The newLoopPtr ❺ traverses the new, copied list, and it always points to the last node we created, which is the node prior to where we'll add the next node. Just as in the removeRecord method, we need a kind of trailing pointer here. Inside the loop ❻, we create a new node, advance newLoopPtr to point to it, copy the data from the old node to the new, and advance oldLoopPtr. After the loop, we terminate the new list by assigning NULL to the next field of the last node ❼ and return the pointer to the new list ❽.

So how does this helper method solve the issue we saw previously? By itself, it doesn't. But with this code in place, we can now overload the assignment operator. *Operator overloading* is a feature of C++ that allows us to change what the built-in operators do with certain types. In this case, we want to overload the assignment operator (=), so that instead of the default shallow copy, it calls our copiedList method to perform a deep copy. In the public section of our class, we add:

```
❶ studentCollection& ❷operator=(❸const studentCollection & ❹rhs);
```

The operator we are overloading is specified by naming the method using the keyword operator followed by the operator we want to overload ❷. The name I've chosen for the parameter (rhs ❹) is a common choice for operator overloads because it stands for *right-hand side*. This helps the programmer keep things straight. So in the assignment statement that started this discussion, s2 = s1, the object s1 would be the right-hand side of the assignment operation, and s2 would be the left-hand side. We reference the right-hand side through the parameter, and we reference the left-hand side by directly accessing class members, the way we would with any other method of the class. So our task in this case is to create a list pointed to by _listHead that is a copy of the list pointed to by the _listHead of rhs. This will have the effect in the call s2 = s1 of making s2 a true copy of s1.

The type of the parameter is always a constant reference to the class in question ❸; the return type is always a reference to the class ❶. You'll see why the parameter is a reference shortly. You might wonder why the method returns anything, since we are manipulating the data member directly in the method. It's because C++ allows chained assignments, like s3 = s2 = s1, in which the return value of one assignment becomes the parameter of the next.

Once all of the syntax is understood, the code for the assignment operator is quite direct:

```
studentCollection& studentCollection::operator=(const studentCollection &rhs) {
  ❶if (this != &rhs) {
      ❷deleteList(_listHead);
      ❸_listHead = copiedList(rhs._listHead);
  }
  ❹return *this;
}
```

To avoid a memory leak, we must first remove all of the nodes from the left-hand side list ❷. (It is for this purpose that we write deleteList as a helper method rather than including its code directly in the destructor.) With the previous left-hand list deleted, we copy the right-hand list using our other helper method ❸. Before performing either of these steps, though, we check that the object on the right-hand side is different from the object on the left-hand side (that is, it's not something like s1 = s1) by checking whether the pointers are different ❶. If the pointers are identical, there's no need to do anything, but this is not just a matter of efficiency. If we performed the deep copy on identical pointers, when we delete the nodes currently in the left-hand side list, we would also be deleting the nodes in the right-hand side list. Finally, we return a pointer to the left-hand side object ❹; this happens whether we actually copied anything or not because although a statement like s2 = s1 = s1 is screwy, we still would like it to work if someone tries it.

As long as we have our list-copying helper method, we should also create a *copy constructor*. This is a constructor that takes another object of the same class as an object. The copy constructor can be invoked explicitly whenever we need to create a duplicate of an existing studentCollection, but copy constructors are also invoked implicitly whenever an object of that class is passed as a value parameter to a function. Because of this, you should consider passing object parameters as const references instead of value parameters unless the function receiving the object needs to modify the copy. Otherwise, your code could be doing a lot of work unnecessarily. Consider a student collection of 10,000 records, for example. The collection could be passed as a reference, a single pointer. Alternatively, it could invoke the copy constructor for a long traversal and 10,000 memory allocations, and this local copy would then invoke the destructor at the end of the function with another long traversal and 10,000 deallocations. This is why the right-hand side parameter to the assignment operator overload uses a const reference parameter.

To add the copy constructor to our class, first we add its declaration to our class declaration in the public section.

```
studentCollection(const studentCollection &original);
```

As with all constructors, there is no return type, and as with the overloaded assignment operator, the parameter is a const reference to our class. The implementation is easy because we already have the helper method.

```
studentCollection::studentCollection(const studentCollection &original) {
    _listHead = copiedList(original._listHead);
}
```

Now we can make a declaration like this:

```
studentCollection s2(s1);
```

This declaration has the effect of declaring s2 and copying the nodes of s1 into it.

The Big Picture for Classes with Dynamic Memory

We've really done a lot to this class since completing the methods specified by the problem description, so let's take a moment to review. Here's what our class declaration looks like now.

```
class studentCollection {
private:
    struct studentNode {
        studentRecord studentData;
        studentNode * next;
    };
public:
    studentCollection();
    ~studentCollection();
    studentCollection(const studentCollection &original);
    studentCollection& operator=(const studentCollection &rhs);
    void addRecord(studentRecord newStudent);
    studentRecord recordWithNumber(int idNum);
    void removeRecord(int idNum);
private:
    typedef studentNode * studentList;
    studentList _listHead;
    void deleteList(studentList &listPtr);
    studentList copiedList(const studentList original);
};
```

The lesson here is that new pieces are required when creating a class with dynamic memory. In addition to the features of our basic class framework—private data, a default constructor, and methods to send data in and out of the object—we have to add additional methods to handle the allocation and cleanup of dynamic memory. At a minimum, we should add a copy constructor and a destructor and also overload the assignment operator if there's any chance someone would use it. The creation of these additional methods can often be facilitated by creating helper methods to copy or delete the underlying dynamic data structure.

This may seem like a lot of work, and it can be, but it's important to note that everything you are adding to the class is something you need to deal with anyway. In other words, if we didn't have a class for our linked-list collection of student records, we're still responsible for deleting the nodes in the list when we're through with them. We would still have to be wary of cross-linking, still have to traverse through a list and copy node by node if we wanted a true copy of the original list, and so on. Putting everything into the class structure is only a little more work up front, and once everything works, the client code can ignore all the memory allocation details. In the end, encapsulation and information hiding make dynamic data structures much easier to work with.

Mistakes to Avoid

We've talked about how to create a good class in C++, so let's round off the discussion by talking about a couple of common pitfalls you should avoid.

The Fake Class

As I mentioned at the beginning of this chapter, I think that C++, as a hybrid language that includes both the procedural and the object-oriented paradigms, is a great language for learning object-oriented programming because the creation of a class is always a positive choice on the part of the programmer. In a language like Java, the question is never, "Should I make a class?" but rather, "How am I going to put this into a class?" The requirement to put everything into a class structure results in what I call a *fake class*, a class without a coherent design that is correct syntactically but has no real meaning. The word *class* as it is used in programming is derived from the sense of the English word meaning a group of things with common attributes, and a good C++ class meets this definition.

Fake classes can happen for several reasons. One type occurs because the programmer really wants to use global variables, not for any defensible reason (such reasons are rare, though they do exist) but out of laziness—just to avoid passing parameters from function to function. While the programmer knows that widespread use of global variables is considered terrible style, he or she thinks the loophole has been found. All or most of the functions of the program are shoveled into a class, and the variables that would have been global are now data members of the class. The main function of the program simply creates one object of the fake class and invokes some "master" method in the class. Technically, the program uses no global variables, but the fake class means that the program has all of the same defects as one that does.

Another type of fake class occurs because the programmer just assumes that object-oriented programming is always "better" and forces it into situations where it doesn't apply. In these cases, the programmer often creates a class that encapsulates very specific functionality that only makes sense in the context of the original program for which it is written. There are two ways to test whether you are writing this type of fake class. The first is by asking, "Can I give the class a specific and reasonably short name?" If you find yourself with a name like *PayrollReportManagerAndPrintSpooler*, you might have a problem.

The other test asks, "If I were to write another program with similar functionality, can I imagine how the class could be reused, with only small modifications? Or would it have to be dramatically rewritten?"

Even in C++, a certain number of fake classes are inevitable, for example, because we have to encapsulate data for use in collection classes. Such classes, however, are usually small and basic. If we can avoid elaborate fake classes, our code will improve.

Single-Taskers

If you've ever seen the television show *Good Eats*, you know that host Alton Brown spends a lot of time discussing how you should outfit your kitchen for maximum efficiency. He often rails against kitchen gadgets he calls *single-taskers*, by which he means tools that do one task well but don't do anything else. In writing our classes, we should strive to make them as general as possible, consistent with including all the specific functionality required for our program.

One way of doing this is with template classes. This is an advanced subject with a somewhat arcane syntax, but it allows us to make classes where one or more of the data members has a type that is specified when an object of the class is created. Template classes allow us to "factor out" general functionality. For example, our studentCollection class contains a lot of code that is common to any class that encapsulates a linked list. We could instead make a template class for a general linked list, such that the type of data within the list nodes is specified when the object of the template class is created, rather than being hardwired as a studentRecord. Then our studentCollection class would have an object of the template linked list class as a data member, rather than a list head pointer, and would no longer manipulate the linked list directly.

Template classes are beyond the scope of this book, but as you develop your abilities as a class designer, you should always strive to make classes that are multitaskers. It's a great feeling when you discover a current problem can be solved using a class you wrote previously, long before you knew the current problem existed.

Exercises

You know what I'm about to say, don't you? Go ahead and try some!

5-1. Let's try implementing a class using the basic framework. Consider a class to store the data for an automobile. We'll have three pieces of data: a manufacturer name and model name, both strings, and a model year, an integer. Create a class with *get/set* methods for each data member. Make sure you make good decisions concerning details like member names. It's not important that you follow my particular naming convention. What's important is that you think about the choices you make and are consistent in your decisions.

5-2.   For our automobile class from the previous exercise, add a support method that returns a complete description of the automobile object as a formatted string, such as, "1957 Chevrolet Impala". Add a second support method that returns the age of the automobile in years.

5-3.   Take the variable-length string functions from Chapter 4 (append, concatenate, and characterAt) and use them to create a class for variable-length strings, making sure to implement all necessary constructors, a destructor, and an overloaded assignment operator.

5-4.   For the variable-length string class of the previous exercise, replace the characterAt method with an overloaded [] operator. For example, if myString is an object of our class, then myString[1] should return the same result as myString.characterAt(1).

5-5.   For the variable-length string class of the previous exercises, add a remove method that takes a starting position and a number of characters and removes that many characters from the middle of the string. So myString.remove(5,3) would remove three characters starting at the fifth position. Make sure your method behaves when the value of either of the parameters is invalid.

5-6.   Review your variable-length string class for possible refactoring. For example, is there any common functionality that can be separated into a private support method?

5-7.   Take the student record functions from Chapter 4 (addRecord and averageRecord) and use them to create a class representing a collection of student records, as before, making sure to implement all necessary constructors, a destructor, and an overloaded assignment operator.

5-8.   For the student record collection class of the previous exercise, add a method RecordsWithinRange that takes a low grade and a high grade as parameters and returns a new collection consisting of the records in that range (the original collection is unaffected). For example, myCollection.RecordsWithinRange(75, 80) would return a collection of all records with grades in the range 75–80 inclusive.

6

SOLVING PROBLEMS WITH RECURSION

This chapter is about *recursion*, which is when a function directly or indirectly calls itself. Recursive programming looks as if it should be simple. Indeed, a good recursive solution often has a simple, almost elegant appearance. However, very often the route to that solution is anything but simple. This is because recursion requires us to think differently than we do with other types of programming. When we process data using loops, we're thinking about processing in a sequential manner, but when we process data using recursion, our normal sequential thinking process won't help. Many good, fledgling programmers struggle with recursion because they can't see a way to apply the problem-solving skills they've learned to recursive problems. In this chapter, we'll discuss how to attack recursive problems systematically. The answer is using what we will call the *Big Recursive Idea*, henceforth referred to as the BRI. It's an idea that's so straightforward it will seem like a trick, but it works.

Review of Recursion Fundamentals

There is not much to know about the *syntax* of recursion; the difficulty arises when you try to use recursion to solve problems. Recursion occurs any time a function calls itself, so the syntax of recursion is just the syntax of a function call. The most common form is *direct recursion*, when a call to a function occurs in the body of that same function. For example:

```
int factorial(int n) {
  ❶if (n == 1) return 1;
    else return n * ❷factorial(n - 1);
}
```

This function, which is a common but highly inefficient demonstration of recursion, computes the factorial of *n*. For example, if *n* is 5, then the factorial is the product of all the numbers from 5 to 1, or 120. Note that in some cases no recursion occurs. In this function, if the parameter is 1, we simply return a value directly without any recursion ❶, which is known as a *base case*. Otherwise, we make the recursive call ❷.

The other form of recursion is *indirect recursion*—for example, if function A calls function B, which later calls function A. Indirect recursion is rarely used as a problem-solving technique, so we won't cover it here.

Head and Tail Recursion

Before we discuss the BRI, we need to understand the difference between head recursion and tail recursion. In *head recursion*, the recursive call, when it happens, comes before other processing in the function (think of it happening at the top, or head, of the function). In *tail recursion*, it's the opposite— the processing occurs before the recursive call. Choosing between the two recursive styles may seem arbitrary, but the choice can make all the difference. To illustrate this difference, let's look at two problems.

PROBLEM: HOW MANY PARROTS?

Passengers on the Tropical Paradise Railway (TPR) look forward to seeing dozens of colorful parrots from the train windows. Because of this, the railway takes a keen interest in the health of the local parrot population and decides to take a tally of the number of parrots in view of each train platform along the main line. Each platform is staffed by a TPR employee (see Figure 6-1), who is certainly capable of counting parrots. Unfortunately, the job is complicated by the primitive telephone system. Each platform can call only its immediate neighbors. How do we get the parrot total at the main line terminal?

Art Belinda Cory Debbie Evan

Figure 6-1: The employees at the five stations can communicate only with their immediate neighbors.

Let's suppose that there are 7 parrots by Art at the main terminal, 5 parrots by Belinda, 3 parrots by Cory, 10 parrots by Debbie, and 2 parrots by Evan at the last station. The total number of parrots is thus 27. The question is, how are the employees going to work together to communicate this total to Art? Any solution to this problem is going to require a chain of communications all the way from the main terminal to the end of the line and back. The staff member at each platform will be requested to count parrots and will then report his or her observations. Even so, there are two distinct approaches to this communications chain, and those approaches correspond to the head recursion and tail recursion techniques in programming.

Approach 1

In this approach, we keep a running total of the parrots as we progress through the outbound communications. Each employee, when making the request of the next employee down the line, passes along the number of parrots seen so far. When we get to the end of the line, Evan will be the first to discover the parrot total, which he will pass up to Debbie, who will pass it to Cory, and so on (as shown in Figure 6-2).

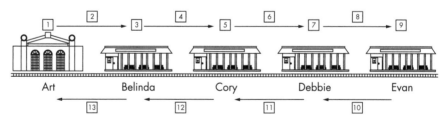

Art Belinda Cory Debbie Evan

Figure 6-2: Numbering of steps taken in Approach 1 for the parrot-counting problem

1. ART begins by counting the parrots around his platform. He counts 7 parrots.
2. ART to BELINDA: "There are 7 parrots here at the main terminal."
3. BELINDA counts 5 parrots around her platform for a running total of 12.
4. BELINDA to CORY: "There are 12 parrots around the first two stations."
5. CORY counts 3 parrots.

6. CORY to DEBBIE: "There are 15 parrots around the first three stations."
7. DEBBIE counts 10 parrots.
8. DEBBIE to EVAN: "There are 25 parrots around the first four stations."
9. EVAN counts 2 parrots and discovers that the total number of parrots is 27.
10. EVAN to DEBBIE: "The total number of parrots is 27."
11. DEBBIE to CORY: "The total number of parrots is 27."
12. CORY to BELINDA: "The total number of parrots is 27."
13. BELINDA to ART: "The total number of parrots is 27."

This approach is analogous to tail recursion. In tail recursion, the recursive call happens after the processing—the recursive call is the last step in the function. In the communications chain above, note that the "work" of the employees—the parrot counting and summation—happens before they signal the next employee down the line. All of the work happens on the outbound communications chain, not the inbound chain. Here are the steps each employee follows:

1. Count the parrots visible from the station platform.
2. Add this count to the total given by the previous station.
3. Call the next station to pass along the running sum of parrot counts.
4. Wait for the next station to call with the total parrot count, and then pass this total up to the previous station.

Approach 2

In this approach, we sum the parrot counts from the other end. Each employee, when contacting the next station down the line, requests the total number of parrots from that station onward. The employee then adds the number of parrots at his or her own station and passes this new total up the line (as shown in Figure 6-3).

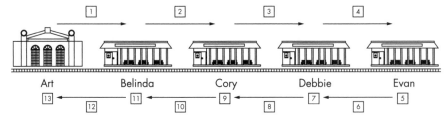

Figure 6-3: Numbering of steps taken in Approach 2 for the parrot-counting problem

1. ART to BELINDA: "What's the total number of parrots from your station to the end of the line?"
2. BELINDA to CORY: "What's the total number of parrots from your station to the end of the line?"

3. CORY to DEBBIE: "What's the total number of parrots from your station to the end of the line?"
4. DEBBIE to EVAN: "What's the total number of parrots from your station to the end of the line?"
5. EVAN is the end of the line. He counts 2 parrots.
6. EVAN to DEBBIE: "The total number of parrots here at the end is 2."
7. DEBBIE counts 10 parrots at her station, so the total from her station to the end is 12.
8. DEBBIE to CORY: "The total number of parrots from here to the end is 12."
9. CORY counts 3 parrots.
10. CORY to BELINDA: "The total number of parrots from here to the end is 15."
11. BELINDA counts 5 parrots.
12. BELINDA to ART: "The total number of parrots from here to the end is 20."
13. ART counts 7 parrots at the main terminal, making a total of 27.

This approach is analogous to head recursion. In head recursion, the recursive call happens before the other processing. Here, the call to the next station happens first, before counting the parrots or the summation. The "work" is postponed until after the stations down the line have reported their totals. Here are the steps each employee follows:

1. Call the next station.
2. Count the parrots visible from the station platform.
3. Add this count to the total given by the next station.
4. Pass the resulting sum up to the previous station.

You may have noticed two practical effects of the different approaches. In the first approach, eventually all of the station employees will learn the overall parrot total. In the second approach, only Art, at the main terminal, learns the full total—but note that Art is the only employee who needs the full total.

The other practical effect will become more important for our analysis when we transition the discussion to actual programming code. In the first approach, each employee passes along the "running total" to the next station down the line when making the request. In the second approach, the employee simply makes the request for information from the next station, without passing any data down the line. This effect is typical of the head recursion approach. Because the recursive call happens first, before any other processing, there is no new information to give the recursive call. In general, the head recursion approach allows the minimum set of data to be passed to the recursive call. Now let's look at another problem.

PROBLEM: WHO'S OUR BEST CUSTOMER?

The manager of DelegateCorp needs to determine which of eight customers produces the most revenue for his company. Two factors complicate this otherwise simple task. First, determining the total revenue for a customer requires going through that customer's whole file and tallying numbers on dozens of orders and receipts. Second, the employees of DelegateCorp, as the name suggests, love to delegate, and each employee passes work along to someone at a lower level whenever possible. To keep the situation from getting out of hand, the manager enforces a rule: When you delegate, you must do some portion of the work yourself, and you have to give the delegated employee less work than you were given.

Tables 6-1 and 6-2 identify the employees and customers of DelegateCorp.

Table 6-1: DelegateCorp Employee Titles and Rank

Title	Rank
Manager	1
Vice manager	2
Associate manager	3
Assistant manager	4
Junior manager	5
Intern	6

Table 6-2: DelegateCorp Customers

Customer Number	Revenue
#0001	$172,000
#0002	$68,000
#0003	$193,000
#0004	$13,000
#0005	$256,000
#0006	$99,000

Following the company rule on delegating work, here's what will happen to the six customer files. The manager will take one file and determine how much revenue that customer has generated for the company. The manager will delegate the other five files to the vice manager. The vice manager will process one file and pass the other four to the associate manager. This process continues until we reach the sixth employee, the intern, who is handed one file and must simply process it, with no further delegation possible.

Figure 6-4 describes the lines of communication and the division of labor. As with the previous example, though, there are two distinct approaches to the communications chain.

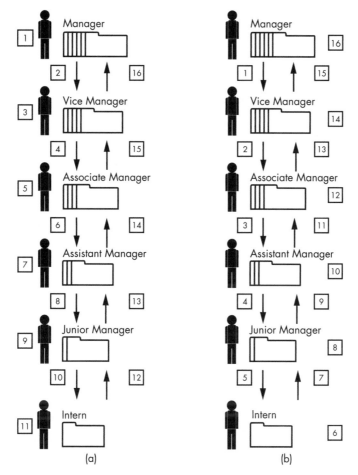

Figure 6-4: The numbering of steps in Approach 1 (a) and Approach 2 (b) for finding the highest-revenue customer

Approach 1

In this approach, when delegating the remaining files, the employee also passes along the highest amount of revenue seen so far. This means that the employee must tally the revenue in one file and compare this to the previous highest amount seen before delegating the remaining files to another employee. Here's an example of how this would proceed in practice.

1. MANAGER tallies the revenue for customer #0001, which is $172,000.

2. MANAGER to VICE MANAGER: "The highest revenue we have seen so far is $172,000, customer #0001. Take these five files and determine the overall highest revenue."

3. VICE MANAGER tallies the revenue for customer #0002, which is $68,000. The highest revenue seen so far is still $172,000, customer #0001.

4. VICE MANAGER to ASSOCIATE MANAGER: "The highest revenue we have seen so far is $172,000, customer #0001. Take these four files and determine the overall highest revenue."

5. ASSOCIATE MANAGER tallies the revenue for customer #0003, which is $193,000. The highest revenue seen so far is now $193,000, customer #0003.

6. ASSOCIATE MANAGER to ASSISTANT MANAGER: "The highest revenue we have seen so far is $193,000, customer #0003. Take these three files and determine the overall highest revenue."

7. ASSISTANT MANAGER tallies the revenue for customer #0004, which is $13,000. The highest revenue seen so far is still $193,000, customer #0003.

8. ASSISTANT MANAGER to JUNIOR MANAGER: "The highest revenue we have seen so far is $193,000, customer #0003. Take these two files and determine the overall highest revenue."

9. JUNIOR MANAGER tallies the revenue for customer #0005, which is $256,000. The highest revenue seen so far is now $256,000, customer #0005.

10. JUNIOR MANAGER to INTERN: "The highest revenue we have seen so far is $256,000, customer #0005. Take this remaining file and determine the overall highest revenue."

11. INTERN tallies the revenue for customer #0006, which is $99,000. The highest revenue seen so far is still $256,000, customer #0005.

12. INTERN to JUNIOR MANAGER: "The highest revenue of all customers is $256,000, customer #0005."

13. JUNIOR MANAGER to ASSISTANT MANAGER: "The highest revenue of all customers is $256,000, customer #0005."

14. ASSISTANT MANAGER to ASSOCIATE MANAGER: "The highest revenue of all customers is $256,000, customer #0005."

15. ASSOCIATE MANAGER to VICE MANAGER: "The highest revenue of all customers is $256,000, customer #0005."

16. VICE MANAGER to MANAGER: "The highest revenue of all customers is $256,000, customer #0005."

This approach, shown in Figure 6-4 (a), uses the tail recursion technique. Each employee processes one customer file and compares the computed revenue for that customer against the highest revenue seen so far. Then the employee passes the result of that comparison to the subordinate employee. The recursion—the passing off of work—happens after the other processing. Each employee's process runs like this:

1. Tally the revenue in one customer file.

2. Compare this total with the highest revenue seen by superiors in other customer files.

3. Pass the remaining customer files to a subordinate employee, along with the highest revenue amount seen so far.

4. When the subordinate employee returns the highest revenue of all the customer files, pass this back to the superior.

Approach 2

In this approach, each employee begins by setting aside one file and then passing the others to the subordinate. In this case, the subordinate isn't asked to determine the highest revenue of all the files, just of the files the subordinate has been given. As with the first sample problem, this simplifies the requests. Using the same data as the first approach, the conversation would be as follows:

1. MANAGER to VICE MANAGER: "Take these five customer files, and tell me the highest revenue."
2. VICE MANAGER to ASSOCIATE MANAGER: "Take these four customer files, and tell me the highest revenue."
3. ASSOCIATE MANAGER to ASSISTANT MANAGER: "Take these three customer files, and tell me the highest revenue."
4. ASSISTANT MANAGER to JUNIOR MANAGER: "Take these two customer files, and tell me the highest revenue."
5. JUNIOR MANAGER to INTERN: "Take this one customer file, and tell me the highest revenue."
6. INTERN tallies the revenue for customer #0006, which is $99,000. This is the only file the INTERN has seen, so that's the highest revenue.
7. INTERN to JUNIOR MANAGER: "The highest revenue in my files is $99,000, customer #0006."
8. JUNIOR MANAGER tallies the revenue for customer #0005, which is $256,000. The highest revenue this employee knows about is $256,000, customer #0005.
9. JUNIOR MANAGER to ASSISTANT MANAGER: "The highest revenue in my files is $256,000, customer #0005."
10. ASSISTANT MANAGER tallies the revenue for customer #0004, which is $13,000. The highest revenue this employee knows about is $256,000, customer #0005.
11. ASSISTANT MANAGER to ASSOCIATE MANAGER: "The highest revenue in my files is $256,000, customer #0005."
12. ASSOCIATE MANAGER tallies the revenue for customer #0003, which is $193,000. The highest revenue this employee knows about is $256,000, customer #0005.
13. ASSOCIATE MANAGER to VICE MANAGER: "The highest revenue in my files is $256,000, customer #0005."
14. VICE MANAGER tallies the revenue for customer #0002, which is $68,000. The highest revenue this employee knows about is $256,000, customer #0005.
15. VICE MANAGER to MANAGER: "The highest revenue in my files is $256,000, customer #0005."
16. MANAGER tallies the revenue for customer #0001, which is $172,000. The highest revenue this employee knows about is $256,000, customer #0005.

This approach, shown in Figure 6-4 (b), uses the head recursion technique. Each employee still has to tally the revenue in one customer file, but that action is postponed until after the subordinate employee determines the highest revenue among the remaining files. The process each employee takes is as follows:

1. Pass all customer files except one to a subordinate employee.
2. Get the highest revenue of those files back from the subordinate employee.
3. Tally the revenue in the one customer file.
4. Pass the larger of those two revenues to the superior.

As in the "counting parrots" problem, the head recursion technique allows each employee to pass the minimum amount of information to the subordinate.

The Big Recursive Idea

We now arrive at the Big Recursive Idea. In fact, if you've read through the steps of the sample problems, you have already seen the BRI in action.

How so? Both of the sample problems follow the form of a recursive solution. Each person in the communications chain performs the same steps on a smaller and smaller subset of the original data. It's important to note, however, that *the problems involve no recursion at all.*

In the first problem, each railway employee makes a request of the next station down the line, and in fulfilling that request, the next employee follows the same steps as the previous employee. But nothing in the wording of the request requires an employee to follow those particular steps. When Art called Belinda using Approach 2, for example, he asked her to count the total number of parrots from her station to the end of the line. He did not dictate a method for discovering this total. If he thought about it, he might have realized that Belinda would have to follow the same steps that he himself was following, but he doesn't have to consider this. To complete his task, all Art required was for Belinda to provide the correct answer to the question he asked.

Likewise, in the second problem, each employee in the management chain hands off as much work as possible to a subordinate. The assistant manager, for example, may know the junior manager well and expect the junior manager to hand all of the files but one to the intern. However, the assistant manager has no reason to care whether the junior manager processes all of the remaining files or passes some of them off to a subordinate. The assistant manager cares only that the junior manager returns the right answer. Because the assistant manager is not going to repeat the work of the junior manager, the assistant manager simply assumes that the result returned by the junior manager is correct and uses that data to solve the overall task that the assistant manager received from the associate manager.

In both problems, when employees make requests of other employees, they are concerned with *what* but not *how*. A question is handed off; an answer is received. This, then, is the Big Recursive Idea: If you follow certain conventions in your coding, *you can pretend that no recursion is taking place.* You can even use a cheap trick (shown below) to move from an iterative implementation to a recursive implementation, without explicitly considering how the recursion is actually solving the problem. Over time, you will develop an intuitive understanding of how recursive solutions work, but before that intuition develops, you can craft recursive implementations and be confident in your code.

Let's put the concept into practice through a code example.

PROBLEM: COMPUTING THE SUM OF AN ARRAY OF INTEGERS

Write a recursive function that is given an array of integers and the size of the array as parameters. The function returns the sum of the integers in the array.

Your first thought may have been that this problem would be trivial to solve iteratively. Indeed, let's start with an iterative solution to this problem:

```
int iterativeArraySum(int integers[], int size) {
    int sum = 0;
    for (int i = 0; i < size; i++) {
        sum += integers[i];
    }
    return sum;
}
```

You saw code very similar to this in Chapter 3, so the function should be simple to understand. The next step is to write code that is halfway between the iterative solution and the final desired recursive solution. We will keep the iterative function and add a second function we will refer to as a *dispatcher*. The dispatcher will hand off most of the work to the previously written iterative function and use this information to solve the overall problem. To write a dispatcher, we have to follow two rules:

1. The dispatcher must completely handle the most trivial case, without calling the iterative function.
2. The dispatcher, when calling the iterative function, must pass a smaller version of the problem.

In applying the first rule to this problem, we must decide what the most trivial case is. If size is 0, then the function has conceptually been passed a "null" array, with a sum of 0. One could also make the argument that the most trivial case should be when size is 1. In that case, there would be only one number in the logical array, and we could return that number as the sum. Either of these interpretations will work, but making the first choice allows the function to handle a special case. Note that the original iterative function will not fail when size is zero, so it would be preferable to maintain that flexibility.

To apply the second rule to this problem, we must figure out a way to pass a smaller version of the problem from the dispatcher to the iterative function. There is no easy way to pass a smaller array, but we can easily pass a smaller value for size. If the dispatcher is given the value of 10 for size, the function is being asked to compute the sum of 10 values in the array. If the dispatcher passes 9 as the value of size to the iterative function, it is requesting the sum of the first 9 values in the array. The dispatcher can then add the value of the one remaining value in the array (the 10th) to compute the sum of all 10 values. Note that reducing size by 1 when calling the iterative function maximizes the work of the iterative function and thereby minimizes the work of the dispatcher. This is always the desired approach—like the managers of DelegateCorp, the dispatcher function avoids as much work as possible.

Putting these ideas together, here's a dispatcher function for this problem:

```
int arraySumDelegate(int integers[], int size) {
  ❶if (size == 0) return 0;
  ❷int lastNumber = integers[size - 1];
    int allButLastSum = ❸iterativeArraySum(integers, size - 1);
  ❹return lastNumber + allButLastSum;
}
```

The first statement enforces the first rule of dispatchers: It checks for a trivial case and handles it completely, in this case, by returning 0 ❶. Otherwise, control passes to the remaining code, which enforces the second rule. The last number in the array is stored in a local variable called lastNumber ❷, and then the sum of all the other values in the array is computed via a call to the iterative function ❸. This result is stored in another local variable, allButLastSum, and finally the function returns the sum of the two local variables ❹.

If we have correctly created a dispatcher function, we have already effectively created a recursive solution. This is the Big Recursive Idea in action. To convert this iterative solution to a recursive solution requires but one further, simple step: have the delegate function call itself where it was previously calling the iterative function. We can then remove the iterative function altogether.

```
int ❶arraySumRecursive(int integers[], int size) {
    if (size == 0) return 0;
    int lastNumber = integers[size - 1];
    int allButLastSum = ❷arraySumRecursive(integers, size - 1);
    return lastNumber + allButLastSum;
}
```

Only two changes have been made to the previous code. The name of the function has been changed to better describe its new form ❶, and the function now calls itself where it previously called the iterative function ❷. The logic of the two functions, arraySumDelegate and arraySumRecursive, is identical. Each function checks for a trivial case in which the sum is already known—in this case, an array of size 0 that has a sum of 0. Otherwise, each function computes the sum of values in the array by making a function call to compute the sum of all of the values, save the last one. Finally, each function adds that last value to the returned sum for a grand total. The only difference is that the first version of the function calls another function, while the recursive version calls itself. The BRI tells us that if we follow the rules outlined above for writing the dispatcher, we can ignore that distinction.

You do not need to literally follow all of the steps shown above to follow the BRI. In particular, you usually would not implement an iterative solution to the problem before implementing a recursive solution. Writing an iterative function as a stepping-stone is extra work that will eventually be thrown away. Besides, recursion is best applied to situations in which an iterative solution is difficult, as explained later. However, you can follow the outline of the BRI without actually writing the iterative solution. The key is thinking of a recursive call as a call to another function, without regards to the internals of that function. In this way, you remove the complexities of recursive logic from the recursive solution.

Common Mistakes

As shown above, with the right approach, recursive solutions can often be very easy to write. But it can be just as easy to come up with an incorrect recursive implementation or a recursive solution that "works" but is ungainly. Most problems with recursive implementations stem from two basic faults: overthinking the problem or beginning implementation without a clear plan.

Overthinking recursive problems is common for new programmers because limited experience and lack of confidence with recursion lead them to think that the problem is more difficult than it really is. Code produced by overthinking can be recognized by its too-careful appearance. For example, a recursive function might have several special cases where it needs only one.

Beginning implementation too soon can lead to overcomplicated "Rube Goldberg" code, where unforeseen interactions lead to fixes that are bolted onto the original code.

Let's look at some specific mistakes and how to avoid them.

Too Many Parameters

As described previously, the head recursion technique can reduce the data passed to the recursive call, while the tail recursion technique can result in passing additional data to recursive calls. Programmers often get stuck in the tail recursion mode because they overthink and start implementation too soon.

Consider our problem of recursively computing the sum of an array of integers. Writing an iterative solution to this problem, the programmer knows a "running total" variable will be needed (in the iterative solution provided, I called this sum) and the array will be summed starting from the first element. Considering the recursive solution, the programmer naturally imagines an implementation that most directly mirrors the iterative solution, with a running total variable and the first recursive call handling the first element in the array. This approach, however, requires the recursive function to pass the running total and the location where the next recursive call should begin processing. Such a solution would look like this:

```
int arraySumRecursiveExtraParams(int integers[], int size, ❶int sum, ❷int currentIndex) {
    if (currentIndex == size) return sum;
    sum += integers[currentIndex];
    return arraySumRecursiveExtraParameters(integers, size, sum, currentIndex + 1);
}
```

This code is as short as the other recursive version but considerably more semantically complex because of the additional parameters, sum ❶ and currentIndex ❷. From the client code's point of view, the extra parameters are meaningless and will always have to be zeroes in the call, as shown in this example:

```
int a[10] = {20, 3, 5, 22, 7, 9, 14, 17, 4, 9};
int total = arraySumRecursiveExtraParameters(a, 10, 0, 0);
```

This problem can be avoided with the use of a *wrapper function*, as described in the next section, but because we can't eliminate those parameters altogether, that's not the best solution. The iterative function for this problem and the original recursive function answer the question, what is the sum of this array with this many elements? In contrast, this second recursive function is being asked, what is the sum of this array if it has this many elements, we are starting with this particular element, and this is the sum of all the prior elements?

The "too many parameters" problem is avoided by choosing your function parameters before thinking about recursion. In other words, force yourself to use the same parameter list you would if the solution were iterative. If you use the full BRI process and actually write the iterative function first, you will avoid this problem automatically. If you skip using the whole process formally, though, you can still use the idea conceptually if you write out the parameter list based on what you would expect for an iterative function.

Global Variables

Avoiding too many parameters sometimes leads programmers into making a different mistake: using global variables to pass data from one recursive call to the other. The use of global variables is generally a poor programming practice, although it is sometimes permissible for performance reasons. Global variables should always be avoided in recursive functions when possible. Let's look at a specific problem to see how programmers talk themselves into this mistake. Suppose we were asked to write a recursive function that counted the number of zeros appearing in an array of integers. This is a simple problem to solve using iteration:

```
int zeroCountIterative(int numbers[], int size) {
❶int count = 0;
   for (int i = 0; i < size; i++) {
      if (numbers[i] == 0) count ++;
   }
   return count;
}
```

The logic of this code is straightforward. We're just running through the array from the first location to the last, counting up the zeroes as we go and using a local variable, count ❶, as a tracker. If we have a function like this in our minds when we write our recursive function, though, we may assume that we need a tracker variable in that version as well. We can't simply declare count as a local variable in the recursive version because then it would be a new variable in each recursive call. So we might be tempted to declare it as a global variable:

```
int count;
int zeroCountRecursive(int numbers[], int size) {
   if (size == 0) return count;
   if (numbers[size - 1] == 0) count++;
   zeroCountRecursive(numbers, size - 1);
}
```

This code works, but the global variable is entirely unnecessary and causes all the problems global variables typically cause, such as poor readability and more difficult code maintenance. Some programmers might attempt to mitigate the problem by making the variable local, but static:

```
int zeroCountStatic(int numbers[], int size) {
❶static int count ❷= 0;
   if (size == 0) return count;
   if (numbers[size - 1] == 0) count++;
   zeroCountStatic(numbers, size - 1);
}
```

In C++, a local variable declared as *static* retains its value from one function call to the next; thus, the local static variable count ❶ would act the same as the global variable in the previous version. So what's the problem? The initialization of the variable to zero ❷ happens only the first time the function is called. This is necessary for the static declaration to be of any use, but it means that the function will return a correct answer only the first time it is called. If this function were called twice—first with an array that had three zeros, then with an array that had five zeros—the function would return an answer of eight for the second array because count would be starting where it had left off.

The solution to avoiding the global variable in this case is to use the BRI. We can assume that a recursive call with a smaller value for size will return the correct result and compute the correct value for the overall array from that. This will lead to a head-recursive solution:

```
int zeroCountRecursive(int numbers[], int size) {
    if (size == 0) return 0;
  ❶int count = zeroCountRecursive(numbers, size - 1);
  ❷if (numbers[size - 1] == 0) count++;
  ❸return count;
}
```

In this function, we still have a local variable, count ❶, but here no attempt is made to maintain its value from one call to the next. Instead, it stores the return value from our recursive call; we optionally increment the variable ❷ before returning it ❸.

Applying Recursion to Dynamic Data Structures

Recursion is often applied to dynamic structures such as linked lists, trees, and graphs. The more complicated the structure, the more the coding can benefit from a recursive solution. Processing complicated structures is often a lot like finding one's way through a maze, and recursion allows us to backtrack to previous steps in our processing.

Recursion and Linked Lists

Let's start, though, with the most basic of dynamic structures, a linked list. For discussions in this section, let's assume we have the simplest of node structures for our linked list, just a single int for data. Here are our type declarations:

```
struct listNnode {
    int data;
    listNode * next;
};
typedef listNode * listPtr;
```

Applying the BRI to a singly linked list follows the same general outline regardless of the specific task. Recursion requires us to divide the problem, to be able to pass a reduced version of the original problem to the recursive call. There is only one practical way to divide a singly linked list: the first node in the list and the rest of the list.

In Figure 6-5, we see a sample list divided into unequal parts: the first node and all of the other nodes. Conceptually, we can view the "rest of" the original list as its own list, starting with the second node in the original list. It is this view that allows the recursion to work smoothly.

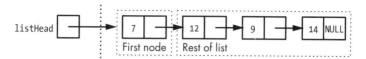

Figure 6-5: A list divided into a first node and "the rest of the list"

Again, though, we are not required to picture all the steps of the recursion to make the recursion work. From the point of view of someone writing a recursive function to process a linked list, it can be conceptualized as the first node, which we have to deal with, and the rest of the list, which we don't and therefore aren't concerned about. This attitude is shown in Figure 6-6.

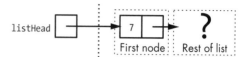

Figure 6-6: The list as a programmer using recursion should picture it: a first node and the rest of the list as a nebulous shape to be passed off to the recursive call

With the division of labor fixed, we can say that recursive processing of singly linked lists will proceed according to the following general plan. Given a linked list L and a question Q:

1. If L is minimal, we directly assign a default value. Otherwise . . .
2. Use a recursive call to produce an answer to Q for the "rest of" list L (the list starting with the second node of L).
3. Inspect the value in the first node of L.
4. Use the results of the previous two steps to answer Q for the whole of L.

As you can see, this is just a straightforward application of the BRI given the practical restrictions on breaking up a linked list. Now let's apply this blueprint to a specific problem.

PROBLEM: COUNTING NEGATIVE NUMBERS IN A SINGLY LINKED LIST

Write a recursive function that is given a singly linked list where the data type is integer. The function returns the count of negative numbers in the list.

The question, Q, we want to answer is, how many negative numbers are in the list? Therefore, our plan can be stated as:

1. If the list has no nodes, the count is 0 by default. Otherwise . . .
2. Use a recursive call to count how many negative numbers are in the "rest of" the list.
3. See whether the value in the first node of the list is negative.

4. Use the results of the previous two steps to determine how many negative numbers are in the whole list.

Here's a function implementation that follows directly from this plan:

```
int countNegative(listPtr head) {
    if (head == NULL) return 0;
    int listCount = countNegative(head->next);
    if (head->data < 0) listCount++;
    return listCount;
}
```

Note how this code follows the same principles as previous examples. It will count the negative numbers "backward," from the end of the list to the front. Also note that the code employs the head recursion technique; we process the "rest of" the list before we process the first node. As before, this allows us to avoid passing extra data in the recursive call or using global variables.

Also notice how linked-list rule 1, "if list L is minimal," is interpreted in the specific implementation of this problem as "if the list has no nodes." That's because it is meaningful to say that a list with no nodes has zero negative values. In some cases, though, there is no meaningful answer for our question Q for a list with no nodes, and the minimal case is a list with one node. Suppose our question was, what's the largest number in this list? That question cannot be answered for a list with no values. If you don't see why, pretend you are an elementary school teacher, and your class happens to be all girls. If your school's principal asked you how many boys in your classroom were members of the boy's choir, you could simply answer zero because you have no boys. If your principal asked you to name the tallest boy in your class, you could not give a meaningful answer to that question—you would have to have at least one boy to have a tallest boy. In the same way, if the question about a data set requires at least one value to be meaningfully answered, the minimal data set is one item. You may still want to return *something* for the "size zero" case, however, if only for flexibility in the use of the function and to guard against a crash.

Recursion and Binary Trees

All of the examples we have explored so far make no more than one recursive call. More complicated structures, however, may require multiple recursive calls. For a taste of how that works, let's consider the structure known as a *binary tree*, in which each node contains "left" and "right" links to other nodes. Here are the types we'll use:

```
struct treeNode {
    int data;
    treeNode * left;
    treeNode * right;
};
typedef treeNode * treePtr;
```

Because each node in the tree points to two other nodes, recursive tree-processing functions require two recursive calls. We conceptualized linked lists as having two parts: a first node and the rest of the list. For applying recursion, we will conceptualize trees as having three parts: the node at the top, known as the *root node*; all of the nodes reached from the left link of the root, known as the *left subtree*; and all of the nodes reached from the right link of the root, known as the *right subtree*. This conceptualization is shown in Figure 6-7. As with the linked list and as developers of a recursive solution, we just focus on the existence of the left and right subtrees, without considering their contents. This is shown in Figure 6-8.

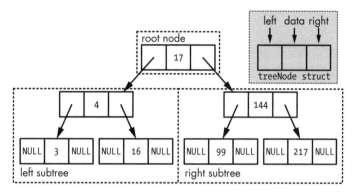

Figure 6-7: A binary tree divided into a root node and left and right subtree

As always, when recursively solving problems involving binary trees, we want to employ the BRI. We will make recursive function calls and assume they return correct results without worrying about how the recursive process solves the overall problem. As with linked lists, we will work with the natural divisions of a binary tree. This produces the following general plan. To answer a question Q for tree T:

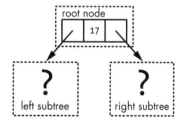

Figure 6-8: A binary tree as a programmer using recursion should picture it: a root node with left and right subtrees of unknown and unconsidered structure

1. If tree T is of minimal size, directly assign a default value. Otherwise . . .

2. Make a recursive call to answer Q for the left subtree of T.

3. Make a recursive call to answer Q for the right subtree of T.

4. Inspect the value in the root node of T.

5. Use the results of the previous three steps to answer Q for all of T.

Now let's apply the general plan to a specific problem.

PROBLEM: FIND THE LARGEST VALUE IN A BINARY TREE

Write a function that, when given a binary tree where each node holds an integer, returns the largest integer in the tree.

Applying the general plan to this specific problem results in the following steps:

1. If the root of the tree has no children, return the value in the root. Otherwise . . .
2. Make a recursive call to find the largest value in the left subtree.
3. Make a recursive call to find the largest value in the right subtree.
4. Inspect the value in the root node.
5. Return the largest of the values in the previous three steps.

With those steps in mind, we can directly write the code for the solution:

```
int maxValue(treePtr root) {
 ❶if (root == NULL) return 0;
 ❷if (root->right == NULL && root->left == NULL)
      return root->data;
 ❸int leftMax = maxValue(root->left);
 ❹int rightMax = maxValue(root->right);
 ❺int maxNum = root->data;
   if (leftMax > maxNum) maxNum = leftMax;
   if (rightMax > maxNum) maxNum = rightMax;
   return maxNum;
}
```

Notice how the minimal tree for this problem is a single node ❷ (although the empty-tree case is covered for safety ❶). This is because the question we are asking can only be meaningfully answered with at least one data value. Consider the practical problem if we tried to make the empty tree the base case. What value could we return? If we return zero, we implicitly require some positive values in the tree; if all of the values in the tree are negative, zero will be erroneously returned as the largest value in the tree. We might solve this problem by returning the lowest (most negative) possible integer, but then we would have to be careful adapting the code for other numeric types. By making a single node the base case, we avoid this decision altogether.

The rest of the code is straightforward. We use recursion to find the maximum values in the left ❸ and right subtrees ❹. Then we find the largest of the three values (value at root, largest in left subtree, largest in right subtree) using a variant of the "King of the Hill" algorithm we've been using throughout this book ❺.

Wrapper Functions

In the previous examples in this chapter, we have discussed only the recursive function itself. In some cases, however, the recursive function needs to be "set up" by a second function. Most commonly, this occurs when we write recursive functions inside of class structures. This can cause a mismatch between the parameters required for the recursive function and the parameters needed for a public method of the class. Because classes typically enforce information hiding, the class client code may not have access to the data or types the recursive function requires. This problem and its solution are shown in the next example.

PROBLEM: FIND THE NUMBER OF LEAVES IN A BINARY TREE

For a class that implements a binary tree, add a publicly accessible method that returns the number of leaves (nodes without children) in the tree. The counting of leaves should be performed using recursion.

Let's sketch the outline of what this class might look like before we try to implement a solution to this problem. For simplicity, we will include only the relevant parts of the class, ignoring the constructors, the destructor, and even the methods that would allow us to build the tree in order to focus on our recursive method.

```
class binaryTree {
    public:
      ❶int leafCount();
    private:
        struct binaryTreeNode {
            int data;
            binaryTreeNode * left;
            binaryTreeNode * right;
        };
        typedef binaryTreeNode * treePtr;
        treePtr _root;
};
```

Note that our leaf-counting function takes no parameters ❶. From an interface point of view, this is exactly correct. Consider a sample call for a previously constructed binaryTree object bt:

```
int numLeaves = bt.leafCount();
```

After all, if we are asking the tree how many leaves it has, what information could we possibly provide to the object that it would not already know about itself? As correct as this is for the interface, it's all wrong for the recursive implementation. If there is no parameter, what changes from one recursive call to the next? Nothing can change in that case, except through global variables, which, as stated earlier, are to be avoided. If nothing changes, there's no way for the recursion to progress or terminate.

The way around this problem is to write the recursive function first, conceptualizing it as a function outside of a class. In other words, we'll write this function to count the leaves in a binary tree in the same style we wrote the function to find the largest value in a binary tree. The one parameter we need to pass is a pointer to our node structure.

This gives us another opportunity to employ the BRI. What is the question Q in this case? It is, how many leaves are in the tree? Applying the general plan for recursively processing binary trees to this specific problem results in the following:

1. If the root of the tree has no children, then the tree has one node total. That node is a leaf by definition, so return 1. Otherwise . . .

2. Make a recursive call to count the leaves in the left subtree.

3. Make a recursive call to count the leaves in the right subtree.

4. In this case, there is no need to inspect the root node because if we get to this step, there is no way the root is a leaf. So . . .

5. Return the sum of steps 2 and 3.

Translating this plan into code results in this:

```
struct binaryTreeNode {
    int data;
    binaryTreeNode * left;
    binaryTreeNode * right;
};
typedef binaryTreeNode * treePtr;
int leafCount(treePtr rootPtr) {
    if (rootPtr == NULL) return 0;
    if (rootPtr->right == NULL && rootPtr->left == NULL)
        return 1;
    int leftCount = leafCount(rootPtr->left);
    int rightCount = leafCount(rootPtr->right);
    return leftCount + rightCount;
}
```

As you can see, the code is a direct translation of the plan. The question is, how do we get from this independent function to something we can use in the class? This is where the unwary programmer could easily get into trouble, thinking that we need to use a global variable or make the root pointer public. But we don't need to do that; we can keep everything inside the class. The trick is to use a *wrapper function*. First, we put the independent function, with the treePtr parameter, in the private section of our class. Then, we write a public function, the wrapper function, which will "wrap" the private function.

Because the public function has access to the private data member _root, it can pass this along to the recursive function and then return the results back to the client like this:

```
class binaryTree {
    public:
        int publicLeafCount();
    private:
        struct binaryTreeNode {
            int data;
            binaryTreeNode * left;
            binaryTreeNode * right;
        };
        typedef binaryTreeNode * treePtr;
        treePtr _root;
        int privateLeafCount(treePtr rootPtr);
};
❶ int binaryTree::privateLeafCount(treePtr rootPtr) {
        if (rootPtr == NULL) return 0;
        if (rootPtr->right == NULL && rootPtr->left == NULL)
            return 1;
        int leftCount = privateLeafCount(rootPtr->left);
        int rightCount = privateLeafCount(rootPtr->right);
        return leftCount + rightCount;
}
❷ int binaryTree::publicLeafCount() {
    ❸return privateLeafCount(_root);
}
```

Although C++ would allow both functions to have the same name, for clarity I've used different names to distinguish between the public and private "leaf count" functions. The code in privateLeafCount ❶ is exactly the same as our previous, independent function leafCount. The wrapper function publicLeafCount ❷ is simple. It calls privateLeafCount, passing the private data member _root, and returns the result ❸. In essence, it "primes the pump" of the recursive process. Wrapper functions are very helpful when writing recursive functions inside classes, but they can be used anytime a mismatch exists between the parameter list required by a function and the desired parameter list of a caller.

When to Choose Recursion

New programmers often wonder why anyone has to deal with recursion. They may have already learned that any program can be constructed using basic control structures, such as selection (if statements) and iteration (for and while loops). If recursion is more difficult to employ than basic control structures and unnecessary, perhaps recursion should just be ignored.

There are several rebuttals to this. First, programming recursively helps programmers think recursively, and recursive thinking is employed throughout the world of computer science in such areas as compiler design. Second, some languages simply require recursion because they lack some basic control structures. Pure versions of the Lisp language, for example, require recursion in almost every nontrivial function.

The question remains, though: If a programmer has studied recursion enough to "get it" and is using a full-featured language such as C++, Java, or Python, should recursion ever be employed? Does recursion have practical use in such languages, or is it just a mental exercise?

Arguments Against Recursion

To explore this question, let's enumerate the bad features of recursion.

Conceptual complexity

For most problems, it's more difficult for the average programmer to solve a problem using recursion. Even once you understand the Big Recursive Idea, it's still going to be easier in most cases to write code using loops.

Performance

Function calls incur significant overhead. Recursion involves lots of function calls and, therefore, can be slow.

Space requirements

Recursion doesn't simply employ many function calls; it also nests them. That is, you can end up with a long chain of function calls waiting for other calls to complete. Each function call that has begun but has yet to end takes additional space on the system stack.

At a glance, this list of features constitutes a strong indictment against recursion as difficult, slow, and wasteful of space. However, these arguments do not hold universally. The most basic rule, then, for deciding between recursion and iteration is, *choose recursion when these arguments do not apply*.

Consider our function that counts the number of leaves in a binary tree. How would you solve this problem without recursion? It's possible, but you would need an explicit mechanism for maintaining the "breadcrumb trail" of nodes for which the left children had already been visited but not the right children. These nodes would need to be revisited at some point so we could travel down the right side. You might store these nodes in a dynamic structure, such as a stack. For comparison, here's an implementation of the function that uses the stack class from the C++ standard template library:

```
int binaryTree::stackBasedCountLeaves() {
    if (_root == NULL) return 0;
    int leafCount = 0;
  ❶stack<❷treePtr> nodes;
  ❸nodes.push(_root);
    while (❹!nodes.empty()) {
        treePtr currentNode = ❺nodes.top();
      ❻nodes.pop();
        if (currentNode->left == NULL && currentNode->right == NULL)
            leafCount++;
```

```
        else {
            if (currentNode->right != NULL) ❸nodes.push(currentNode->right);
            if (currentNode->left != NULL) ❸nodes.push(currentNode->left);
        }
    }
    return leafCount;
}
```

This code follows the same pattern as the original, but if you've never used the stack class before, a few comments are in order. The stack class works like the system stack we discussed in Chapter 3; you can add and remove items only at the top. Note that we could perform our leaf count operation using any data structure that doesn't have a fixed size. We could have used a vector, for example, but the use of the stack most directly mirrors the original code. When we declare the stack ❶, we specify the type of items we will store there. In this case, we would store pointers to our binaryTreeNode structure ❷. We make use of four stack class methods in this code. The push method ❸ places an item (a node pointer, in this case) on the top of the stack. The empty method ❹ tells us whether there are any items left on the stack. The top method ❺ gives us a copy of the item on top of the stack, and the pop method ❻ removes the top item from the stack.

The code solves the problem by placing a pointer to the first node on the stack and then repeatedly removing a pointer to a node from the stack, checking whether it's a leaf, incrementing our counter if it is, and placing pointers to child nodes, if they exist, on the stack. So the stack keeps track of the nodes we have discovered, but have yet to process, in the same way that the chain of recursive calls in the recursive version keeps track of nodes we must revisit. In comparing this iterative version to the recursive version, we see that none of the standard objections to recursion applies with much vigor in this case. First, this code is longer and more complicated than the recursive version, so there is no argument against the recursive version on the basis of conceptual complexity. Second, look how many function calls stackBasedCountLeaves makes—for each visit to an interior node (i.e., not a leaf), this function makes up to five function calls: one each to empty, top, and pop, and one or two to push. The recursive version makes only the two recursive calls for each interior node. (Note that it is possible for us to avoid the function calls to the stack object by incorporating the logic of the stack within the function. This, however, would increase the complexity of the function even further.) Third, while this iterative version doesn't use additional system stack space, it makes explicit use of a private stack. In fairness, this is less space than the system stack overhead of the recursive calls, but it's still an expenditure of system memory in proportion to the maximum depth of the binary tree we are traversing.

Because the objections against recursion are mitigated or minimized in this case, recursion is a good choice for the problem. Put more generally, if a problem is simple to solve iteratively, then iteration should be your first choice. Recursion should be used when iteration would be complicated. Often this involves the necessity of the "breadcrumb trail" mechanism shown here.

Traversals of branching structures, such as trees and graphs, are inherently recursive. Processing linear structures, such as arrays and linked lists, usually does not require recursion, but there are exceptions. You will never go wrong making a first stab at a problem using iteration and seeing how far you get. As a last set of examples, consider the following linked-list problems.

PROBLEM: DISPLAY A LINKED LIST IN ORDER

Write a function that is passed the head pointer of a singly linked list where the data type of each node is an integer and that displays those integers, one per line, in the order they appear in the list.

PROBLEM: DISPLAY A LINKED LIST IN REVERSE ORDER

Write a function that is passed the head pointer of a singly linked list where the data type of each node is an integer and that displays those integers, one per line, in the reverse order they appear in the list.

Because these problems are mirror images of each other, it's natural to assume that their implementations would likewise be mirror images. That is indeed the case for recursive implementations. Using the listNode and listPtr type given previously, here are recursive functions to solve both of these problems:

```
void displayListForwardsRecursion(listPtr head) {
    if (head != NULL) {
        ❶cout << head->data << "\n";
        ❷displayListForwardsRecursion(head->next);
    }
}
void displayListBackwardsRecursion(listPtr head) {
    if (head != NULL) {
        ❸displayListBackwardsRecursion(head->next);
        ❹cout << head->data << "\n";
    }
}
```

As you can see, the code in these functions is identical except for the order of the two statements inside the if statement. That makes all the difference. In the first case, we display the value in the first node ❶ before making the recursive call to display the rest of the list ❷. In the second case, we make the call to display the rest of the list ❸ before we display the value in the first node ❹. This results in an overall backward display.

Because both of these functions are equally succinct, one might assume that recursion is properly used to solve both of these problems, but that's not the case. To see that, let's look at iterative implementations of both of these functions.

```
void displayListForwardsIterative(listPtr head) {
  ❶for (listPtr current = head; current != NULL; current = current->next)
    cout << current->data << "\n";
}
void displayListBackwardsIterative(listPtr head) {
  ❷stack<listPtr> nodes;
  ❸for (listPtr current = head; current != NULL; current = current->next)
    nodes.push(current);
  ❹while (!nodes.empty()) {
    ❺nodePtr current = nodes.top();
    ❻nodes.pop();
    ❼cout << current->data << "\n";
  }
}
```

The function to display the list in order is nothing more than a straight-forward traversal loop ❶, such as those we saw back in Chapter 4. The function to display the list in reverse order, though, is more complicated. It suffers from the same requirement for a "breadcrumb trail" as our binary tree problems. Displaying the nodes in a linked list in reverse order requires returning to prior nodes by definition. In a singly linked list, there's no way to do that using the list itself, so a second structure is required. In this case, we need another stack. After declaring the stack ❷, we push all of the nodes in our linked list onto the stack using a for loop ❸. Because this is a stack, where each item is added on top of previous items, the first item in the linked list will be on the bottom of the stack, and the last item in the linked list will be on the top. We enter a while loop that continues until the stack is empty ❹, repeatedly grabbing a pointer to the top node on the stack ❺, removing that node pointer from the stack ❻, and then displaying the data in the referenced node ❼. Because the data on the top is the last data in the linked list, this has the effect of displaying the data in the linked list in reverse order.

As with the iterative binary tree function shown earlier, it would be possible to write this function without using a stack (by building a second list within the function that is a reverse of the original). There is no way, however, to make the second function as simple as the first or to avoid effectively traversing two structures instead of one. Comparing the recursive and iterative implementations, it's easy to see that the iterative "forward" function is so simple that there is no practical advantage in employing recursion, and there are several practical disadvantages. In contrast, the recursive "backward" function is simpler than the iterative version and should be expected to perform approximately as well as the iterative version. Therefore, the "backward" function is a reasonable use of recursion, while the "forward" function, though a good recursive programming exercise, is not a good practical use of recursion.

Exercises

As always, trying out the ideas presented in the chapter is imperative!

6-1. Write a function to compute the sum of just the positive numbers in an array of integers. First, solve the problem using iteration. Then, using the technique shown in this chapter, convert your iterative function to a recursive function.

6-2. Consider an array representing a binary string, where every element's data value is 0 or 1. Write a bool function to determine whether the binary string has odd parity (an odd number of 1 bits). Hint: Remember that the recursive function is going to return true (odd) or false (even), not the count of 1 bits. Solve the problem first using iteration, then recursion.

6-3. Write a function that is passed an array of integers and a "target" number and that returns the number of occurrences of the target in the array. Solve the problem first using iteration, then recursion.

6-4. Design your own: Find a problem processing a one-dimension array that you have already solved or that is trivial for you at your current skill level, and solve the problem (or solve it again) using recursion.

6-5. Solve exercise 6-1 again, using a linked list instead of an array.

6-6. Solve exercise 6-2 again, using a linked list instead of an array.

6-7. Solve exercise 6-3 again, using a linked list instead of an array.

6-8. Design your own: Try to discover a linked-list processing problem that is difficult to solve using iteration but can be solved directly using recursion.

6-9. Some words in programming have more than one common meaning. In Chapter 4, we learned about the heap, from which we get memory allocated with new. The term *heap* also describes a binary tree in which each node value is higher than any in the left or right subtree. Write a recursive function to determine whether a binary tree is a heap.

6-10. A *binary search tree* is a binary tree in which each node value is greater than any value in that node's left subtree but less than any value in the node's right subtree. Write a recursive function to determine whether a binary tree is a binary search tree.

6-11. Write a recursive function that is passed a binary search tree's root pointer and a new value to be inserted and that creates a new node with the new value, placing it in the correct location to maintain the binary search tree structure. Hint: Consider making the root pointer parameter a reference parameter.

6-12. Design your own: Consider basic statistical questions you can ask of a set of numerical values, such as average, median, mode, and so forth. Attempt to write recursive functions to compute those statistics for a binary tree of integers. Some are easier to write than others. Why?

7

SOLVING PROBLEMS
WITH CODE REUSE

This chapter is very different from those that came before. In previous chapters, I stressed the importance of finding your own solution to problems. That's what the book is about, after all: writing original solutions to programming problems. Even in previous chapters, though, we talked about how you are always learning from what you've written before, and that's why you should retain all the code that you write for future reference. In this chapter, we'll go one step further and discuss how to use code and ideas from other programmers to solve our problems.

If you remember how this book started, this topic may seem like an odd inclusion. At the beginning, I talked about what a mistake it was to try to solve complex problems by modifying someone else's code. Not only does this have a low chance of success, but even when it succeeds, it provides no learning experience for you. And if this is all you ever do, you never actually become a programmer and are of limited use in software development. That said, once any programming problem reaches a respectable size, it's not reasonable to expect a programmer to develop a solution entirely from scratch. That's an inefficient use of the programmer's time, and it relies too heavily on the programmer being an expert in all things. Plus, it's more likely to lead to a buggy or difficult-to-maintain program.

Good Reuse and Bad Reuse

We must therefore distinguish between good reuse, which allows us to write better programs and write them more quickly, and bad reuse, which may allow us to impersonate a programmer for a while but ultimately leads to poor development, of both the code and the programmer. Table 7-1 summarizes the differences. The left column shows the properties of good reuse and the right column shows the properties of bad reuse. When considering whether or not to attempt a reuse of code, ask yourself whether you are more likely to produce the properties in the left column or the right column.

Table 7-1: Good and Bad Code Reuse

Good Reuse	Bad Reuse
Following a blueprint	Copying someone else's work
Magnifies and extends your capabilities	Falsifies your capabilities
Helps you learn	Helps you avoid learning
Saves time in the short term and the long term	May save time in the short term but may lengthen time in the long term
Results in a working program	May result in a program that doesn't work anyway

It's important to note that the difference between good reuse and bad reuse doesn't reside in what code you reuse or how you reuse it but in your relationship to the code and concepts that you are borrowing. Once, in writing a term paper in a literature class, I discovered that something I had learned in a previous course was relevant to my paper's topic, so I included it. When I submitted a draft of my paper to the professor, she told me I needed a citation for that information. Frustrated, I asked my professor at what point I could simply state my knowledge in a paper without providing a reference. Her answer was that I could stop referencing others for what was in my head when I became such an expert that others were referencing me.

In programming terms, good reuse occurs when you write code yourself based on reading someone's description of a general concept or when you make use of code that you could have written yourself. Throughout this chapter, we're going to talk about how you can take ownership of coding concepts so that you can be sure that your reuse is helping you become a better programmer, not a lazier one.

Let me also draw attention to the last row in Table 7-1. Attempts at bad reuse often fail altogether. This is not surprising, because it involves a programmer using code that he or she doesn't actually understand. In some situations, the borrowed code will work initially, but when the programmer attempts to modify or expand the borrowed code base, the lack of deep comprehension removes the possibility of an organized approach. The programmer then resorts to flailing about and trial and error, thus violating the first and most important of our general problem-solving rules: Always have a plan.

Review of Component Fundamentals

Now that we know the kind of reuse we are aiming for, let's categorize the different ways in which code can be reused. In this book, I'm going to use the term *component* to refer to anything created by one programmer that can be reused by another to help solve a programming problem. Components can exist anywhere on the continuum from abstract to concrete, from an idea to fully implemented code. If we think of solving a programming problem as analogous to tackling a handyman project, the techniques we've learned for solving problems are like tools, and components are like specialty parts. Each of the following components is a different way of reusing prior work of programmers.

Code Block

A *code block* is just that: a block of code that has been copied from one program listing to another. More colloquially, we would call this a *copy-and-paste job*. This is the lowest form of component use and is often bad reuse, with all of the problems that implies. Of course, if the code you are copying is your own, there's no real harm done, except that you might consider packaging the existing code as a class library or other structure to allow it to be reused in a cleaner and more easily maintained way.

Algorithms

An *algorithm* is a programming recipe; it's a particular method of accomplishing a goal and is expressed either in plain language or pictorially as in a flowchart. For example, back in Chapter 3, we discussed the *sort* operation for arrays and different ways this sort could be accomplished. One method of sorting an array is the insertion-sort algorithm, and I showed a sample implementation of the algorithm. It's important to note that the given code was one implementation of the insertion sort, but insertion sort is the algorithm itself—that way of sorting an array—and not the particular code. Insertion sort works by repeatedly taking the next unsorted value in the array and shifting the sorted values "up" one position until we've made a hole in the correct position for the value we're currently inserting. Any code that uses this method to sort an array is an insertion sort.

Algorithms are a high-level form of reuse and generally lead to good reuse properties. Algorithms are essentially just ideas, and you, the programmer, must implement the ideas, calling upon your programming skills and your deep understanding of the algorithm itself. The algorithms you will commonly use are well studied and have predictable performance in various situations. With an algorithm as a blueprint, you can have confidence in the correctness of your code and in its performance.

There are some potential downsides to basing code on an algorithm, though. When you use an algorithm, you are starting at the conceptual level. Therefore, you have a long road ahead to the finished code for that section of the program. The algorithm certainly saves time, because the problem-solving aspect is essentially complete, but depending on the algorithm and its particular application in your programming, the implementation of the algorithm can be nontrivial.

Patterns

In programming, a *pattern* (or *design pattern*) is a template for a particular programming technique. The concept is related to an algorithm but distinguishable. Algorithms are like recipes for solving particular problems, while patterns are general techniques used in particular programming situations. The problems that patterns solve are typically within the structure of the code itself. For example, in Chapter 6 we discussed the problem presented by a recursive function in a linked-list class: The recursive function needed the "head" pointer to the first node in the list as a parameter, but that data needed to remain private. The solution was to create a *wrapper*, a function that would adapt one parameter list to another. The wrapper technique is a design pattern. We can use this pattern to solve the problem of a recursive function in a class, but it can be used in other ways as well. For example, suppose we had a linkedList class that allowed items to be inserted or removed at any point in the list, but what we needed was a stack class—that is, a list that allowed insertion and removal only at one end. We could create a new class stack that had public methods for the typical stack operations, such as push and pop. These methods would just call member functions on the linkedList object that was a private data member of our stack class. In this way, we would reuse the functionality of a linked-list class while providing the interface of a stack class.

Like algorithms, patterns are a high-level form of component use, and learning patterns is a great way to build up your programming tool chest. Patterns share some of the potential problems of algorithms, though. Knowing that a pattern exists is not the same as knowing how to implement a pattern in the particular language you have chosen for a programming solution, and patterns are often tricky to implement correctly or with maximum performance. For example, there is a pattern known as a *singleton*, which is a class that allows only one object of the class to be created. Creating a singleton class is straightforward, but creating a singleton class that does not create the one allowed instance object until it is actually needed can be surprisingly difficult, and the best technique may vary from language to language.

Abstract Data Types

An *abstract data type*, as we discussed in Chapter 5, is a type defined by its operations, not by how those operations are implemented. The stack type, which we have used several times in this book, is a good example. Abstract data types are like patterns in that they define the effects of operations, but they do not specifically define how those operations are implemented. As with algorithms, however, there are well-known implementation techniques for these operations. For example, a stack can be implemented using any number of underlying data structures, such as a linked list or an array. Once we make the decision to use a particular data structure, though, the implementation decisions are sometimes already made. Suppose we implemented a stack using a linked list and are unable to wrap around an existing linked list, but we must write our own list code. Because the stack is a last-in-first-out structure, it only makes sense for us to insert and remove items at one end of the linked list. Furthermore, it only makes sense to insert and remove at the front of the list. Theoretically, you could insert and remove at the end, but this would result in an inefficient traversal of the entire list for every insertion or removal. To avoid those traversals would require a doubly linked list with a separate pointer to the last node in the list. Inserting and removing at the beginning of the list allows the simplest, most efficient implementation, so linked-list implementations of stacks are almost all implemented the same way.

Thus, even though the *abstract* in *abstract data type* means the type is conceptual and without implementation detail, in practice, when you choose to implement an abstract data type in your code, you won't be figuring out the implementation from scratch. Rather, you will have existing implementations of the type as guides.

Libraries

In programming, a *library* is a collection of related pieces of code. A library typically includes the code in compiled form, along with needed source code declarations. Libraries can include stand-alone functions, classes, type declarations, or anything else that can appear in code. In C++, the most obvious examples are the standard libraries. The strcmp function we used in previous chapters comes from the old C library *cstring*, the container classes such as vector come from the C++ Standard Template Library, and even the NULL we have used in all of our pointer-based code is not part of the C++ language itself but defined in a library header file, *stdlib.h*. Because so much core functionality is contained within libraries, library use is inevitable in modern programming.

Generally, library use is good code reuse. Code is included in a library because it provides functionality that is commonly needed in a variety of programs—library code helps programmers avoid "reinventing the wheel." Nevertheless, as developing programmers, when we use library code, we must strive to learn from the experience and not merely take a shortcut. We'll see an example of this later in the chapter.

Note that while many libraries are general purpose, others are designed as *application programming interfaces (APIs)* providing the high-level language programmer with a simplified or more coherent view of an underlying platform. For example, the Java language includes an API called JDBC, which provides classes that allow programs to interact with relational databases in a standard way. Another example is DirectX, which provides Microsoft Windows game programmers extensive functionality with sound and graphics. In both cases, the library provides a connection between the high-level program and foundation-level hardware and software—the database engine in the case of JDBC and the graphics and sound hardware in the case of DirectX. Moreover, in both cases, the code reuse is not just good—it is, for all practical purposes, required. A database programmer in Java or a graphics programmer writing C++ code for Windows is going to make use of an API—if not these APIs, then something else, but the programmer isn't going to cook up a new connection to the platform from scratch.

Building Component Knowledge

Components are so helpful that programmers make use of them whenever possible. In order to use a component to aid in solving a problem, though, a programmer must know of its existence. Depending on how finely you define them, available components might number into the hundreds or even thousands, and a beginning programmer is going to be exposed to only a few of them. A good programmer must therefore always be adding component knowledge to his or her toolkit. Such knowledge gathering occurs in two different ways: A programmer may explicitly allot time for learning new components as a general task, or the programmer may search for a component to solve a specific problem. We'll call the first approach *exploratory learning* and the second approach *as-needed learning*. To develop as a programmer, you will need to employ both approaches. Once you have mastered the syntax of your chosen programming language, discovering new components is one of the primary ways for you to better yourself as a programmer.

Exploratory Learning

Let's start with an exploratory learning example. Suppose we wanted to learn more about design patterns. Fortunately, there is general agreement about which design patterns are the most useful or frequently used, so we could begin with any number of resources on this topic and be fairly sure that we aren't missing anything important. We would benefit by simply finding a list of design patterns and studying it, but we would gain more insight if we implemented some of the patterns.

One pattern we'll find in a typical list is called *strategy* or *policy*. This is the idea of allowing an algorithm, or part of an algorithm, to be chosen at runtime. In the purest form, the strategy form, this pattern allows changing how a function or method operates but does not alter the result. For example, a method of a class that sorts its data, or involves sorting data, might allow the sort methodology (quicksort or insertion sort, for example) to be chosen. The result is the same in any case—sorted data—but allowing the client to choose the sort methodology could offer performance benefits. For example, the client could avoid using quicksort for data with a high rate of duplicates. In the policy form, the client's choice affects the outcome. For example, suppose a class represents a hand of playing cards. The sorting policy could determine whether aces are considered high (above a king) or low (less than a 2).

Putting Learning into Practice

Reading that paragraph, you now know what the strategy/policy pattern is, but you haven't made it your own. It's the difference between browsing tools at the hardware store and actually buying one and using it. So let's take this design pattern down from the shelf and put it to use. The fastest way to try out a new technique is to incorporate it into code you've already written. Let's create a problem that can be solved using this pattern and that is built upon code we've already written.

PROBLEM: THE FIRST STUDENT

At a particular school, each class has a designated "first student" who is responsible for maintaining order in the classroom if the teacher has to leave the room. Originally, this title was bestowed upon the student with the highest grade, but now some teachers think the first student should be the student with the greatest seniority, which means the lowest student ID number, as they are assigned sequentially. Another faction of teachers thinks the first student tradition is silly and intends to protest by simply choosing the student whose name appears first in the alphabetical class roll. Our task is to modify the student collection class, adding a method to retrieve the first student from the collection, while accommodating the selection criteria of the various teacher groups.

As you can see, this problem is going to employ the policy form of the pattern. We want our method that returns the first student to return a different student based on a chosen criterion. In order to make this happen in C++, we're going to use function pointers. We've briefly seen this concept in action in Chapter 3 with the qsort function, which takes a pointer to a function that compares two items in the array to be sorted. We'll do something similar here; we'll have a set of comparison functions that takes two of our studentRecord objects and determines whether the first student is "better" than the second by looking at the grades, ID numbers, or names of the students.

To get started, we need to define a type for our comparison functions:

```
typedef bool ❶(* firstStudentPolicy)(studentRecord r1, studentRecord r2);
```

This declaration creates a type named firstStudentPolicy as a pointer to a function that returns a bool and takes two parameters of type studentRecord. The parentheses around * firstStudentPolicy ❶ are necessary to prevent the declaration from being interpreted as a function that returns a pointer to a bool. With this declaration in place, we can create our three policy functions:

```
bool higherGrade(studentRecord r1, studentRecord r2) {
    return r1.grade() > r2.grade();
}
bool lowerStudentNumber(studentRecord r1, studentRecord r2) {
    return r1.studentID() < r2.studentID();
}
bool nameComesFirst(studentRecord r1, studentRecord r2) {
    return ❶strcmp(r1.name().c_str()❷, r2.name().c_str()❷) ❸< 0;
}
```

The first two functions are very simple: higherGrade returns true when the first record has the higher grade, and lowerStudentNumber returns true when the first record has the lower student number. The third function, nameComesFirst, is essentially the same, but it requires the strcmp ❶ library function, which expects two "C-style" strings—that is, null-terminated character arrays instead of string objects. So we have to invoke the c_str()❷ method on the name strings in both student records. The strcmp function returns a negative number when the first string comes before the second alphabetically, so we check the return value to see whether it's less than zero ❸. Now we are ready to modify the studentCollection class itself:

```
class studentCollection {
private:
    struct studentNode {
        studentRecord studentData;
        studentNode * next;
    };
public:
    studentCollection();
    ~studentCollection();
    studentCollection(const studentCollection &copy);
    studentCollection& operator=(const studentCollection &rhs);
    void addRecord(studentRecord newStudent);
    studentRecord recordWithNumber(int IDnum);
    void removeRecord(int IDnum);
  ❶void setFirstStudentPolicy(firstStudentPolicy f);
  ❷studentRecord firstStudent();
private:
  ❸firstStudentPolicy _currentPolicy;
    typedef studentNode * studentList;
    studentList _listHead;
    void deleteList(studentList &listPtr);
    studentList copiedList(const studentList copy);
};
```

This is the class declaration we saw back in Chapter 5 with three new members: a private data member, _currentPolicy ❸, to store a pointer to one of our policy functions; a setFirstStudentPolicy ❶ method to change this policy; and the firstStudent method itself ❷, which will return the first student according to the current policy. The code for setFirstStudentPolicy is simple:

```
void studentCollection::setFirstStudentPolicy(firstStudentPolicy f) {
    _currentPolicy = f;
}
```

We also need to modify the default constructor to initialize the current policy:

```
studentCollection::studentCollection() {
    _listHead = NULL;
    _currentPolicy = NULL;
}
```

Now we are ready to write firstStudent:

```
studentRecord studentCollection::firstStudent() {
❶if (_listHead == NULL || _currentPolicy == NULL) {
        studentRecord dummyRecord(-1, -1, "");
        return dummyRecord;
    }
    studentNode * loopPtr = _listHead;
❷studentRecord first = loopPtr->studentData;
❸loopPtr = loopPtr->next;
    while (loopPtr != NULL) {
        if (❹_currentPolicy(loopPtr->studentData, first)) {
            first = loopPtr->studentData;
        }
    ❺loopPtr = loopPtr->next;
    }
    return first;
}
```

The method begins by checking for special cases. If there is no list to review or no policy in place ❶, we return a dummy record. Otherwise, we traverse the list to find the student who best meets the current policy, using the basic searching techniques we've been using throughout this book. We assign the record at the beginning of the list to first ❷, start our loop variable at the second record in the list ❸, and begin the traversal. Inside the traversal loop, a call to the current policy function ❹ tells us whether the student we're currently looking at is "better" than the best student we've found so far, based on the current criterion. When the loop is over, we return the "first student" ❺.

Analysis of First Student Solution

Having solved a problem using the strategy/policy pattern, we're much more likely to recognize situations in which the technique can be employed than if we had just read about the technique once and never used it. We can also analyze our sample problem to start forming our own opinion about the worth of the technique, when it can be properly employed, and when it might be a mistake, or at least more trouble than it's worth. One thought that may have occurred to you about this particular pattern is that it weakens encapsulation and information hiding. For example, if the client code is providing the policy functions, it requires access to types that would normally remain internal to the class, in this case, the studentRecord type. (We'll consider a way around this problem in the exercises.) This means the client code could break if we ever modify that type, and we must weigh this concern against the benefits of the pattern before applying it in other projects. In previous chapters, we discussed how knowing when to use a technique—or when not to use it—is as important as knowing how to use it. By examining your own code, you gain insight into this critical question.

For further practice, you can review your library of completed projects in search of code that could be refactored using this technique. Remember that much "real world" programming involves supplementing or modifying an existing code base, so this is excellent practice for such modifications, in addition to developing your skill with the particular component. Moreover, one of the benefits of good code reuse is that we learn from it, and this practice maximizes learning.

As-Needed Learning

The previous section described what we might call "learning through wandering." While such journeys are valuable to programmers, there are other times where we must move toward a particular goal. If you're working on a particular problem, especially if you're working against any kind of deadline, and you suspect that a component could be of great help to you, you don't want to wander randomly through the world of programming and hope that you stumble upon what you need. Instead, you want to find the component or components that directly apply to your situation as quickly as possible. That sounds very tricky, though—how do you find what you need when you don't know exactly what you're looking for? Consider the following sample problem:

PROBLEM: EFFICIENT TRAVERSAL

A programming project will use your studentCollection class. The client code needs the ability to traverse all of the students in the collection. Obviously, to maintain information hiding, the client code cannot be given direct access to the list, but it's a requirement that the traversals are efficient.

Because the key word in this description is *efficient*, let's be precise about what that means in this case. Let's suppose that a particular object of our studentCollection class has 100 students. If we had direct access to the linked list, we could write a loop to traverse the list that would loop 100 times. That's the most efficient any list traversal can be. Any solution that requires us to loop more than 100 times to determine the result would be inefficient.

Without the requirement for efficiency, we might try to solve the problem by adding a simple recordAt method to our class that would return the student record at a particular position in the collection, numbering the first record as 1:

```
studentRecord studentCollection::recordAt(int position) {
    studentNode * loopPtr = _listHead;
    int i = 1;
 ❶while (loopPtr != NULL && i < position) {
        i++;
        loopPtr = loopPtr->next;
    }
    if (loopPtr == NULL) {
      ❷studentRecord dummyRecord(-1, -1, "");
        return dummyRecord;
    } else {
      ❸return loopPtr->studentData;
    }
}
```

In this method, we use a loop ❶ to traverse the list until we reach the desired position or we reach the end of the list. At the end of the loop, if the end of the list has been reached, we create and return a dummy record ❷, or we return the record at the specified position ❸. The problem is that we are performing a traversal merely to find one student record. This is not necessarily a full traversal, because we will stop when we reach the desired position, but it is a traversal nonetheless. Suppose the client code is attempting to average student grades:

```
int gradeTotal = 0;
for (int recNum = 1; recNum <= numRecords; recNum++) {
    studentRecord temp = sc.recordAt(recNum);
    gradeTotal += temp.grade();
}
double average = (double) gradeTotal / numRecords;
```

For this code segment, assume that sc is a previously declared and populated studentCollection and recNum is an int storing the number of records. Suppose recNum is 100. If you just glance at this code, it might appear that computing the average takes just 100 trips through the loop, but since each call to recordAt is itself a partial list traversal, this code involves 100 traversals, each of which will involve looping about 50 times for the average case. So instead of 100 steps, which would be efficient, this could require about 5,000 steps, which is very inefficient.

When to Search for a Component

We have now arrived at the real problem. Providing client access to collection members for traversals is easy; providing such access efficiently is not. We could, of course, try to solve this problem using only our own problem-solving ability, but we would reach the solution much faster if we could use a component. The first step in finding a previously unknown component that can aid our solution is assuming that such a component actually exists. Put another way, you won't find a component unless you start searching for one. Therefore, to maximize the benefit of components, you need to be on the lookout for situations where they can help. When you find yourself stuck on some aspect of the problem, try the following:

1. Restate the problem generically.
2. Ask yourself: Is this likely to be a common problem?

The first step is important because if we state our problem as "Allow client code to efficiently compute the average student grade in a linked list of records encapsulated in a class," it sounds like it's specific to our situation. If, however, we state the problem as "Allow client code to efficiently traverse a linked list without providing direct access to the list's pointers," then we begin to understand that this might be a common problem. Surely, we might ask ourselves, as often as programs store linked lists and other sequentially accessed structures within classes, other programmers must have figured out ways to allow efficient access to every item in the structure?

Finding a Component

Now that we've agreed to look, it's time to find our component. To make things clear, let's restate the original programming problem as a research problem: "Find a component we can use to modify our studentCollection class to allow client code to efficiently traverse the internal list." How do we solve *this* problem? We could start by looking at any of our component types: patterns, algorithms, abstract data types, or libraries.

Suppose we started by looking at the standard C++ libraries. We would not necessarily be looking for a class to "plug in" to our solution, but we instead could mine a library class that was similar to our studentCollection class for ideas. This employs the analogy strategy we used to solve programming problems. If we find a class that has an analogous problem, we can borrow its analogous solution. Our previous exposure to the C++ library has brought us into contact with its container classes, such as vector, and we should look for the container class that's most like our student collection class. If we go to a favorite C++ reference, be that a book or a site on the Web, and review the C++ container classes, we see there is a "sequence container" called list that fits the bill. Does the `list` class allow efficient traversal by client code? It does, using an object known as an *iterator*. We see that the list class provides methods `begin` and `end` that produce iterators, which are objects that can reference a particular item in the list and be incremented to make the iterator reference the next object in the list. If `intList` is a `list<int>`, populated with integers, and `iter` is a `list<int>::iterator`, then we could display all of the integers in the list with the following:

```
iter = intList.begin();
while (iter != intList.end()) {
    cout << *iter << "\n";
    iter++;
}
```

Through the use of the iterator, the `list` class has solved the problem of providing a mechanism to the client for efficiently traversing the list. At this point, we might think to drop the `list` class itself into our `studentCollection` class, replacing our home-built linked list. We could then create `begin` and `end` methods for our class that would wrap the same methods from the embedded list object, and the problem would be solved. This, however, runs straight into the issue of good versus bad reuse. Once we fully understand the iterator concept and can reproduce it on our own in our own code, plugging an existing class from the Standard Template Library into our code will be a good option—perhaps the best option. If we're not able to do that, using the `list` class becomes a shortcut that doesn't help us grow as programmers. Sometimes, of course, we must avail ourselves of components that we couldn't reproduce, but if we fall into the habit of depending on other programmers to solve our problems, we risk never becoming problem solvers ourselves.

So let's implement the iterator ourselves. Before we do that, though, let's briefly look at other ways we could have arrived at the same place. We began the search in the standard template libraries, but we could have begun elsewhere. For example, we could have searched through a list of common design patterns. Under the heading of "behavioral patterns," we would find the *iterator* pattern, in which the client is allowed sequential access to a collection of items without exposing the underlying structure of the collection. This is exactly what we need, but we could have found it only by searching through a list of patterns or remembering it from previous investigations of patterns. We could have started our search with abstract data types because *list* in general, and *linked list* in particular, are common abstract data types. However, many discussions and implementations of the list abstract data type do not consider client list traversal to be a basic operation, so the iterator concept never comes up. Finally, if we begin our search in the algorithms area, we would be unlikely to find anything helpful. Algorithms tend to describe tricky code, and the code to create an iterator is fairly simple, as we will soon see. In this case, then, the class library was the quickest route to our destination, followed by patterns. As a general rule, however, you must consider all component types when searching for a helpful component.

Applying the Component

We now know we're going to make an iterator for our `studentCollection` class, but all the `list` standard library class has shown us is how the iterator methods work externally. If we got stuck on implementation, we might consider reviewing the source code `list` and its ancestor classes, but given the difficulty of reading large swaths of unfamiliar code, that's a measure of last resort. Instead, let's just think our way through this. Using the previous code example as a guide, we can say that an iterator is defined by four central operations:

1. A method in the collection class that provides an iterator that references the first item in the collection. In the `list` class, this was `begin`.

2. A mechanism to test whether the iterator has advanced past the last item in the collection. In the previous example, this was a method called `end` in the `list` class that produced a special iterator object to test against.

3. A method in the iterator class that moves the iterator so that it references the next item in the collection. In the previous example, this was the overloaded ++ operator.

4. A method in the iterator class that returns the currently referenced item in the collection. In the previous example, this was the overloaded * (prefixed) operator.

In terms of writing the code, nothing here looks difficult. It's just a question of putting everything in the right place. So let's get started. From the descriptions above, our iterator, which we'll call `scIterator`, needs to store a reference to an item in the `studentCollection` and needs to be able to advance to the next item. Thus, our iterator should store a pointer to a `studentNode`. That will allow it to return the `studentRecord` contained within, as well as advance to the next `studentNode`. Therefore, the private section of iterator class will have this data member:

```
studentCollection::studentNode * current;
```

Right away, we've got a problem. The `studentNode` type is declared within a private section of `studentCollection`, and therefore the line above won't work. Our first thought is that perhaps `studentNode` shouldn't have been declared privately, but that's not the right answer. The node type is inherently private because we don't want random client code to depend upon a particular implementation of the node type, thus creating code that could break if we modify our class. Nevertheless, we need to allow `scIterator` access to our private type. We do that with a `friend` declaration. In the public section of `studentCollection`, we add:

```
friend class scIterator;
```

Now scIterator can access the private declarations within studentCollection, including the declaration for studentNode. We can also declare some constructors:

```
scIterator::scIterator() {
    current = NULL;
}
scIterator::scIterator(studentCollection::studentNode * initial) {
    current = initial;
}
```

Let's hop over to the studentCollection for a second and write our *begin* method—a method that returns an iterator that references the first item in our collection. Following the naming scheme I have used in this book, this method should have a noun for a name, such as firstItemIterator:

```
scIterator studentCollection::firstItemIterator() {
    return scIterator(_listHead);
}
```

As you can see, all we need to do here is stuff the head pointer of the linked list into a scIterator object and return it. If you're anything like me, seeing the pointers flying around here may make you a little nervous, but note that scIterator is just going to hold onto a reference to an item in the studentCollection list. It's not going to allocate any memory of its own, and therefore we don't need to worry about deep copy and overloaded assignment operators.

Let's return to scIterator and write our other methods. We need a method to advance the iterator to the next item, as well as a method to determine whether we are past the end of the collection. We should think about both of these at the same time. In advancing the iterator, we need to know what value the iterator should have when it passes beyond the last node in the list. If we do nothing special, the iterator would naturally get the value of NULL, so that would be the easiest value to use. Note that we have initialized our iterator to NULL in the default constructor, so when we use NULL to indicate past-the-end we lose any distinction between these two states, but for this current problem that's not an issue. The code for the methods is:

```
❶ void scIterator::advance() {
    ❷if (current != NULL)
        ❸current = current->next;
}
❹ bool scIterator::pastEnd() {
    return current == NULL;
}
```

Remember that we are just using the iterator concept to solve the original problem. We are not trying to duplicate the exact specification of a C++

Standard Template Library iterator, so we don't have to use the same interface. In this case, rather than overloading the ++ operator, I have a method called advance ❶, which checks to see that the current pointer isn't NULL ❷ before advancing it to the next node ❸. Similarly, I find having to create a special "end" iterator to compare against cumbersome, so I just have a bool method called pastEnd ❹ that determines whether we've run out of nodes.

Lastly, we need a way to get the currently referenced studentRecord object:

```
studentRecord scIterator::student() {
 ❶if (current == NULL) {
      studentRecord dummyRecord(-1, -1, "");
      return dummyRecord;
 ❷} else {
      return current->studentData;
   }
}
```

As we've done previously, for safety, if our pointer is NULL, we create and return a dummy record ❶. Otherwise, we return the currently referenced record ❷. This completes the implementation of the iterator concept with our studentCollection class. For clarity, here's the complete declaration of the scIterator class:

```
class scIterator {
public:
    scIterator();
    scIterator(studentCollection::studentNode * initial);
    void advance();
    bool pastEnd();
    studentRecord student();
private:
    studentCollection::studentNode * current;
};
```

With the code all in place, we can test our code with a sample traversal. Let's implement that average grade computation for comparison:

```
  scIterator iter;
  int gradeTotal = 0;
  int numRecords = 0;
❶ iter = sc.firstItemIterator();
❷ while (!iter.pastEnd()) {
     numRecords++;
   ❸gradeTotal += iter.student().grade();
   ❹iter.advance();
  }
  double average = (double) gradeTotal / numRecords;
```

This listing makes use of all of our iterator-related methods, so it's a good test of our code. We call firstItemIterator to initialize our scIterator object ❶. We call pastEnd as our loop termination test ❷. We call the student method of the iterator object to get the current studentRecord so that we can extract the grade ❸. Finally, to move the iterator to the next record, we call the advance method ❹. When this code works, we can be reasonably confident that we have implemented the various methods correctly, and more than that, that we have a firm understanding of the iterator concept.

Analysis of Efficient Traversal Solution

As before, just because the code works doesn't mean the potential for learning from this event is over. We should carefully consider what we have done, its positive effects and negative effects, and contemplate expansions of the basic idea we have just implemented. In this case, we can say that the iterator concept definitely solves the original problem of inefficient client traversal of our collection, and once implemented, the use of the iterator is elegant and highly readable. On the downside, there's no denying that the inefficient approach based on the recordAt method was much easier to write. In deciding whether or not the implementation of an iterator is valuable for a particular situation, we have to ask ourselves how often traversals would occur, how many items would typically be in our list, and so on. If traversals are infrequent and the list is small, the inefficiency is probably not important, but if we expect the list to grow large or cannot guarantee that it will not, the iterator may be required.

Of course, if we had decided to use a list object from the Standard Template Library, we would no longer worry about the difficulty of implementing the iterator because we would not be implementing it ourselves. The next time a situation like this arises, we can make use of the list class without feeling we are shortchanging ourselves or setting ourselves up for later difficulties, because we have investigated both lists and iterators to the point where we understand what must be going on behind the scenes, even if we never reviewed the actual source code.

Going further, we can think about broader applications of iterators and their possible limitations. Suppose, for example, we needed an iterator that could efficiently move not just to the next item in our studentCollection but also to the previous item. Now that we know how the iterator works, we can see that there is really no way to do this with our current studentCollection implementation. If the iterator maintains a link to a particular node in the list, advancing to the next node requires merely following the link in the node. Retreating to the previous node, however, requires traversing the list again up to that point. Instead, we would need a doubly linked list, where the nodes have pointers in both directions, to both the next node and the previous one. We can generalize this thought and start to consider different data structures and what kinds of traversals or data access can be efficiently offered to clients. For example, in the previous chapter on recursion, we briefly encountered the binary tree structure. Is there some way to allow an efficient client traversal of this structure in its standard form? If not, how would we have to modify it to allow efficient reversals? What is even the right order for the nodes in a binary tree to be traversed? Thinking through questions like these helps us to become better programmers. Not only will we teach ourselves new skills, but we'll also learn more about the strengths and weaknesses of different components. Knowing the pros and cons of a component will allow us to use it wisely. Failing to consider the limitations of a particular approach can lead to dead ends, and the more we know about the components we use, the less likely this will happen to us.

Choosing a Component Type

As we've seen in these examples, the same problem can be solved using different types of components. A pattern may express the idea of a solution, an algorithm may outline an implementation of that idea or another idea that will solve the same problem, an abstract data type may encapsulate the concept, and a class in a library may contain a fully tested implementation of the abstract data type. If each of these is an expression of the same concept that we need to solve our problem, how do we know which component type to pull out of our toolbox?

One primary consideration is how much work may be required to integrate the component into our solution. Linking a class library into our code is often a fast way to solve a problem, whereas implementing an algorithm from a pseudocode description may take a lot of time. Another important consideration is how much flexibility the proposed component offers. Often, a component will come in a nice, prepackaged form, but when it is integrated into the project, the programmer discovers that while the component does most of what he or she needs, it doesn't do everything. Perhaps the return value of one method is in the wrong format and requires additional processing, for example. If the component is used anyway, more trouble may be discovered down the road before the component is eventually discarded altogether and new code for that part of the problem is developed from scratch. If the programmer had chosen a component at a higher conceptual level, such as a pattern, the resulting code implementation would fit the problem perfectly because it was created specifically for that problem.

Figure 7-1 summarizes the interplay of these two factors. Generally, code from a library comes ready to use, but it cannot be directly modified. It can only be indirectly modified either through the use of C++ templates or if the code in question implements something like the *strategy* pattern we saw earlier in this chapter. At the other end of the scale, a pattern may be presented as nothing more than an idea ("a class that can have only one instance"), offering maximum implementation flexibility but requiring a lot of work from the programmer.

Of course, this is just a general guideline, and individual cases will differ. Perhaps the class we're using from the library is at such a low level in our program that flexibility won't suffer. For example, we might wrap a collection class of our own design around a basic container class like list, which is broad enough in capabilities that even if we have to expand the functionality of our container class, we can expect the list class to handle it. Before using a pattern, perhaps we've already implemented a particular pattern before, so we're not so much creating new code as adapting previously written code.

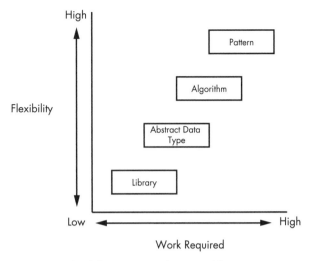

Figure 7-1: Flexibility versus work required for component types

The more experience you have in using components, the more confident you can be that you are starting in the right place. Until you develop that experience, you can use the trade-off between flexibility and work required as a rough guide. For each specific situation, ask yourself questions such as the following:

- Can I use the component as is, or does it require additional code to bolt it into my project?
- Am I confident that I understand the full extent of the problem, or the part that relates to this component, and that it will not change in the future?
- Will I increase my programming knowledge by choosing this component?

Your answers to these questions will help you estimate how much work will be involved and how much benefit you receive from each possible approach.

Component Choice in Action

Now that we understand the general idea, let's run through a quick example to demonstrate the specifics.

PROBLEM: SORTING SOME, LEAVING OTHERS ALONE

A project requires you to sort an array of studentRecord objects by grade, but there's a catch. Another part of the program is using a special grade value of –1 to indicate a student whose record cannot be moved. So while all the other records must be moved around, those with –1 grades should be left exactly where they are, resulting in an array that is sorted except for –1 grades interspersed throughout.

This is a tricky problem, and there are lots of ways we could attempt to solve it. To keep things simple, let's reduce our choices to two: Either we choose an algorithm—that is, a sorting routine like insertion sort—and modify it to ignore the studentRecord objects with −1 grades, or we figure out a way to use the qsort library routine to solve this problem. Both of these options are possible. Because we're comfortable with the insertion-sort code, it shouldn't be too difficult to throw in some if statements to explicitly check and skip over records with −1 grades. Making qsort do the work for us will take a bit of a workaround. We could copy the student records with the real grades into a separate array, sort them using qsort, and then copy them back, making sure we don't copy over any of the −1 grade records.

Let's follow through with both options to see how the choice of component type affects the resulting code. We'll start with the algorithm component, writing our own modified insertion sort to solve the problem. As usual, we'll approach this problem in stages. First, let's reduce the problem by removing the whole −1 grade issue and just sorting an array of studentRecord objects without any special rules. If sra is an array containing arraySize objects of type studentRecord, the resulting code looks like this:

```
int start = 0;
int end = arraySize - 1;
for (int i = start + 1; i <= end; i++) {
    for (int j = i; j > start && ❶sra[j-1].grade() > sra[j].grade(); j--) {
    ❷studentRecord temp = sra[j-1];
      sra[j-1] = sra[j];
      sra[j] = temp;
    }
}
```

This code is very similar to the insertion sort for integers. The only differences are that the comparison requires calls to the grade method ❶, and our temporary object used for swap space has changed type ❷. This code works fine, but there is one caveat for testing this and other code blocks that follow in this section: Our studentRecord class validates data, and as previously written, it will not accept a −1 grade, so make sure you make the necessary changes. Now we're ready to complete this version of the solution. We need the insertion sort to ignore records with −1 grades. This is not as simple as it sounds. In the basic insertion-sort algorithm, we are always swapping adjacent locations in the array, j and j - 1 in the code above. If we are leaving records with −1 grades in place, though, the locations of the next records to be swapped could be an arbitrary distance apart.

Figure 7-2 illustrates this problem with an example. If this shows the array in its original configuration, then the arrows indicate the locations of the first records to be swapped, and they are not adjacent. Furthermore, eventually the last record (for Art) will have to be swapped from location [5] to [3] and then from [3] to [0], so all the swaps required to sort this array (as much as we are sorting it) involve nonadjacent records.

[0]	[1]	[2]	[3]	[4]	[5]
Tom	Gladys	Sam	Jane	John	Art
87	–1	–1	84	–1	72
11523	83764	65342	11523	11764	77663

Figure 7-2: Arbitrary distance between records to be swapped in modified insertion sort

In considering how to solve this problem, I looked out for an analogy and found one in the processing of linked lists. In many linked-list algorithms, we have to maintain a pointer not only to the current node in our list traversal but also to the previous node. So at the end of loop bodies, we often assign the current pointer to the previous pointer before advancing the current pointer. Something similar needs to go on here. We need to keep track of the last "real" student record as we progress linearly through the array to find the next "real" record. Putting this idea into practice results in the following code:

```
for (int i = start + 1; i <= end; i++) {
  ❶if (sra[i].grade() != -1) {
    ❷int rightswap = i;
      for (int leftswap = i - 1;
         leftswap >= start
         && (sra[leftswap].grade() > sra[rightswap].grade()
         ❸|| sra[leftswap].grade() == -1);
         leftswap--)
      {
        ❹if(sra[leftswap].grade() != -1) {
            studentRecord temp = sra[leftswap];
            sra[leftswap] = sra[rightswap];
            sra[rightswap] = temp;
          ❺rightswap = leftswap;
        }
      }
  }
}
```

In the basic insertion-sort algorithm, we repeatedly insert unsorted items into an ever-growing sorted area within the array. The outer loop selects the next unsorted item to be placed in sorted order. In this version of the code, we start by checking that the grade in location i is not –1 ❶ inside the outer loop body. If it is, we will just skip to the next record, leaving this record in place. Once we have established that the student record at location i can be moved, we initialize rightswap to this location ❷. Then we begin the inner loop. In the basic insertion-sort algorithm, each iteration of the inner loop swaps an item with its neighbor. In our version, though, because we are leaving records with –1 grades in place, we perform a swap only when location j does not contain a grade of –1 ❹. We then swap between locations leftswap and rightswap and assign leftswap to rightswap ❺, setting up the next swap in the inner loop if there is one. Finally, we have to modify our inner loop condition. Normally the inner loop in an insertion sort stops when we reach the front end of the array or when we find a value that is less than the value we are inserting. Here, we have to make a compound condition using logical *or* so that the loop continues past –1 grades ❸ (because –1 will be less than any legitimate grade, thus stopping the loop prematurely).

This code solves our problem, but it's possible that it may be giving off some "bad smells." The standard insertion-sort code is easy to read, especially if you understand the gist of what it's doing, but this modified version is hard on the eyes and probably needs some comment lines if we want to be able to understand it later. Perhaps a refactoring is in order, but let's try the other approach for solving this problem and see how that reads.

The first thing we'll need is a comparison function for use with qsort. In this case, we'll be comparing two studentRecord objects, and our function will subtract one grade from the other:

```
int compareStudentRecord(const void * voidA, const void * voidB) {
    studentRecord * recordA = (studentRecord *) voidA;
    studentRecord * recordB = (studentRecord *) voidB;
    return recordA->grade() - recordB->grade();
}
```

Now we're ready to sort the records. We'll do this in three phases. First, we will copy all of the records that don't have a –1 grade to a secondary array, leaving no gaps. Then, we'll call qsort to sort the secondary array. Finally, we will copy the records from the secondary array back to the original array, skipping over the records with the –1 grades. The resulting code looks like this:

```
❶ studentRecord * sortArray = new studentRecord[arraySize];
❷ int sortArrayCount = 0;
  for (int i = 0; i < arraySize; i++) {
  ❸if (sra[i].grade() != -1) {
        sortArray[sortArrayCount] = sra[i];
        sortArrayCount++;
    }
  }
❹ qsort(sortArray, sortArrayCount, sizeof(studentRecord), compareStudentRecord);
❺ sortArrayCount = 0;
❻ for (int i = 0; i < arraySize; i++) {
    ❼if (sra[i].grade() != -1) {
        sra[i] = sortArray[sortArrayCount];
        sortArrayCount++;
    }
  }
```

Although this code is about the same length as the other solution, it's more straightforward and easier to read. We begin by declaring our secondary array, sortArray ❶, of the same size as the original array. The variable sortArrayCount is initialized to zero ❷; in the first loop, we'll use this to track how many records we have copied into the secondary array. Inside that loop, each time we encounter a record without a –1 grade ❸, we assign it to the next available slot in sortArray and increment sortArrayCount. When the loop is over, we sort the secondary array ❹. The variable sortArrayCount is reset to 0 ❺; we'll use it in the second loop to track how many records we have copied from the secondary array back to the original array. Note that the second loop traverses the *original* array ❻, looking for slots that need to be filled ❼. If we approach this the other way, trying to loop through the secondary array and pushing the records over to the original array, we would need a double loop, with the inner loop searching for the next real-grade slot in the original array. This is another example of how the problem can be made easy or difficult based on our conceptualization of it.

Comparing the Results

Both solutions work and are reasonable approaches. For most programmers, the first solution, in which we modified insertion sort to leave some records in place as we sorted around them, is harder to write and harder to read. The second solution, though, appears to introduce some inefficiency because it requires copying the data to the secondary array and back again. Here's where a little knowledge of algorithm analysis comes in handy. Suppose we were sorting 10,000 records—if we were sorting much fewer, we wouldn't really care about the efficiency. We can't know for sure what algorithm underlies the qsort call, but the worst case for a general-purpose sort would require 100 million record swaps, and the best case would be around 130,000. Regardless of where along the range we end up, copying 10,000 records back and forth isn't going to be a major performance drain compared to the sorting. Also, we have to consider that whatever algorithm is used by qsort may be more efficient than our simple insertion sort, wiping out any benefit we may have gained from avoiding copying the data to and from the secondary array.

So in this scenario, the second approach, using qsort, appears to be the winner. It's simpler to implement, simpler to read and therefore more easily maintained, and we can expect its performance to be as good as, or possibly better than, the first solution. The best thing we can say about the first approach is that we may have learned skills that we can apply to other problems, whereas the second approach, by virtue of its simplicity, offers no such insights. As a general rule, when you are at the stage of programming where you are trying to maximize your learning, you should favor higher-level components such as algorithms and patterns. When you are at the stage of trying to maximize your efficiency as a programmer (or are under a hard deadline), you should favor lower-level components, choosing prebuilt code when possible. Of course, if time permits, trying several different approaches, as we have done here, provides the best of all worlds.

Exercises

Try out as many components as you can. Once you get a handle on how to learn new components, your abilities as a programmer will start to grow quickly.

7-1. A complaint offered against the *policy/strategy* pattern is that it requires exposing some internals of the class, such as types. Modify the "first student" program from earlier in this chapter so that the policy functions are all stored within the class and are chosen by passing a code value (of a new, enumerated type, for example), instead of passing the policy function itself.

7-2. Rewrite our `studentCollection` functions from Chapter 4 (`addRecord` and `averageRecord`) so that instead of directly implementing a linked list, you use a class from the C++ library.

7-3. Consider a collection of `studentRecord` objects. We want to be able to quickly find a particular record based on student number. Store the student records in an array, sort the array by student number, and investigate and implement the *interpolation search* algorithm.

7-4. For the problem in 7-3, implement a solution by implementing an abstract data type that allows an arbitrary number of items to be stored and individual records to be retrieved based on a key value. A generic term for a structure that can efficiently store and retrieve items based on a key value is a *symbol table*, and common implementations of the symbol table idea are *hash tables* and *binary search trees*.

7-5. For the problem in 7-3, implement a solution using a class from the C++ library.

7-6. Suppose you are working on a project in which a particular `studentRecord` may need to be augmented with one of the following pieces of data: term paper title, year of enrollment, or a `bool` indicating whether the student is auditing the class. You don't want to include all of these data fields in the base `studentRecord` class, knowing that in most cases they won't be used. Your first thought is to create three subclasses, each having one of the data fields, with names such as `studentRecordTitle`, `studentRecordYear` and `studentRecordAudit`. Then you are informed that some student records will contain two of these additional data fields or perhaps all three. Creating subclasses for each possible variation is impractical. Find a design pattern that addresses this conundrum, and implement a solution.

7-7. Develop a solution to the problem described in 7-6 that does not make use of the pattern you discovered but instead solves the problem using C++ library classes. Rather than focusing on the three particular data fields described in the previous question, try to make a general solution: a version of the `studentRecord` class that allows arbitrary extra fields of data to be added to particular objects. So, for example, if `sr1` is a `studentRecord`, you might want client code to make the call `sr1.addExtraField("Title", "Problems of Unconditional Branching")`, and then later `sr1.retrieveField("Title")` would return "Problems of Unconditional Branching."

7-8. Design your own: Take a problem you have already solved, and solve it again using a different component. Remember to analyze the results in comparison to your original solution.

8

THINKING LIKE A PROGRAMMER

It's time for us to bring together everything we've experienced over the previous chapters to complete the journey from fledgling coder to problem-solving programmer.

In previous chapters, we've solved problems in a variety of areas. I believe these areas are the most beneficial for the developing programmer to master, but of course there are always more things to learn, and many problems will require skills not covered in this book. So in this chapter, we're going to come full circle to general problem-solving concepts, taking the knowledge we've gained in our journey to develop a *master plan* for attacking any programming problem. Although we might call this a general plan, in one way it's actually a very specific plan: It will be *your* plan, and no one else's. We'll also look at the many ways you can add to your knowledge and skills as a programmer.

Creating Your Own Master Plan

Way back in the first chapter, we learned the first rule of problem solving was that you should always have a plan. A more precise formulation would be to say you should always follow *your* plan. You should construct a master plan that maximizes your strengths and minimizes your weaknesses and then apply this master plan to each problem you must solve.

Over many years of teaching, I've seen students of all different abilities. By that I don't simply mean that some programmers have more ability than others, although of course this is true. Even among programmers with the same level of ability, there is great diversity. I've lost track of how often I've been surprised by a formerly struggling student who quickly masters a particular skill or a talented student who displays a weakness in a new area. Just as no two fingerprints are the same, no two brains are the same, and lessons that are easy for one person are difficult for another.

Suppose you're a football coach, planning your offense for the next game. Because of an injury, you're not sure which of two quarterbacks will be able to start. Both quarterbacks are highly capable professionals, but like any individuals in any endeavor, they have their strengths and weaknesses. The game plan that creates the best opportunity for victory with one quarterback might be terrible for the other.

In creating your master plan, you are the coach and your skill set is your quarterback. To maximize your chances for success, you need a plan that recognizes both your strengths and your weaknesses.

Playing to Your Strengths and Weaknesses

The key step in making your own master plan, then, is identifying your strengths and weaknesses. This is not difficult, but it requires effort and a fair degree of honest self-appraisal. In order to benefit from your mistakes, you must not only correct them in programs in which they appear, but you must also note them, at least mentally, or better yet, in a document. In this way, you can identify patterns of behavior that you would have otherwise missed.

I'm going to describe weaknesses in two different categories: coding and design. *Coding weaknesses* are areas where you tend to repeat mistakes when you're actually writing the code. For example, many programmers frequently write loops that iterate one time too many or one time too few. This is known as a *fencepost error*, from an old puzzle about how many fenceposts are needed to build a 50-foot fence with 10-foot-long rails between posts. The immediate response from most people is five, but if you think about it carefully, the answer is six, as shown in Figure 8-1.

Most coding weaknesses are situations in which the programmer creates semantic errors by coding too quickly or without enough preparation. *Design weaknesses*, in contrast, are problems you commonly have in the problem-solving or design stage. For example, you might discover you have trouble getting started or trouble integrating previously written subprograms into a complete solution.

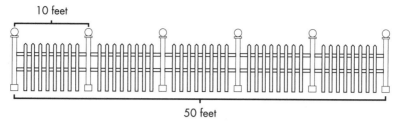

Figure 8-1: The fencepost puzzle

Although there is some overlap between these two categories, the two types of weaknesses tend to create different sorts of problems and must be defended against in different ways.

Planning Against Coding Weaknesses

Perhaps the most frustrating activity in programming is spending hours tracking down a semantic error that turns out to be a simple thing to fix once identified. Because no one is perfect, there's no way to completely eliminate these situations, but a good programmer will do all he or she can to avoid making the same mistakes over and over again.

I knew a programmer who had tired of making what is perhaps the most common semantic error in C++ programming: the substitution of the assignment operator (=) for the equality operator (==). Because conditional expressions in C++ are integer, not strictly Boolean, a statement such as the following is syntactically legal:

```
if (number = 1) flag = true;
```

In this case, the integer value 1 is assigned to number, and then the value 1 is used as the result of the conditional statement, which C++ evaluates as true. What the programmer meant to do, of course, was:

```
if (number == 1) flag = true;
```

Frustrated at making this type of mistake over and over, the programmer taught himself to always write equality tests the other way, with the numerical literal on the left side, such as:

```
if (1 == number) flag = true;
```

By doing this, if the programmer slips up and substitutes the equality operator, the expression 1 = number would no longer be legal C++ syntax, and would produce a syntax error that would be caught at compile time. The original error is legal syntax, so it's only a semantic error, which would be caught at compile time or not caught at all. Since I had made this mistake many times myself (and driven myself crazy trying to track the bug down), I employed this method, putting the numerical literal on the left side of the equality operator. In doing so, I discovered something curious. Because this ran counter to my usual style, putting the literal on the left forced me to pause momentarily when writing conditional statements. I would think, "I need to remember to put the literal on the left so that I'll catch myself if I use the assignment operator." As you might expect, by having that thought run through my head, I never actually used the assignment operator but always correctly used the equality operator. Now, I no longer put the literal on the left side of the equality operator, but I still pause and let those thoughts run through my head, which keeps me from using the wrong operator.

The lesson here is that being aware of your coding-level weaknesses is often all that is necessary to avoid them. That's the good news. The bad news is that you still have to put in the work to be aware of your coding weaknesses in the first place. The key technique is asking yourself why you made a particular mistake, rather than just fixing the mistake and moving on. This will allow you to identify the general principle you failed to follow. For example, suppose you had written the following function to compute the average of the positive numbers in an array of integers:

```
double averagePositive(int array[ARRAYSIZE]) {
    int total = 0;
    int positiveCount = 0;
    for (int i = 0; i < ARRAYSIZE; i++) {
        if (array[i] > 0) {
            total += array[i];
            positiveCount++;
        }
    }
  ❶return total / (double) positiveCount;
}
```

At a glance, this function looks fine, but upon closer inspection, it has a problem. If there are no positive numbers in the array, then the value of positiveCount will be zero when the loop ends, and this will result in a division by zero at the end of the function ❶. Because this is floating-point division, the program may not actually crash but rather produce odd behavior, depending on how the value of this function is used in the overall program.

If you were quickly trying to get your code running and you discovered this problem, you might add some code to handle the case where positiveCount is zero and move on. But if you want to grow as a programmer, you should ask yourself what mistake you made. The specific problem, of course, is that you didn't account for the possibility of dividing by zero. If that's as deep as the analysis goes, though, it won't help you very much in the future. Sure, you might catch another situation where a divisor might turn out to be zero, but that is not a very common situation. Instead, we should ask what general principle has been violated. The answer: that we should always look for special cases that can blow up our code.

By considering this general principle, we'll be more likely to see patterns in our mistakes and therefore more likely to catch those mistakes in the future. Asking ourselves, "Any chance of dividing by zero here?" is not nearly as useful as asking ourselves, "What are the special cases for this data?" By asking the broader question, we'll be reminded to check not just for division by zero but also for empty data sets, data outside the expected range, and so on.

Planning Against Design Weaknesses

Design weaknesses require a different approach to circumvent. The first step, though, is the same: You identify the weaknesses. A lot of people have trouble with this step because they don't like to turn such a critical eye on themselves. We're conditioned to conceal personal failings. It's like when a job interviewer asks you what your biggest weakness is, and you are expected to answer with some nonsense about how you care too much about the quality of your work instead of providing an *actual* weakness. But just as Superman has his Kryptonite, even the best programmers have real weaknesses.

Here's a sample (and certainly not exhaustive) list of programmer weaknesses. See whether you recognize yourself in any of these descriptions.

Convoluted designs

> The programmer with this weakness creates programs that have too many parts or too many steps. While the programs work, they don't inspire confidence—like worn clothing that looks as if it would fall apart at the first tug of a thread—and they are clearly inefficient.

Can't get started

> This programmer has a high degree of inertia. Whether from a lack of confidence in problem solving or plain procrastination, this programmer takes too long to make any initial progress on a problem.

Fails to test

> This programmer doesn't like to formally test the code. Often the code will work for general cases, but not for special cases. In other situations, the code will work fine but won't "scale up" for larger problem sets that the programmer hasn't tested.

Overconfident

> Confidence is a great thing—this book is intended to increase the confidence of its readers—but too much confidence can sometimes be as much a problem as too little. Overconfidence manifests itself in various ways. The overconfident programmer might attempt a more complicated solution than necessary or allow too little time to finish a project, resulting in a rushed, bug-ridden program.

Weak area

> This category is a bit of a catchall. Some programmers work smoothly enough until they hit certain concepts. Consider the topics discussed in previous chapters of this book. Most programmers, even after completing the exercises, will be more confident in some of the areas we've covered than others. For example, perhaps the programmer gets lost with pointer programs, or recursion turns the programmer's head inside out. Maybe the programmer has trouble designing elaborate classes. It's not that the programmer can't muddle through and solve the problem, but it's rough work, like driving through mud.

There are different ways you can confront your large-scale weaknesses, but once you recognize them, it's easy to plan around them. If you're the kind of programmer who often skips testing, for example, make testing an explicit part of your plan for writing each module, and don't move onto the next module until you put a check in that box. Or consider a design paradigm called *test-driven development*, in which the testing code is written first, and then the code is written to fill those tests. If you have trouble getting started, use the principles of dividing or reducing problems, and start writing code as soon as you can, with the understanding that you may have to rewrite that code later. If your designs are often too complicated, add an explicit refactoring step to your master plan. The point is, no matter what weaknesses you have as a programmer, if you recognize them, you can plan around them. Then your weaknesses are no longer weaknesses—just obstacles in the road that you will steer around on the way to successful project completion.

Planning for Your Strengths

Planning for your weaknesses is largely about avoiding mistakes. Good planning, though, isn't just about avoiding mistakes. It's about working toward the best possible result given your current abilities and whatever restraints you may be operating under. This means you must also incorporate your strengths into your master plan.

You might think that this section isn't for you, or at least not yet. After all, if you are reading this book, then you are still becoming a programmer. You might wonder whether you even have any strengths at this stage of your development. I'm here to tell you that you do, even if you haven't recognized them yet. Here's a list of common programmer strengths, by no means exhaustive, with descriptions of each and hints to help you recognize whether the term applies to you:

Eye for detail

This type of programmer can anticipate special cases, see potential performance issues before they arise, and never lets the big picture cloud over the important details that must be handled for the program to be a complete and correct solution. Programmers with this strength tend to test their plans on paper before coding, code slowly, and test frequently.

Fast learner

A fast learner picks up new skills quickly, whether that's learning a new technique in an already-known language or working with a new application framework. This type of programmer enjoys the challenge of learning new things and may choose projects based on this preference.

Fast coder

The fast coder doesn't need to spend a lot of time with a reference book to hammer out a function. Once it's time to start typing, the code flows off the ends of the fast coder's fingers without much effort and with few syntactical errors.

Never gives up

For some programmers, a pesky bug is a personal affront that can't be ignored. It's like the program has slapped the programmer across the mouth with a leather glove, and it's up to the programmer to respond. This type of programmer always seems to stay levelheaded, determined but never very frustrated, and confident that with enough effort, victory is assured.

Super problem-solver

Presumably you were not a super problem-solver when you bought this book, but now that you've gotten some guidance, perhaps it's all starting to come easily. The programmer with this trait is starting to envision potential solutions to a problem even as he or she is reading it.

Tinkerer

To this sort of programmer, a working program is like a wonderful toy box. The tinkerer has never lost the thrill of making the computer do his or her bidding and loves to keep finding something else for the computer to do. Maybe the tinkering means adding more and more functionality to a working program—a symptom known as *creeping featurism.* Maybe the program can be refactored for improved performance. Maybe the program can just be made prettier for the programmer or the user.

Few programmers will exhibit more than a couple of these strengths—in fact, some of them tend to cancel each other out. But every programmer has strengths. If you don't recognize yourself in any of these, it just means you have yet to learn enough about yourself or your strength is something that doesn't fit into one of my categories.

Once you've identified your strengths, you need to factor them into your master plan. Suppose you're a fast coder. Obviously this will help get any project across the finish line, but how can you leverage this strength in a systematic way? In formal software engineering, there is an approach called *rapid prototyping,* in which a program is initially written without extensive planning and then improved through successive iterations until the results meet the problem requirements. If you're a fast coder, you might try adopting this method, coding as soon as you have a basic idea and letting your rough prototype guide the design and development of the final program code.

If you're a rapid learner, maybe you should start every project by hunting for new resources or techniques to solve the current problem. If you're not a rapid learner, but you are the sort of programmer who doesn't easily get frustrated, maybe you should start the project with the areas you think will be the most difficult to give yourself the most time to tackle them.

So whatever strengths you have, make sure you are taking advantage of them in your programming. Design your master plan so that you spend as much time as possible doing what you do best. Not only will you produce the best results this way, but you'll also have the most fun, too.

Putting the Master Plan Together

Let's look at constructing a sample master plan. The ingredients include all the problem-solving techniques we have developed, plus our analysis of our strengths and weaknesses. For this example, I'll use my own strengths and weaknesses.

In terms of problem-solving techniques, I use all of the techniques I share in this book, but I'm especially fond of the "reduce the problem" technique because using that technique allows me to feel that I'm always making concrete progress toward my goal. If I'm currently unable to figure out a way to write code that meets the full specification, I just throw out part of the specification until I gain momentum.

My biggest coding weakness is excessive eagerness. I love to program because I love to see computers following my instructions. Sometimes this leads me to think, "Let's give this thing a rip and see what happens," when I should still be analyzing the correctness of what I just wrote. The danger here isn't that the program will fail—it's that the program will either appear to succeed but not cover all the special cases, or succeed but not be the best possible solution I could write.

I love elegant program designs that are easy to expand and reuse. Often when I code larger projects, I spend a lot of time developing alternative designs. On the whole, this is a good trait, but sometimes this results in me spending too much time in the design phase, not leaving enough time to actually implement the selected design. Also, this can sometimes result in a solution that is over-designed. That is, sometimes the solution is more elegant, expandable, and robust than it really needs to be. Because every project is limited in time and money, the best solution must balance the desire for high software quality with the need to conserve resources.

My best programming strength, I think, is that I pick up new concepts well, and I love to learn. While some programmers like using the same skills over and over, I love a project where I can learn something new, and I'm always exhilarated by that challenge.

With all that in mind, here is my master plan for a new project.

To fight my primary design weakness, I will strictly limit my time spent in the design phase or, alternatively, limit the number of distinct designs I will consider before moving on. This might sound like a dangerous idea to some readers. Shouldn't we spend as much time as we can in the design phase before jumping into coding? Don't most projects fail because not enough time was spent on the front end, leading to a cascade of compromises on the back end? These concerns are valid, but remember that I'm not creating a general guidebook for software development. I'm creating my own personal master plan for tackling programming problems. My weakness is over-designing, not under-designing, so a rule limiting design time makes sense for me. For another programmer, such a rule could be disastrous, and some programmers may need a rule to force them to spend more time on design.

After I complete my initial analysis, I'm going to consider whether the project presents opportunities to learn new techniques, libraries, and so forth. If it does, I'm going to write a small test-bed program to try out these new skills before attempting to incorporate them into my developing solution.

To fight excessive eagerness, I could incorporate a miniature code-review step when I finish coding each module. However, that will require an exercise of willpower on my part—when I complete each module, I'm going to want to go ahead and try it out. Simply hoping that I can talk myself out of it each time is like leaving an open bag of potato chips next to a hungry man and being surprised when the bag is emptied. It's better to subvert weaknesses with a plan that doesn't require the programmer to fight his or her instincts. So what if I create two versions of the project: a crusty, anything-goes version and a polished version for delivery? If I allow myself to play with the first version at will but prevent myself from incorporating code into the polished version until it's been fully vetted, I'm much more likely to overcome my weakness.

Tackling Any Problem

Once we have a master plan, we're ready for anything. That's what this book is ultimately all about: starting with a problem, any problem, and finding a way through to the solution. In all the previous chapters, the problem descriptions pushed us in a particular initial direction, but in the real world, most problems don't come with a requirement to use an array or recursion or to encapsulate some part of the program's functionality into a class. Instead, the programmer makes those decisions as part of the problem-solving process.

At first, fewer requirements might seem to make problems easier. After all, a design requirement is a constraint, and don't constraints make problems harder? While this is true, it's also true that all problems have constraints—it's just that in some cases they are more explicitly spelled out than in others. For example, not being told whether a particular problem requires a dynamically allocated structure doesn't mean that the decision has no effect. The broad constraints of the problem—whether for performance, modifiability, speed of development, or something else—may be more difficult, or perhaps impossible, to meet if we make the wrong design choices.

Imagine a group of friends has asked you to select a movie for everyone to watch. If one friend definitely wants a comedy, another doesn't like older films, and another lists five films she's just seen and doesn't want to see again, these constraints will make the selection difficult. However, if no one has any suggestions beyond "just pick something good," your work is even harder, and you're highly likely to pick something that at least one member of the group won't like at all.

Therefore larger, broadly defined, weakly constrained problems are the most difficult of all. However, they are susceptible to the same problem-solving techniques we've used throughout this book; they just take more time to solve. With your knowledge of these techniques and your master plan in hand, you will be able to solve any problem.

To demonstrate what I'm talking about, I'm going to walk you through the first steps of a program that plays hangman, the classic children's game, but with a twist.

Before we get to the problem description, let's review the basic rules of the game. The first player selects a word and tells a second player how many letters are in the word. The second player then guesses a letter. If the letter is in the word, the first player shows where the letter appears in the word; if the letter appears more than once, all appearances are indicated. If the letter is not in the word, the first player adds a piece to a stick-figure drawing of a man being hanged. If the second player guesses all the letters in the word, the second player wins, but if the first player completes the drawing, the first player wins. Different rules exist for how many pieces make up the drawing of the hanged man, so more generally we can say that the players agree ahead of time how many "misses" will win the game for the first player.

Now that we've covered the basic rules, let's look at the specific problem, including the challenging twist.

PROBLEM: CHEATING AT HANGMAN

Write a program that will be Player 1 in a text-based version of hangman (that is, you don't actually have to draw a hanged man—just keep track of the number of incorrect guesses). Player 2 will set the difficulty of the game by specifying the length of the word to guess as well as the number of incorrect guesses that will lose the game.

The twist is that the program will cheat. Rather than actually picking a word at the beginning of the game, the program may avoid picking a word, so long as when Player 2 loses, the program can display a word that matches all the information given to Player 2. The correctly guessed letters must appear in their correct positions, and none of the incorrectly guessed letters can appear in the word at all. When the game ends, Player 1 (the program) will tell Player 2 the word that was chosen. Therefore, Player 2 can never prove that the game is cheating; it's just that the likelihood of Player 2 winning is small.

This is not a monster-sized problem by real-world standards, but it's large enough to demonstrate the issues we face when dealing with a programming problem that specifies results but no methodology. Based on the problem description, you could fire up your development environment and begin to write code in one of dozens of different places. That, of course, would be a mistake because we always want to program with a plan, so I need to apply my master plan to this specific situation.

The first part of my master plan is limiting the amount of time I spend in the design phase. In order to make that a reality, I need to think carefully about the design before I work on the production code. However, I believe that some experimentation will be necessary in this case for me to work out a solution to the problem. My master plan also allows me to create two projects, a rough-and-ready prototype and a final, polished solution. So I'm going to allow myself to begin coding for the prototype at any time, prior to any real design work, but not allow any coding in the final solution until I believe my design is set. That won't guarantee I'll be entirely satisfied with the design in the second project, but it offers the best opportunity for that to be so.

Now it's time to start picking this problem apart. In previous chapters, we would sometimes list all of the subtasks needed to complete a problem, so I'd like to make an inventory of the subtasks. At this point, though, this would be difficult because I don't know what the program will actually do to accomplish the cheating. I need to investigate this area further.

Finding a Way to Cheat

Cheating at hangman is specific enough that I don't expect to find any help in the normal sources of components; there is no *NefariousStrategy* pattern. At this point, I have a vague idea how the cheating could be accomplished. I'm thinking that I'll choose an initial puzzle word and hang on to that as long as Player 2 chooses letters that aren't actually in that word. Once Player 2 hits upon a letter that's actually in the word, though, I'll switch to another word if it's possible to find one that has none of the letters selected thus far. In other words, I'll deny a match to Player 2 as long as possible. That's the idea, but I need more than an idea—I need something I can implement.

In order to firm up my ideas, I'm going to work through an example on paper, taking on the role of Player 1, working from a word list. To keep things simple, I'm going to assume that Player 2 has requested a three-letter word and that the complete list of three-letter words that I know are shown in the first column of Table 8-1. I'll assume that my first choice "puzzle word" is the first word on the list, *bat*. If Player 2 guesses any letter besides *b*, *a*, or *t*, I'll say "no," and we'll be one step closer to completing the gallows. If Player 2 guesses a letter in the word, then I'll pick another word, one that doesn't contain that letter.

Looking at my list, though, I'm not so sure this strategy is the best. In some situations, it probably makes sense. Suppose Player 2 guesses *b*. No other word in the list contains *b*, so I can switch the puzzle word to any of them. This also means that I've minimized the damage; I've eliminated only one possible word from my list. But what happens if Player 2 guesses *a*? If I just say "no," I eliminate all words containing an *a*, which leaves just the three words in the second column of Table 8-1 for me to choose from. If I decided instead to admit the presence of letter *a* in the puzzle word, I would have five words left I could choose from, as shown in the third column. Note, though, that this extended selection exists only because all five of the words have the *a* in the same position. Once I declare a guess correct, I have to show exactly where the letter appears in the word. I'll feel a lot better about my chances for the rest of the game if I have more word choices remaining to react to future guesses.

Table 8-1: Sample Word List

All Words	Words Without *a*	Words with *a*
bat	dot	bat
car	pit	car
dot	top	eat
eat		saw
pit		tap
saw		
tap		
top		

Also, even if I managed to avoid revealing letters early in the game, I have to expect that Player 2 will eventually make a correct guess. Player 2 could start with all of the vowels, for example. Therefore, at some point I will have to decide what to do when a letter is revealed, and from my experiment with the sample list, it looks like I will have to find the location (or locations) where the letter appears most often. From this observation, I realized that I have been thinking about cheating in the wrong way. I should never actually pick a puzzle word, even temporarily, but just keep track of all the possible words I could choose if I have to.

With this idea in mind, I can now define cheating in a different way: Keep as many words as possible in the list of candidate puzzle words. For each guess that Player 2 makes, the program has a decision to make. Do we claim that the guess was a miss or a match? If it was a match, in which positions does the guessed letter appear? I'll have my program keep an ever-dwindling list of candidate puzzle words and, after each guess, make the decision that will leave the greatest number of words in that list.

Required Operations for Cheating at Hangman

Now I understand the problem well enough to create my list of subtasks. In a problem of this size, there's a good chance that a list made at this early stage will leave some operations out. This is okay, because my master plan anticipates that I will not create a perfect design the first time around.

Store and maintain a list of words.

This program must have a list of valid English words. The program will therefore have to read a list of words from a file and store them internally in some format. This list will be reduced, or extracted from, during the game as the program cheats.

Create a sublist of words of a given length.

Given my intention to maintain a list of candidate puzzle words, I have to start the game with a list of words of the length specified by Player 2.

Track letters chosen.

The program will need to remember which letters have been guessed, how many of those were incorrect, and for any that were deemed correct, where they appear in the puzzle word.

Count words in which a letter does not appear.

In order to facilitate cheating, I'll need to know how many words in the list do not contain the most recently guessed letter. Remember that the program will decide whether the most recently guessed letter appears in the puzzle word with the goal of leaving the maximum number of words in the candidate word list.

Determine the largest number of words based on letter and position.

This looks like the trickiest operation. Let's suppose Player 2 has just guessed the letter *d* and the current game has a puzzle-word length of three. Perhaps the current candidate word list as a whole contains 10 words that include *d*, but that's not what's important because the program will have to state where the letter occurs in the puzzle word. Let's call the positioning of letters in a word a pattern. So *d??* is a three-letter pattern that specifies the first letter is a *d* and the other two letters are anything other than a *d*. Consider Table 8-2. Suppose that the list in the first column contains every three-letter word containing *d* known to the program. The other columns break this list down by pattern. The most frequently occurring pattern is *??d*, with 17 words. This number, 17, would be compared with the number of words in the candidate list that do not contain a *d* to determine whether to call the guess a match or a miss.

Create a sublist of words matching a pattern.

When the program declares that a Player 2 guess is a match, it will create a new candidate word list with only those words that match the letter pattern chosen. In the previous example, if we declared *d* a match, the third column in Table 8-2 would become the new candidate word list.

Keep playing until the game is over.

After all the other operations are in place, I need to write the code that glues everything together and actually play the game. The program should repeatedly request a guess from Player 2 (the user), determine whether the candidate word list would be longer by rejecting or accepting that guess, reduce the word list accordingly, and then display the resulting puzzle word, with any correctly guessed letters revealed, along with a review of all previously guessed letters. This process would continue until the game was over, having been won by one player or the other—the conditions for which I also need to figure out.

Table 8-2: Three-Letter Words

All Words	?dd	??d	d??	d?d
add	add	aid	day	did
aid	odd	and	die	
and		bad	doe	
bad		bed	dog	
bed		bid	dry	
bid		end	due	
day		fed		
did		had		
die		hid		
doe		kid		
dog		led		
dry		mad		
due		mod		
end		old		
fed		red		
had		rid		
hid		sad		
kid				
led				
mad				
mod				
odd				
old				
red				
rid				
sad				

Initial Design

Although it may appear that the previous list of required operations merely lists raw facts, design decisions are being made. Consider the operation "Create a sublist of words matching a pattern." That operation is going to appear in my solution, or at least this initial version of it, but strictly speaking, it's not a *required* operation at all. Neither is "Create a sublist of words of a given length." Rather than maintaining a list of candidate puzzle words that keeps getting smaller, I could keep the original master list of words throughout the game. This would complicate most of the other operations, though. The operation to "Count words in which a letter does not appear" could not merely iterate through the candidate puzzle-word list and count all words without the specified letter. Because it would be searching through the master list, it would also have to check the length of each word and whether the word matches the letters revealed so far in the puzzle word. I think the path I have chosen is easier overall, but I have to be aware that even these early choices are affecting the final design.

Beyond the initial breakdown of the problem into subtasks, though, I have other decisions to make.

How to store the lists of words

The key data structure of the program will be the list of words, which the program will reduce throughout the game. In choosing a structure, I make the following observations. First, I don't believe I will require random access to the words in the list but instead will always be processing the list as a whole, from front to back. Second, I don't know the size of the initial list I require. Third, I'm going to be reducing the list frequently. Fourth and finally, the methods of the standard `string` class will probably come in handy in this program. Putting all of these observations together, I decide that my initial choice for this structure will be the standard template `list` class, with an item type of `string`.

How to track letters guessed

The chosen letters are conceptually a set—that is, a letter has either been chosen or it hasn't, and no letter can be chosen more than once. Thus, it's really a question of whether a particular letter of the alphabet is a member of the "chosen" set. I'm therefore going to represent chosen letters as an array of `bool` of size 26. If the array is named `guessedLetters`, then `guessedLetters[0]` is true if *a* has been guessed during the game so far and false otherwise; `guessedLetters[1]` is for *b*, and so on. I'll use the range conversion techniques we've been employing throughout this book to convert between a lowercase alphabet letter and its corresponding position in the array. If `letter` is a char representing a lowercase letter, then `guessedLetters[letter - 'a']` is the corresponding location.

How to store patterns

One of the operations I'll be coding, "Create a sublist of words matching a pattern," is going to use the pattern of a letter's positions in a word. This pattern will be produced by another operation, "Determine the largest number of words based on letter and position." So what format will I use for that data? The pattern is a series of numbers representing the positions in which a particular letter appears. There are a lot of ways I could store these numbers, but I'm going to keep things simple and use another `list`, this one with an item type of `int`.

Am I writing a class?

Because I am coding this program in C++, I can use object-oriented programming or not, at my discretion. My first thought is that many of the operations in my list could naturally coalesce into a class, called `wordList` perhaps, with methods to remove words based on specified criteria (that is, length and pattern). However, because I'm trying to avoid making design decisions now that I'll have to revoke later, I'm going to make my first, rough-and-ready program entirely procedural. Once I've worked out all of the tricky aspects of the program and actually written code for all of the operations in my list, I'll be in a great position to determine the applicability of object-oriented programming for the final version.

Initial Coding

Now the fun begins. I fire up my development environment and get to work. This program is going to use a number of classes from the standard library, so for clarity, let me set all of those up first:

```
#include <iostream>
using std::cin;
using std::cout;
using std::ios;
#include <fstream>
using std::ifstream;
#include <string>
using std::string;
#include <list>
using std::list;
using std::iterator;
#include <cstring>
```

Now I'm ready to start coding the operations on my list. To some extent, I could code the operations in any order, but I'm going to start with a function to read a plain text file of words into my chosen list<string> structure. At this point, I realize I need to find an existing master file of words—I don't want to type it up myself. Luckily, Googling *word list* reveals a number of sites that have lists of English words in plain-text format, one word per line of the file. I'm already familiar with reading text files in C++, but if I weren't, I would write a small test program just to play around with that skill first and then integrate that ability into the cheating hangman program, a practice I discuss later in this chapter.

With the file in hand, I can write the function:

```
list<string> readWordFile(char * filename) {
    list<string> wordList;
 ❶ifstream wordFile(filename, ios::in);
 ❷if (wordFile == NULL) {
        cout << "File open failed. \n";
        return wordList;
    }
    char currentWord[30];
 ❸while (wordFile >> currentWord) {
     ❹if (strchr(currentWord, '\'') == 0) {
            string temp(currentWord);
            wordList.push_back(temp);
        }
    }
    return wordList;
}
```

This function is straightforward, so I'll make just a few brief comments. If you've never seen one before, an ifstream object ❶ is an input stream that works just like cin, except that it reads from a file instead of standard input. If the constructor is unable to open the file (usually this means the file wasn't found), the object will be NULL, something I explicitly check for ❷. If the file exists, it's processed in a loop ❸ that reads each line of the file into a character array, converts the array to a string object, and adds it to a list. The file of English words I ended up using included words with apostrophes, which aren't legal for our game, so I explicitly exclude them ❹.

Next, I write a function to display all the words in my list<string>. This isn't on my required list of operations, and I wouldn't use it in the game (that would only help Player 2, whom I'm trying to cheat, after all), but it's a good way to test whether my readWordFile function is working correctly:

```
void displayList(❶const list<string> & wordList) {
  ❷list<string>::const_iterator iter;
    iter = wordList.begin();
    while (iter != wordList.end()) {
       cout << ❸iter->c_str() << "\n";
       iter++;
    }
}
```

This is essentially the same list traversal code introduced in the previous chapter. Note that I have declared the parameter as a const reference ❶. Because the list may be quite large at the beginning, having a reference parameter reduces the overhead of the function call, while a value parameter would have to copy the entire list. Declaring that reference parameter a const signals that the function won't change the list, which aids the readability of the code. A const list requires a const iterator ❷. The cout stream can't output a string object, so this method produces the equivalent null-terminated char array using c_str()❸.

I use this same basic structure to write a function that counts the words in the list that do not contain a specified letter:

```
int countWordsWithoutLetter(const list<string> & wordList, char letter) {
    list<string>::const_iterator iter;
    int count = 0;
    iter = wordList.begin();
    while (iter != wordList.end()) {
    ❶if (iter->find(letter) == string::npos) {
         count++;
      }
      iter++;
    }
    return count;
}
```

As you can see, this is the same basic traversal loop. Inside, I call the find method of the string class ❶, which returns the position of its char parameter in the string object, returning the special value npos when the character isn't found.

I use this same basic structure to write the function that removes all the words from my word list that don't match the specified length:

```
void removeWordsOfWrongLength(list<string> & wordList,
                                  int acceptableLength)
{
   list<string>::iterator iter;
   iter = wordList.begin();
   while (iter != wordList.end()) {
      if (iter->length() != acceptableLength) {
       ❶iter = wordList.erase(iter);
      } else {
       ❷iter++;
      }
   }
}
```

This function is a good example of how every program you write is an opportunity to deepen your understanding of how programs work. This function was straightforward for me to write because I understood what was happening "under the hood" from previous programs that I had written. This function employs the basic traversal code of the previous functions, but the code gets interesting inside the loop. The erase() method removes an item, specified by an iterator, from a list object. But from our experience implementing the iterator pattern for a linked list in Chapter 7, I know that the iterator is almost certainly a pointer. From our experience with pointers back in Chapter 4, I know that a pointer is useless, and often dangerous, when it's a dangling reference to something that's been deleted. Therefore, I know I need to assign a valid value to iter after this operation. Fortunately, the designers of erase() have anticipated this problem and have the method return a new iterator that points to the item immediately following the one we just erased, so I can assign that value back to iter ❶. Also note that I explicitly advance iter ❷ only when I have not deleted the current string from the list, because the assignment of the erase() return value effectively advances the iterator, and I don't want to skip any items.

Now for the tough part: finding the most common pattern of a specified letter in the remaining word list. This is another opportunity to use the divide-the-problem technique. I know one of the subtasks of this operation is determining whether a particular word matches a particular pattern. Remember that a pattern is a list<int>, with each int representing a position where the letter appears in the word, and that for a word to match a pattern, not only must the letter appear in the specified positions in the word, but the letter must *not* appear anywhere else in the word. With that thought in mind, I'm going to test a string for a match by traversing it; for each position in the string, if the specified letter appears, I'll make sure that position is in the pattern, and if some other letter appears, I'll make sure that position is not in the pattern.

To make things even simpler, I'll first write a separate function to check whether a particular position number appears in a pattern:

```
bool numberInPattern(const list<int> & pattern, int number) {
   list<int>::const_iterator iter;
   iter = pattern.begin();
   while (iter != pattern.end()) {
      if (*iter == number) {
         return true;
      }
      iter++;
   }
   return false;
}
```

This code is pretty simple to write based on the previous functions. I simply traverse the list, searching for number. Either I find it and return true or I get to the end of the list and return false. Now I can implement the general pattern-matching test:

```
bool matchesPattern(string word, char letter, list<int> pattern) {
   for (int i = 0; i < word.length(); i++) {
      if (word[i] == letter) {
         if (!numberInPattern(pattern, i)) {
            return false;
         }
      } else {
         if (numberInPattern(pattern, i)) {
            return false;
         }
      }
   }
   return true;
}
```

As you can see, this function follows the plan outlined earlier. For each character in the string, if it matches letter, the code checks that the current position is in the pattern. If the character doesn't match letter, the code checks that the position is not in the pattern. If a single position doesn't match the pattern, the word is rejected; otherwise, the end of the word is reached, and the word is accepted.

At this point, it occurs to me that finding the most frequent pattern will be easier if every word in the list contains the specified letter. So I write a quick function to chop out the words without the letter:

```
void removeWordsWithoutLetter(list<string> & wordList,
                              char requiredLetter) {
   list<string>::iterator iter;
   iter = wordList.begin();
```

```
      while (iter != wordList.end()) {
         if (iter->find(requiredLetter) == string::npos) {
            iter = wordList.erase(iter);
         } else {
            iter++;
         }
      }
   }
}
```

This code is just a combination of the ideas used in the previous functions. Now that I think about it, I'm going to need the opposite function as well, one that chops out all the words that *have* the specified letter. I'll use this to reduce the candidate word list when the program calls the latest guess a miss:

```
void removeWordsWithLetter(list<string> & wordList, char forbiddenLetter) {
   list<string>::iterator iter;
   iter = wordList.begin();
   while (iter != wordList.end()) {
      if (iter->find(forbiddenLetter) != string::npos) {
         iter = wordList.erase(iter);
      } else {
         iter++;
      }
   }
}
```

Now I'm ready to find the most frequent pattern in the word list for the given letter. I considered a number of approaches and picked the one that I thought I could most easily implement. First, I'll use a call to the function above to remove all the words without the specified letter. Then, I'll take the first word in the list, determine its pattern, and count how many other words in the list have the same pattern. All of these words will be erased from the list as I count them. Then the process will repeat again with whatever word is now at the head of the list and so on until the list is empty. The result looks like this:

```
void mostFreqPatternByLetter(❶list<string> wordList, char letter,
                             ❷list<int> & maxPattern,
                             ❸int & maxPatternCount) {
❹removeWordsWithoutLetter(wordList, letter);
   list<string>::iterator iter;
   maxPatternCount = 0;
❺while (wordList.size() > 0) {
      iter = wordList.begin();
      list<int> currentPattern;
   ❻for (int i = 0; i < iter->length(); i++) {
         if ((*iter)[i] == letter) {
            currentPattern.push_back(i);
         }
      }
      int currentPatternCount = 1;
      iter = wordList.erase(iter);
```

```
❼while (iter != wordList.end()) {
    if (matchesPattern(*iter, letter, currentPattern)) {
        currentPatternCount++;
        iter = wordList.erase(iter);
    } else {
        iter++;
    }
}
❽if (currentPatternCount > maxPatternCount) {
    maxPatternCount = currentPatternCount;
    maxPattern = currentPattern;
}
currentPattern.clear();
    }
}
```

The list arrives as a value parameter ❶ because this function is going to whittle the list down to nothing during processing, and I don't want to affect the parameter passed by the calling code. Note that maxPattern ❷ and maxPatternCount ❸ are outgoing parameters only; these will be used to send the most regularly occurring pattern and its number of occurrences back to the calling code. I remove all of the words without letter ❹. Then I enter the main loop of the function, which continues as long as the list isn't empty ❺. The code inside the loop has three main sections. First, a for loop constructs the pattern for the first word in the list ❻. Then, a while loop counts how many words in the list match that pattern ❼. Finally, we see whether this count is greater than the highest count seen so far, employing the "King of the Hill" strategy first seen back in Chapter 3 ❽.

The last utility function I should need will display all of the letters guessed so far. Remember that I am storing these as an array of 26 bool values:

```
void displayGuessedLetters(bool letters[26]) {
    cout << "Letters guessed: ";
    for (int i = 0; i < 26; i++) {
        if (letters[i]) cout << ❶(char)('a' + i) << " ";
    }
    cout << "\n";
}
```

Note that I am adding the base value of one range, in this case, the character a, to a value from another range ❶, a technique we first employed back in Chapter 2.

Now I have all the key subtasks completed, and I'm ready to try solving the whole problem, but I have a lot of functions here that haven't been fully tested, and I would like to get them tested as soon as possible. So, rather than tackle the rest of the problem in one step, I'm going to reduce the problem. I'll do this by making some of the variables, such as the size of the puzzle word, into constants.

Because I'm going to be throwing this version away, I'm comfortable with putting the entire game-playing logic into the main function. Because the result is lengthy, though, I'm going to present the code in stages.

```
int main () {
❶list<string> wordList = readWordFile("wordlist.txt");
  const int wordLength = 8;
  const int maxMisses = 9;
❷int misses = 0;
❸int discoveredLetterCount = 0;
❹removeWordsOfWrongLength(wordList, wordLength);
❺char revealedWord[wordLength + 1] = "********";
❻bool guessedLetters[26];
  for (int i = 0; i < 26; i++) guessedLetters[i] = false;
❼char nextLetter;
  cout << "Word so far: " << revealedWord << "\n";
```

This first section of code sets up the constants and variables we'll need to play the game. Most of this code is self-explanatory. The word list is created from a file ❶ and then pared down to the specified word length, in this case, the constant value 8 ❹. The variable misses ❷ stores the number of wrong guesses by Player 2, while discoveredLetterCount ❸ tracks the number of positions revealed in the word (so if *d* appears twice, guessing *d* increases this value by two). The revealedWord variable stores the puzzle word as currently known to Player 2, with asterisks for letters that have not yet been guessed ❺. The guessedLetters array of bool ❻ tracks the specific letters guessed so far; a loop sets all the values to false. Finally, nextLetter ❼ stores the current guess of Player 2. I output the initial revealedWord, and then I'm ready for the main game loop.

```
❶ while (discoveredLetterCount < wordLength && misses < maxMisses) {
    cout << "Letter to guess: ";
    cin >> nextLetter;
  ❷guessedLetters[nextLetter - 'a'] = true;
  ❸int missingCount = countWordsWithoutLetter(wordList, nextLetter);
    list<int> nextPattern;
    int nextPatternCount;
  ❹mostFreqPatternByLetter(wordList, nextLetter, nextPattern, nextPatternCount);
    if (missingCount > nextPatternCount) {
    ❺removeWordsWithLetter(wordList, nextLetter);
      misses++;
    } else {
    ❻list<int>::iterator iter = nextPattern.begin();
      while (iter != nextPattern.end()) {
        discoveredLetterCount++;
        revealedWord[*iter] = nextLetter;
        iter++;
      }
      wordList = reduceByPattern(wordList, nextLetter, nextPattern);
    }
    cout << "Word so far: " << revealedWord << "\n";
    displayGuessedLetters(guessedLetters);
}
```

There are two conditions that can end the game. Either Player 2 discovers all of the characters in the word, so that discoveredLetterCount reaches wordLength, or Player 2's bad guesses complete the hangman, in which case misses will equal maxMisses. So the loop continues as long as neither condition has occurred ❶. Inside the loop, after the next guess is read from the user, the corresponding position in guessedLetters is updated ❷. Then the cheating begins. The program determines how many candidates would be left in the word list if the guess were declared a miss using countWordsWithoutLetter ❸, and it determines the maximum that could be left if the guess were declared a hit using mostFreqPatternByLetter ❹. If the former is larger, the words with the guessed letter are culled and misses is incremented ❺. If the latter is larger, we'll take the pattern given by mostFreqPatternByLetter and update revealedWord, while also removing all words from the list that don't match the pattern ❻.

```
    if (misses == maxMisses) {
        cout << "Sorry. You lost. The word I was thinking of was '";
        cout << ❶(wordList.cbegin())->c_str() << "'.\n";
    } else {
        cout << "Great job. You win. Word was '" << revealedWord << "'.\n";
    }
    return 0;
}
```

The remainder of the code is what I call a *loop postmortem*, where the post-loop action is determined by the condition that "killed" the loop. Here, either our program successfully cheated its way to a victory or Player 2, against all odds, forced the program to reveal the entire word. Note that when the program wins, at least one word must remain in the list, so I just display the first word ❶ and claim that was the one I was thinking of all along. A more devious program might randomly select one of the remaining words to reduce the chance of the opponent detecting the cheating.

Analysis of Initial Results

I've put all this code together and tested it, and it works, but clearly there are a lot of improvements to be made. Beyond any design considerations, the program is missing a lot of functionality. It doesn't allow the user to specify the size of the puzzle word or the number of allowable wrong guesses. It doesn't check to see whether the guessed letter has been guessed before. For that matter, it doesn't even check that the input character is a lowercase letter. It's missing a lot of interface pleasantries, like telling the user how many more misses are available. I think it would also be nice if the program could offer to play again, rather than making the user re-run the program.

As for the design, when I begin to think about the finished version of the program, I'm going to seriously consider an object-oriented design. A wordlist class now seems like a natural choice. The main function looks too large to me. I like a modular, easy-to-maintain design, and that should result in a main function that is short and merely directs traffic among the subprograms that do the real work. So my main function needs to be broken up into several functions. Some of my initial design choices might need rethinking. For example, in hindsight, storing patterns as list<int> looks cumbersome. Perhaps I could try an array of bool, in a manner analogous to guessedLetters?

Or perhaps I should look for another structure entirely. Now is also the time for me to step back to see whether there are any opportunities to learn new techniques in solving this problem. I'm wondering whether there are specialized data structures that I have not yet considered that could be helpful. Even if I end up sticking with my original choices, I could learn a lot from the investigation.

Though all of these decisions are still looming, I feel like I'm well on my way with this project. Having a working program that meets the essential requirements of the problem is a great place to be. I can easily experiment with the different design ideas in this rough version, with the confidence that comes from knowing I already have a solution, and I'm only looking for a better solution.

CREATE A RESTORE POINT

The Microsoft Windows operating system creates what it calls a *restore point* before installing or modifying system components. The restore point contains backup copies of key files, such as the registry. If an installation or update results in a serious problem, it can effectively be "rolled back," or undone by copying back the files from the restore point.

I highly recommend taking the same approach with your own source code. When you have a working program that you expect to later modify, make a copy of the entire project, and modify only the copy. It's quick to do and can save you considerable time later if your modifications go awry. Programmers can easily fall into the trap of thinking, "I accomplished this once; therefore, I can do it again." That's usually true, but there's a big difference between knowing that you can do something again and being able to bring up the old source code for instant reference.

You can also use *version control software*, which automates the copying and storage of project files. Version control software performs more than the "restore point" function; it also may allow multiple programmers to work independently on the same files, for example. While such tools are beyond the scope of this book, they're something you should investigate as you develop as a programmer.

The Art of Problem Solving

Did you recognize all the problem-solving techniques I employed in my solution so far? I had a plan for solving the problem. As always, this is the most crucial of all problem-solving techniques. I decided to start with what I knew for the first version of my solution, employing a couple of data structures with which I was very familiar, arrays and the list class. I reduced the functionality to make it easier to write my rough-and-ready version and to allow me to test my code earlier than I could otherwise. I divided the problem into operations and made each operation a different function, allowing me to work on pieces of the program separately. When I was unsure how to cheat, I experimented, allowing me to restate "cheating" as "maximizing the size of the candidate word list," which was a concrete concept for me to code. In the particulars of coding the operations, I employed techniques analogous to those used throughout this book.

I also successfully avoided getting frustrated, although I suppose you'll have to take my word for that.

Before we move on, let me be clear that I have demonstrated the steps *I* took to get to this stage in the process of solving this problem. These are not necessarily the same steps you would take to solve this problem. The code shown above is not the best solution to the problem and is not necessarily better than what you would come up with. What I hope it demonstrates is that any problem, no matter the size, can be solved using variations of the same basic techniques used throughout this book. If you were tackling a problem twice as large as this one, or 10 times as large, it might test your patience, but you could solve it.

Learning New Programming Skills

There's one more topic to discuss. In mastering the problem-solving techniques of this book, you are taking the key step down the road of life as a programmer. However, as with most professions, this is a road without a destination, for you must always be striving to better yourself as a programmer. As with everything else in programming, you should have a plan for how you will learn new skills and techniques, rather than just trusting that you will pick up new things here and there along the way.

In this section, we'll discuss some of the areas in which you may want to acquire new skills and some systematic approaches for each. The common thread running through all of the areas is that you must put what you want to learn into practice. That's why each chapter in this book ends with exercises— and you have been working through those exercises, right? To read about new ideas in programming is a vital first step in actually learning them, but it is only the first step. To reach the point where you can confidently employ a new technique in the solution for a real-world problem, you should first try out the technique in a smaller, synthetic problem. Remember that one of our basic problem-solving techniques is to break complex problems down, by either dividing the problem or temporarily reducing the problem so that each state we're dealing with has just one nontrivial element. You don't want to try to solve a nontrivial problem at the same time that you're learning the skill that will be central to your solution because then your attention will be divided between two difficult problems.

New Languages

I think C++ is a great programming language for production code, and I explained in the first chapter why I think it's also a great language to learn with. That said, no programming language is superior in all situations; therefore, good programmers must learn several.

Take the Time to Learn

Whenever possible, you should give yourself time to study a new language before attempting to write production code with one. If you attempt to solve a nontrivial problem in the language you have never used before, you are quickly going to run counter to an important problem-solving rule: Avoid frustration. Set yourself the task of learning a language, and complete the task before you assign yourself any "real" programs in that language.

Of course, in the real world, sometimes we are not completely in control of when we are assigned projects. At any moment, someone could request that we write a program in a particular language, and that request could be accompanied by a deadline that would prevent us from leisurely studying the language before tackling the actual problem. The best defense against encountering this situation is to begin studying other programming languages *before* you are absolutely required to know them. Investigate languages that interest you or that are used for areas in which you expect to program during your career. This is another situation in which an activity that seems like a poor use of time in the short term will pay large dividends in the long term. Even if it turns out that you don't require the language you have studied in the near future, studying another language can improve your skills with the other languages you already know because it forces you to think in new and different ways, breaking you out of old habits and giving you fresh perspectives on your skills and techniques. Think of it as the programming equivalent of cross-training.

Start with What You Know

When you begin learning a new programming language, by definition you know nothing about it. If it's not your first programming language, though, you do know a lot about programming. So a good first step in learning a new language is to understand how code that you already know how to write in another language can be written in the new language.

As stated before, you want to learn this by doing, not just by reading. Take programs you have written in other languages, and rewrite them in the new language. Systematically investigate individual language elements, such as control statements, classes, other data structures, and so on. The goal is to transfer as much of your previous knowledge as possible to the new language.

Investigate What's Different

The next step is to study what is different about the new language. While two high-level programming languages may have extensive similarities, *something* must be different with the new language, or there would be no reason to choose this language over any other. Again, learn by doing. Just reading, for example, that a language's multiple-selection statement allows ranges (instead of the individual values of a C++ switch statement) isn't as helpful to your development as actually writing code that meaningfully employs the capability.

This step is obviously important for languages that are noticeably dissimilar but is equally important for languages that have a common ancestor, such as C++, C#, and Java, which are all object-oriented descendents of C. Syntax similarities can trick you into believing you know more about the new language than you really do. Consider the following code:

```
integerListClass numberList;
numberList.addInteger(15);
```

If these lines were presented to you as C++ code, you would understand that the first line constructed an object, numberList, of a class, integerListClass, and the second line invoked an addInteger method on that object. If that class actually exists and has a method of that name that takes an int parameter, this code makes perfect sense. Now suppose I told you this code had been written in Java, not C++. Syntactically, there is nothing illegal about these two lines. However, in Java, a mere variable declaration of a class object does not actually construct the object because object variables are actually references—that is, they behave in a manner analogous to pointers. To perform the equivalent steps in Java, the correct code would be:

```
integerListClass numberList = new integerListClass;
numberList.addInteger(15);
```

You would likely catch on to this particular difference between Java and C++ quickly, but many other differences could be quite subtle. If you don't take the time to discover them, they can make debugging very difficult in the new language. As you scan your code, your internal programming language interpreter will be feeding you incorrect information about what you are reading.

Study Well-Written Code

I've made a point throughout this book that you shouldn't try to learn programming by taking someone else's code and modifying it. There are times, however, when the study of someone else's code is vital. While you can build up your skills in a new language by writing a series of original programs, to reach a level of mastery, you will want to seek out code written by a programmer skilled in that language.

You're not looking to "crib" this code; you're not going to borrow this code to solve a specific problem. Instead, you're looking at existing code to discover the "best practices" in that language. Look at an expert programmer's code and ask yourself not just *what* the programmer is doing but *why* the programmer is doing it. If the code is accompanied by the programmer's explanations, all the better. Differentiate between style choices and benefits to performance. By completing this step, you will avoid a common pitfall. Too often, programmers will learn just enough in a new language to survive, and the result is weak code that doesn't use all of the features of the language. If you are a C++ programmer required to write code in Java, for example, you don't want to settle for writing code in pidgin C++; instead, you want to learn to write actual Java code the way a Java programmer would.

As with everything else, put what you learn into practice. Take the original code and modify it to do something new. Put the code out of sight and try to reproduce it. The goal is to become comfortable enough with the code that you could answer questions about it from another programmer.

It's important to emphasize that this step comes after the others. Before we reach the stage of studying someone else's code in a new language, we have already learned the syntax and grammar of the new language and applied the problem-solving skills we learned in another language to the new language. If we try to shorten the process by starting the study of the new language with the study of long program samples and the modification of those samples, there's a real risk that that's all we'll ever be able to do.

New Skills for a Language You Already Know

Just because you reach the point where you can say that you "know" a language, doesn't mean you know everything about that language. Even once you have mastered the syntax of the language, there will always be new ways to combine existing language features to solve problems. Most of these new ways will fall under one of the "component" headings of the previous chapter, in which we discussed how to build component knowledge. The important factor is effort. Once you get good at solving problems in certain ways, it's easy to rely on what you already know and cease growing as a programmer. At that point, you're like a baseball pitcher who throws a mean fastball but doesn't know how to throw anything else. Some pitchers have had successful professional careers with only one pitch, but the pitcher who wants to go from being a reliever to a starter needs more.

To be the best programmer you can be, you need to seek new knowledge and new techniques and put them into practice. Look for challenges and overcome them. Investigate the work of expert programmers of your chosen languages.

Remember that necessity is the mother of invention. Seek out problems that cannot satisfactorily be solved with your current skill set. Sometimes you can modify problems you have already solved to provide new challenges. For example, you may have written a program that works fine when the data set is small, but what happens when you allow the data to grow to gargantuan proportions? Or what if you have written a program that stores its data on the local hard drive, but you wanted the data to be stored remotely? What if you need multiple executions of the program that could access and update the remote data concurrently? By starting with a working program and adding new functionality, you can focus on just the new aspects of the programming.

New Libraries

Modern programming languages are inseparable from their core libraries. When you learn C++, you'll inevitably learn something about the standard template libraries, for example, and when you study Java, you will learn about standard Java classes. Beyond the libraries bundled with the language, though, you'll need to study third-party libraries. Sometimes these are general application frameworks, such as Microsoft's .NET framework, that can be used with several different high-level languages. In other cases, the library is specific to a particular area, like OpenGL for graphics, or is part of a third-party proprietary software package.

As with learning a new language, you should not try to learn a new library during a major project that requires that library. Instead, learn the main components of the library separately in a test project of zero importance before employing them in a real project. Assign yourself a progression of increasingly difficult problems to solve. Remember that the goal is not necessarily to complete any of those problems, only to learn from the process, so you don't need to polish the solutions or even complete them once you have successfully employed that part of the library in your program. These programs can then serve as references for later work. When you find yourself stuck because you're unable to remember how to, let's say, superimpose a 2D display over a 3D scene in OpenGL, there's nothing better than being able to open up an old program that was created just to demonstrates that very technique and is written in your own style because it was written by you.

Also, as with learning a new language, once you are comfortable with the basics of a library, you should review the code written by experts in the use of that library. Most large libraries have idiosyncrasies and caveats that aren't exposed by the official documentation and that, outside of long experience, can only be discovered from other programmers. In truth, to make much headway with some libraries requires the initial use of a framework provided by another programmer. The important thing is not to rely on others' code any more than you have to and to quickly get to the stage where you re-create the code you were originally shown. You might be surprised how much you learn from the process of re-creating someone else's existing code. You may see a call to a library function in the original code and understand that the arguments passed in this call produce a certain result. When you set that code aside, though, and try to reproduce that effect on your own, you'll be forced to investigate the function's documentation, all the particular values the arguments could take, and why they have to be what they are to get the desired effect.

Take a Class

As a longtime educator, I feel I have to conclude this section by talking about classes—not in the object-oriented programming sense, but in the sense of a course at a school. Whatever area of programming you want to learn about, you'll find someone offering to teach you, whether in a traditional classroom or in some online environment. However, a class is a catalyst for learning, not the learning itself, especially in an area like programming. No matter how knowledgeable or enthusiastic a programming instructor is, when you actually learn new programming abilities, it will happen as you're sitting in front of your computer, not as you're sitting in a lecture hall. As I reiterate throughout this book, you have to put programming ideas into practice, and you have to make them your own to truly learn them.

This isn't to suggest that classes have no value—because they often have tremendous value. Some concepts in programming are inherently difficult or confusing, and if you have access to an instructor with a talent for explaining difficult concepts, that may save you loads of time and frustration. Also, classes provide an evaluation of your learning. If you are again fortunate with your instructor, you may learn much from the evaluation of your code, which would streamline the learning process. Finally, the successful completion of a class provides some evidence to current or future employers that you understand the subjects taught (if you are unfortunate and have a poor instructor, you can at least take solace in that).

Just remember that your programming education is your responsibility, even when you take a class. A course will provide a framework for acquiring a grade and credit at the end of the term, but that framework doesn't limit you in your learning. Think of your time in the class as a great opportunity to learn as much about the subject as possible, beyond any objectives listed in the course syllabus.

Conclusion

I fondly remember my first programming experience. I wrote a short, text-based simulation of a pinball machine, and no, that doesn't make any sense to me either, but it must have at the time. I didn't own a computer then—who did in 1976?—but at my father's office was a teletype terminal, essentially an enormous dot-matrix printer with a click-clack keyboard, that communicated with the mainframe at the local university via acoustic modem. (You picked up the phone to dial by hand, and when you heard electronic screaming, you dropped the handset into a special cradle connected to the terminal.) As primitive and pointless as my pinball simulation was, the moment the program worked and the computer was acting under my instructions, I was hooked.

The feeling I had that day—that a computer was like an infinite pile of Legos, Erector Sets, and Lincoln Logs, all for me to build anything I could imagine—is what drives my love of programming. When my development environment announces a clean build and my fingers reach for the keystroke that will begin execution of my program, I'm always excited, in anticipation of success or failure, and anxious to see the results of my efforts, whether I am writing a simple test project or putting the finishing touches on a large solution, or whether I am creating beautiful graphics or just constructing the front end of a database application.

I hope you have similar feelings when you program. Even if you are still struggling with some of the areas covered in this book, I hope you now understand that as long as programming excites you so much that you always want to stick with it, there is no problem you can't solve. All that is required is the willingness to put in the effort and to go about the process the right way. Time takes care of the rest.

Are you thinking like a programmer yet? If you've solved the exercises at the ends of these chapters, then you should be thinking like a programmer and be confident in your problem-solving ability. If you haven't solved many of the exercises, then I have a suggestion for you, and I'll bet you can guess what it is: Solve more exercises. If you've skipped some in previous chapters, don't start with the exercises in this chapter—go back to where you left off, and work your way forward from there. If you don't want to do more exercises because you don't enjoy programming, then I can't help you.

Once you are thinking like a programmer, be proud of your skills. If someone calls you a coder rather than a programmer, say that a well-trained bird could be taught to peck out code—you don't just write code, you use code to solve problems. When you're sitting across an interview table from a future employer or client, you'll know that whatever the job requires, you can figure it out.

Exercises

You had to know that there would be one last set of exercises. These are, of course, tougher and more open-ended than any from previous chapters.

8-1. Write a complete implementation for the cheating hangman problem that's better than mine.

8-2. Expand your hangman program so that the user can choose to be Player 1. The user still selects the number of letters in the word and the number of missed guesses, but the program does the guessing.

8-3. Rewrite your hangman program in another language, one that you currently know little or nothing about.

8-4. Make your hangman game graphical, actually displaying the gallows and the hangman as he is being constructed. You're trying to think like a programmer, not like an artist, so don't worry about the quality of the art. You must make an actual graphical program, though. Don't draw the hangman using ASCII text—that's too easy. You might want to investigate 2D graphics libraries for C++ or choose a different platform that's more graphically oriented to begin with, like Flash. Having a graphical hangman might require constraining the number of wrong guesses, but there may be a way to offer at least a range of choices for this number.

8-5. Design your own exercise: Employ the skills you learned in the hangman problem to solve something completely different that involves manipulating a list of words, such as another game that uses words—like Scrabble, a spellchecker, or whatever else you can think of.

8-6. Design your own exercise: Search for a C++ programming problem of such size or difficulty that you are sure you would have once considered it impossible for you to solve with your skills, and solve it.

8-7. Design your own exercise: Find a library or API that interests you but that you have yet to use in a program. Then investigate that library or API and use it in a useful program. If you're interested in general programming, consider the Microsoft .NET library or an open-source database library. If you like low-level graphics, consider OpenGL or DirectX. If you'd like to try making games, consider an open-source game engine like Ogre. Think about the kinds of programs you'd like to write, find a library that fits, and go at it.

8-8. Design your own exercise: Write a useful program for a new platform (one that's new to you)—for example, mobile or web programming.

INDEX

avoiding frustration, 21–22, 95–96,
201, 220, 224
by dividing problems, 41

B

bad_alloc exception, 89
bad smells, 65, 97, 192
base case, 144, 162
Big Recursive Idea (BRI), 143,
152–155
binary tree
empty, testing for, 162
leaf, 163
recursive processing, 160–165,
166–167
root node, 161
subtree, 161

C

C++
array declaration, 55
array initialization, 57
as choice for this book, xvii
cin standard stream, 26
class declaration, 112–113
cout standard stream, 26
delete operator, 83
exception, 130
file processing, 210–211
free function, 88
friend keyword, 184
get method, 34
header files for input/output, 26
list class, 182–183, 210–214,
216, 218
malloc function, 88
new operator, 75, 82, 97, 98
pointer declaration, 82
prerequisites, xv
reference parameters, 84
short-circuit evaluation, 129,
132, 133
Standard Template Library, 175
this keyword, 120
typedef keyword, 91, 101, 127,
160, 177
character codes, 34–35

checksum validation, 31–32
cin standard stream, 26
class
access specifier, 112, 119,
125, 127
basic framework, 119–122
composition, 126
constructor, 112–113, 119,
121–122, 126–127
data member, 112
declaration, 112–113
deep copy, 134–137
destructor, 133–134
dynamic data structures,
125–140
encapsulation, 114, 126, 180
expressiveness, 117–118, 121, 128
fake, 140–141
friend method, 184
get and *set*, 119–121
goals of use, 113–118
information hiding, 115, 180
interface, 115
method, 112
method names, choosing, 117,
119–120
operator overloading, 137
private member, 112
protected member, 112
public member, 112
shallow copy, 135
single-tasker, 141
subclass, 112
support method, 122
template, 141
validation, 121, 124
wrapper function, 163–165
classic puzzles
the Fox, the Goose, and the
Corn, 3–7, 15, 17, 20
sliding number puzzle, 7–11, 18
sudoku, 11–13
Quarrasi Lock, 13–15, 20
code block, 173
code reuse, 53, 172–173
abstract data type, 175
algorithm, 173–174
as-needed learning, 180–188

struct, 69

structure deference (->), 102, 128

subclass, 122

subscript, 56

sudoku, 11–13

support method, 122–125

T

tail recursion, 144, 145–146, 149–150

template class, 141

test-driven development, 200

testing, 124, 190, 199–200, 215

    memory leaks, 95

    promoting ease of, 34, 57, 66, 70, 218

    storing test programs, 44

    test cases, coding, 93, 98–100, 130–134, 186–187

this keyword, 120

thrashing, 89

tracking state, 50-51

traversal, linked list, 106–108, 129, 168–169, 179, 181

typedef keyword, 91, 101–102, 127, 160, 177

V

validation

    checksum 31–32

    code (*see* testing)

    data, 61–62, 92, 96, 121, 124–125

vectors, 55

    vs. arrays, 75–76

    declaring, 76

    push_back method, 76

W

weaknesses

    coding weaknesses, 196, 197–199

    design weaknesses, 196, 199–200

whitespace, 34

wrapper function, 163–165, 174

The Electronic Frontier Foundation (EFF) is the leading organization defending civil liberties in the digital world. We defend free speech on the Internet, fight illegal surveillance, promote the rights of innovators to develop new digital technologies, and work to ensure that the rights and freedoms we enjoy are enhanced — rather than eroded — as our use of technology grows.

EFF.ORG

ELECTRONIC FRONTIER FOUNDATION

Protecting Rights and Promoting Freedom on the Electronic Frontier

Think Like a Programmer is set in New Baskerville, TheSansMono Condensed, Futura, and Dogma.

This book was printed and bound at Edwards Brothers Malloy in Ann Arbor, Michigan. The paper is 70# Williamsburg Smooth, which is certified by the Sustainable Forestry Initiative (SFI). The book uses a RepKover binding, which allows it to lie flat when open.